£150·00

ORAL TRADITION

ORAL TRADITION

A Study in
Historical Methodology

by

JAN VANSINA

translated by

H. M. WRIGHT

ROUTLEDGE & KEGAN PAUL
LONDON

First published 1961 as
DE LA TRADITION ORALE
ESSAI DE METHODE HISTORIQUE
in 'Annales du Musée Royal de l'Afrique Centrale,
Sciences humaines, No. 36'
© *Jan Vansina 1961*

This translation first published 1965
by Routledge & Kegan Paul Limited
Broadway House, 68-74 Carter Lane
London, E.C.4

Printed in Great Britain
by R. & R. Clark Limited, Edinburgh

Contents

CONTENTS

CONTENTS

CONTENTS

Preface

Verba volent, scripta manent, says the proverb; but it is given the lie by those peoples the world over whose behaviour and institutions prove that the word is not quite so transitory as might be supposed. It is enough to have witnessed the guardians of oral traditions solemnly reciting the texts stored in their memory to be convinced of this. The listeners, motionless and intent, follow every word that is spoken, and there can be no doubt that to them these words bring the past back to life, for they are venerable words that provide the key to the storehouse of wisdom of the ancestors who worked, loved, and suffered in times gone by. There can be no doubt that to them oral traditions are a source of knowledge about the past.

Among the various kinds of historical sources, traditions occupy a special place. Yet little has been done towards analysing their special features as historical documents. This is all the more astonishing in view of the fact that they are constantly being used as source material, for not only are traditions the most important sources for the history of peoples without writing, but they are known to be the basis of many written sources too, especially those of classical antiquity and of the early Middle Ages.

This study hopes to draw attention to this lacuna in the theoretical analysis of historical sources and to remedy it by examining the value of oral traditions as a historical source. By oral traditions, I mean all oral testimonies concerning the past which are transmitted from one person to another. It is of course impossible, with the limited amount of information so far at our disposal, to deal exhaustively in this one book with a subject so vast and so unexplored, and all I can attempt to do is to point out the problems involved. This book is therefore no more than an introduction. But it will have fulfilled its purpose if it leads to further studies, whether they be of a theoretical nature, or whether they treat oral sources in a properly scientific manner.

Since my treatment of the subject lies in the field of theory, I could not *a priori* limit my field of investigations to any particular time or place, but in practice most of the traditions on which this study is based come from present-day pre-literate peoples. This is because there is sufficient information about some of these sources to enable the historian to estimate their value as historical evidence, which is far from being the case with traditions which have reached us by means of written records made in the distant past. In spite of my efforts to give as wide a field of reference as possible, the reader will notice that it is mainly African traditions I have made use of, the reason for this being that I am better acquainted with the literature on Africa than with any other. The sources I have chiefly relied upon are those which I myself collected in Belgian colonial territory, among the Kuba of the Kasai (Congo) and in Rwanda and Burundi. This was unavoidable, because the literature on oral traditions does not contain the kind of information required for dealing with the problems that are raised in this study. This attempt to evaluate oral traditions as a historical source developed out of the fieldwork I carried out among the Kuba from 1953 to 1956, and in Ruanda-Urundi from 1957 to 1960, so that the material collected there has naturally influenced the way in which my theories have been arrived at.

I am very well aware that the approach to the subject which I have chosen is not the only one possible, and that the plan of arrangement which I have adopted is not the only one that could have been followed. Since almost all the problems dealt with raise a whole host of other problems, a large number of other possible plans of arrangement suggested themselves; but after trying out several of them, I decided that the one I have chosen was best suited for a clear exposition of the subject. I have had to leave out numerous examples which were to have illustrated various points in my argument, for fear of overloading this book, but I hope to publish, within the next two years or so, a history of the Kuba, a history of Burundi, and a book on the problems of Rwanda history, which will form complementary volumes to this one.

Many people have been of help to me in my work, either directly or indirectly, and I should like to express my thanks to them here. Among the professors who gave me my training in history and anthropology, I should like to make special mention of the late Canon Prof. Dr. and Mag. A. de Meyer of the Catholic University of Louvain, who taught me historical methodology and encouraged me to take up this subject; Canon Prof. Dr. J. M. Desmet of the same university, who directed my studies in it and who was my promoter when this work in its first form was presented as a doctoral thesis at the University of Louvain, under the title: 'De historische waarde der mondelinge over-leveringen met toepassing op de geschiedenis der Kuba'; the members of the jury, and particularly Dr. A. Maesen, lecturer at the Catholic University of Louvain and keeper at the Musée Royal du Congo Belge, who helped me on many ethnological points, and Dr. A. E. Meeussen, lecturer at the Catholic University of Louvain and keeper at the Musée Royal du Congo Belge, who initiated me in linguistic problems and in general scientific methodology. My thanks also go to Professor D. Forde of the Department of Social Anthropology at University College, London, and to his assistants, especially Dr. M. Douglas and Dr. P. Kaberry. I also owe a great deal to the late Prof. Dr. F. M. Olbrechts, Director of the Musée Royal du Congo Belge, who made it possible for me to undertake research, and to the keepers in the departments of 'sciences humaines' at this museum.

Finally, I owe a special debt of gratitude to the Institut pour la Recherche Scientifique en Afrique Centrale, where, like many others, I was able to attain a high degree of specialization, and under the auspices of which I have been able to carry out fieldwork in Africa since 1953.

I must also mention here all those who, in Africa, have helped me, advised me, or taken an interest in my work, and take this opportunity of extending to them my warmest thanks. I wish also to thank M. R. Schillings, at that time District Officer in Mweka, who initiated me in Africa's practical problems.

Many Africans have also collaborated with me in this work. Whether as clerks or as informants, Kuba, Rundi, and Rwanda have brought devotion and intelligence to their task and made it possible for me to collect the materials on which this work is based.

It is impossible to mention by name and thank individually all those who have, either directly or indirectly, helped and advised me during the preparation of this book. There have been so many helpers that it could indeed be described as a piece of group research.

Astrida,
29th April 1960.

NOTE. The spelling of proper names in the vernacular has been very much simplified for the convenience of the non-specialist reader. Thus the tones in tonal languages have not been indicated, and the phonological systems have been represented by restricting the signs used to the ordinary five vowels.

TRANSLATOR'S NOTE. The words *témoignage* and *témoin*, which are used as technical terms, have been translated as 'testimony' and 'informant'. (For their definition, see p. 22.) The verb 'to testify' has also been used in the technical sense of 'to make a testimony'.

CHAPTER I

Oral Tradition and Historical Methodology

1. AIMS AND PLAN OF THE WORK

ORAL traditions are historical sources of a special nature. Their special nature derives from the fact that they are 'unwritten' sources couched in a form suitable for oral transmission, and that their preservation depends on the powers of memory of successive generations of human beings. These special features pose a problem for the historian. Do they *a priori* deprive oral tradition of all validity as a historical source? If not, are there means for testing its reliability? These are precisely the questions to which the present study seeks to find an answer, and I hope to show that oral tradition is not necessarily untrustworthy as a historical source, but, on the contrary, merits a certain amount of credence within certain limits.

In those parts of the world inhabited by peoples without writing, oral tradition forms the main available source for a reconstruction of the past, and even among peoples who have writing, many historical sources, including the most ancient ones, are based on oral traditions. Thus a claim for the practical utility of research on the specific characteristics of oral tradition, and on the methods for examining its trustworthiness, is doubly substantiated.

The results of my researches are discussed in five chapters. The first deals with the main characteristic of oral tradition— its transmission by word of mouth—and with the relations obtaining between each successive testimony and the tradition itself. In the following chapter, I analyse the characteristic features, the form, and the content of the testimony as such, which should be of help when we come to try to understand any particular testimony. Next comes a survey of the various ways in which error or deliberate falsification may occur in a testimony, thus making it no more than a mirage of reality. The fourth chapter is devoted to an examination of how testimonies originate, and of how the amount of weight to be attached to any one testimony may be established by comparing it with others. Finally there is a chapter devoted to a discussion on the historical information that can be obtained from oral traditions with the aid of auxiliary source material. Each type of material enables us to catch a glimpse of one particular aspect of the past, although each has its limitations. These findings lead, in conclusion, to a general discussion on the essential features of historical methodology as a whole. Material concerning the practical problems arising during the search for and collection of sources has been gathered together in an appendix.

I should like to make it clear that my examination of the topic is primarily based on traditions still alive among peoples without writing, since sources of this kind preserve the essential nature of oral tradition better than traditions found in literate societies. Among peoples without writing, oral tradition continues to exist at the very heart of the environment that gave rise to it. It has not yet been supplanted, nor had its main functions taken over, by written documents, as is the case in a society where writing has taken pride of place. Nor has it yet been torn from its natural context, as happens once traditions have been committed to writing. For these reasons, and also because of the opportunities open to me, I have based this study mainly on the oral traditions of the Kuba, the Rundi, and the Rwanda, among whom I carried out field researches from 1955 to 1956, and from 1957 to 1960.

2. THE RELATION OF ORAL TRADITION TO WRITTEN HISTORY

1. Few historians have gone into the methodological problems raised by oral tradition. Research has, of course, been carried out

on the reliability of certain categories of traditional material, such as historical or hagiographic legends[1]; but such attempts as have been made to study oral tradition as a whole have been conducted in a manner that could scarcely be regarded as satisfactory.

Those writers who have discussed the value of the traditions of classical antiquity have worked with defective sources which lacked the essential features of oral tradition, for they were not transmitted to them by live informants, and there is a paucity of information, not to say complete ignorance, about the way in which they were originally transmitted. It is thus easy to understand why most of these writers maintain that oral traditions can only be regarded as reliable when corroborated by archaeological finds or linguistic evidence.[2] G. Dumezil's assessment of the situation led him to divide classicists into two kinds: those who emphasize the validity of tradition, holding that a tradition always has a kernel of truth, but that it is usually impossible to establish what is true and what is false; and those who accentuate the alterations and falsifications which traditions undergo, while at the same time conceding that a record of real events, duly established by other means, can also be preserved by tradition.[3] There is nothing surprising about this. The writers in question had at that time no means of judging the reliability of the traditions they were examining.

The main research work on oral tradition in general with regard to its value as historical source material has been done by E. Bernheim, A. Feder, and W. Bauer.

Bernheim distinguishes between the following categories of oral traditions: narratives, legends, anecdotes, proverbs, and historical lays.[4] He further distinguishes between the narrative which is a first-hand, eyewitness report, and all other sources consisting of second-hand, hearsay reports of events, which must be treated as if they were legends. He makes exception, however, of the historical narrative, because of the part played by free poetic inspiration in the elaboration of the material.[5] Thus, from the point of view of historical methodology, second-hand traditions can be equated with the reported narrative. The freer the manner of transmission, the greater will the number of divergent versions be, whereas the more mechanical the transmission, the more trustworthy will the tradition be.[6] In order to establish whether an oral tradition contains a kernel of historical truth or not, it is necessary to discover the oldest attested form in which the tradition was handed down. It will then be possible to assess its trustworthiness by applying the accepted rules of textual criticism.[7] Should a tradition contain some internal contradiction, or go against facts established from other sources, it must be regarded as unreliable.[8]

He then proceeds to examine the various types of distortion of historical truth that may occur,[9] and concludes that some second-hand traditional material can be subjected to scrutiny by the methods employed in historical criticism. This amounts to saying that if the reliability of a tradition has been established, it can be regarded as valid source material.[10]

Feder supplies an additional distinction to that established by Bernheim between first-hand and second-hand traditions: that between anonymous traditions and traditions of which the authorship is known. Under second-hand traditions he has one group containing sources such as rumours, anecdotes, historical proverbs, and pithy sayings, and another group of sources referring to more remote periods of the past, which he calls folk tradition or oral tradition in the strict sense of the term.

To this second group belong historical lays and spoken traditions or sagas. While first-hand traditions may be regarded as reliable, second-hand traditions must be treated with the greatest reserve.

As for oral tradition *sensu stricto*, it is always anonymous. It can never be relied upon with any certainty as a true account of events, because nothing is known of the first eyewitnesses nor of those who subsequently transmitted it. Oral tradition can only be regarded as reliable if it refers to comparatively recent events, if an adequate capacity for critical judgment existed at the time when it was handed down, and if other sources of information existed which would enable persons possessing this capacity to exercise it, in which case, the tradition must be trustworthy if it has not been questioned by such persons. Furthermore, pre-literate peoples have highly developed powers of memory, and hand down their traditions in a form made suitable for oral transmission by the use of rhyme or other formulae for linking the material together.[11] A final point made by Feder is that a

4

tradition must not be accepted as trustworthy merely on the grounds that its origins are known, and, in support of this rule, he gives instances of the way in which oral tradition becomes imperceptibly distorted.[12]

Bauer divides oral traditions into two groups. The first comprises all sources—regardless of whether they have survived intact or have become distorted in the process of transmission—which can be traced back to a particular individual and which have been handed down for some definite purpose, either public or private. To the second group belong those sources for which no personal authorship can be discovered, and which have spread more or less of their own accord. This is the group to which rumours, myths, sagas, legends, anecdotes, proverbs, and folk-songs must be assigned. When dealing with sources of this kind, it is important to establish immediately whether they have been composed or concocted for propaganda purposes, or with some autobiographical aim in view.

All such anonymous oral traditions share the common characteristic of being transmitted spontaneously from one person to another, and during this process the original form is lost and the content becomes fluctuating and blurred. Certain types of changes which are liable to occur must be attributed to the need to create an 'atmosphere'—to the imaginative inventiveness of the narrator and his desire to improve upon his material so as to pander to the love of the sensational felt by his audience, and increase the pleasure which he himself experiences in recounting what he has to say. It may be added that all this is done with the open intention of producing the desired effect, and audience-reaction affects the course of the recital, so that everything combines to create an atmosphere in which the recital takes on the character of an original stroke of inspiration.

He then proceeds to discuss the various types of oral traditions. Rumour is only useful as a historical source if it can be corroborated by other sources. With sagas, legends, and anecdotes, the mode of transmission must be examined, and they must be rejected if they contain internal contradictions or give accounts of events which are not in accord with fact as otherwise established. With regard to the sagas of classical antiquity, linguistic or archaeological evidence may be a determinative

5

factor in assessing their factual accuracy. Historical lays are always propagandist in intention, and moreover suffer from distortion of the original version owing to the omission of allusions which no longer have any meaning or which are simply not understood. Proverbs express moral attitudes and likewise arouse a moral response. But general information transmitted orally can be treated in the same way as written sources.[13]

This summary of the views put forward by these three writers plainly shows that they have based their researches on European oral traditions and on traditions which have been handed down from classical times. They have not, in fact, had any genuine sources at their disposal, particularly as regards oral tradition proper, such as it is still to be found today in pre-literate societies. I have mentioned above, the drawbacks of using traditional material that survives only in written form. It should be noted that all surviving traditions in Europe are traditions which have been preserved in a society that uses writing for recording all the events of the past that have a more than anecdotal interest.

As a result, oral tradition in such societies is limited to the exchanges that take place in the course of everyday conversation, and consists of traditions which are handed down from generation to generation in a random fashion, without the aid of any special techniques. Moreover, they all serve aesthetic, moral, or didactic purposes. These are by no means the purposes common to all types of oral tradition. I shall come back to this point later.

Neither the conclusions which these writers feel justified in drawing nor the rules which they formulate can be regarded as of general validity, because they are based on sources of inferior quality; and their ideas will be challenged throughout this study, when confronted with the traditions of pre-literate peoples, among whom oral tradition at its best is to be found.

2. For several years now, however, professional historians have been paying closer attention to oral history. J. D. Fage and R. Oliver are outstanding examples of historians who have made use of oral traditions, although they have not developed any theories as to their validity or as to the manner in which such sources should be handled. The former, influenced by modern social anthropology, lays emphasis on the relation of

oral tradition to its social environment, and considers that no assessment can be made of the worth of a tradition unless it is known what function it fulfils, and hence what distortions are likely to ensue. He is, moreover, of the opinion that the distortions are usually such as to render traditions quite worthless.[14] Oliver thinks that oral traditions are often worth investigating, and that they are not affected by the functions they fulfil to the point of losing all value as historical sources. But their historical value can only be judged if comparative use is made of archaeological evidence which may either corroborate or invalidate them.[15]

3. Long before the appearance of professional historians such as these, amateurs living among pre-literate peoples collected oral traditions, and, although not in the least interested in the theoretical aspect of the question, used them to reconstruct the past of these peoples. It may be said that the first historical writings based on oral traditions all date from the time when the first European explorers arrived upon the scene, and very nearly all that we know today about the early history of these pre-literate peoples is due to such amateur historians.

It is, however, only recently that contact has been established between these practitioners and their professional colleagues. It dates, in fact, from no earlier than 1953, at least as far as Africa is concerned. This was the year in which the first conference on African history and archaeology was held, which brought together professional historians and amateur collectors of traditions. A glance at the volume which resulted from their discussions will show the importance ascribed to oral tradition by the participants.[16] The attitude adopted towards the reliability of traditions recalls that of Fage and Oliver, as well as that of American ethnohistorians. R. A. Hamilton summarizes it as follows:

> Such work as has so far been done makes it clear that oral tradition ought never to be used alone and unsupported. It has to be related to the social and political structure of the peoples who preserve it, compared with the traditions of neighbouring peoples, and linked with the chronological indications of genealogies and age-set

cycles, of documented contacts with literate peoples, of dated natural phenomena such as famines and eclipses, and of archaeological finds.[17]

In other words, oral tradition can be of real value, but doubts must be entertained about it unless it can be substantiated by other historical sources.

4. Thus both amateur historians and present-day professional historians such as those mentioned above believe that it is possible to rely to some extent on oral traditions. But they have not so far made any attempt to apply the methods of historical criticism to these sources in a manner that would enable a more rational assessment to be made both of the actual nature of these sources, and of their comparative reliability.

3. THE TREATMENT OF ORAL TRADITION IN ETHNOLOGICAL LITERATURE

Ethnologists who have attempted to study the past of peoples without writing have been faced with the problem of how much worth to attach to oral tradition. Hence a number of them have devoted a certain amount of attention to the problem. The following are the six main attitudes adopted:

1. Oral traditions are never reliable.
2. Oral traditions may contain a certain amount of truth.
3. It is impossible to assess the amount of truth contained in oral tradition.
4. All oral traditions contain a kernel of historical truth.
5. All factors affecting the reliability of traditions should be thoroughly examined.
6. The reliability of these sources should be examined according to the usual canons of historical methodology.

It will perhaps be useful if I say something about the various ways oral traditions have been treated in monographs devoted to the history of pre-literate peoples.

1. A. Van Gennep is sceptical about the reliability of oral traditions.[18] He holds that the very method of transmission rapidly results in the tradition becoming altered as it is spontaneously handed down from one generation to the next. He also

mentions the distortions a tradition may undergo, basing his findings mainly on present-day oral traditions in Europe, although he also quotes instances from the traditions of peoples without writing.[19] E. S. Hartland likewise attaches little value to traditions as historical evidence. Apart from certain indications as to the direction of migrations and cultural diffusion, he regards all the information they provide as worthless.[20]

The opinion held by Lowie is that oral tradition is *a priori* without any historical value whatsoever. Primitive tribes have no sense of history, nor any sense of historical perspective.[21] In the words of this American anthropologist: 'The point is, not whether they recollect happenings, but whether they recollect happenings that are historically significant. Otherwise a perfectly true statement may be as dangerous as a wholly false one.'[22]

This comes from an article in which Lowie concluded a discussion that had been carried on in the *American Anthropologist* in 1914 and 1915, throughout which he had vigorously opposed an article by R. B. Dixon and J. R. Swanton, in which these writers had expressed their faith in the information to be derived from oral tradition.[23] In his first reply, Lowie made his position clear by saying: 'I cannot attach to oral tradition any historical value whatsoever under any conditions whatsoever'.[24] This statement was then attacked by Dixon and Swanton, and also by A. A. Goldenweiser.

2. These last three writers, and others as well, such as E. Sapir, D. Tait, and W. Muehlmann, vindicate the importance of oral tradition as a historical source, and quote examples showing that traditions can indeed contain authentic information. Dixon and Swanton maintain that the reliability of oral tradition cannot be contested if the information it contains is in line with evidence derived from archaeology, linguistics, physical anthropology, and ethnology.[25] The former was finally forced to express the opinion that oral tradition could be said always to provide accurate information concerning the origins of a tribe.[26] Goldenweiser states his position by saying that 'the ethnologist, in the absence of better evidence, follows the lead of tradition until further data, of higher evidential value, serve to confirm or to refute his preliminary conjectures and hypotheses'.[27] As for Sapir,

he is convinced that reliance may be placed on traditions, although he stipulates that 'when they refer to the distant past, they must be handled with a good deal of reserve'. He proves, by means of linguistic and cultural evidence, that certain traditions of the Pueblo Indians are well founded, and in addition he quotes examples from Nahuatl- and Tsimshian-speaking Aztec peoples. He concludes by expressing the opinion that there is a 'ring of history' in the Indian accounts of migration and tribal or clan movements.[28] The position adopted by these American writers, and the interest evinced, from Boas onwards, by the various schools of American anthropology in cultural history (which they have for some time now termed 'ethnohistory'), have led them to include, more or less tacitly, oral traditions among the possible sources available to the ethnohistorian. M. Herskovits states that the ethnohistorian draws on four different kinds of resources: on those of history, archaeology, oral traditions, and ethnology. The first two may be thought of as giving him 'hard' materials—that is, materials which give reliable information. The last two are 'soft'. They can only lead us to probabilities.[29] Later in this same article the writer warns the ethnohistorian against the tendency to assign too much validity to oral traditions.[30] C. E. Fuller, who was a pupil of Herskovits, has studied the history of the Gwambe, and he, too, regards oral tradition as an authentic historical source. The use of oral traditions, when checked against written documents and compared with present-day ethnographical data, has enabled him to reconstruct a detailed picture of Gwambe culture and of the changes it has undergone over quite an extensive period of time.[31]

Both Herskovits and Fuller come very close to Sapir's point of view. They maintain that traditions have the 'ring of history', but insist that they must be checked against other historical sources before valid use can be made of them.

The importance of taking linguistic and ethnographic evidence into account for testing the reliability of Dagomba and Konkomba traditions is also underlined by Tait, and he states that a historian cannot work among primitive peoples without having first been trained in linguistics and ethnography.[32]

Muehlmann thinks that oral traditions are trustworthy

sources, and that it is because of a European prejudice against them that so little use has so far been made of them. In West Africa, for instance, they give an account of historical events which can be compared with other versions of the same account found among neighbouring tribes. Their value chiefly lies in the light they throw on cultural history.[33]

3. There is a group of writers, among whom may be included F. Graebner, W. Schmidt, and G. Van Bulck, who, in contradistinction to the positions adopted by the writers mentioned above, maintain that it is impossible to decide whether a tradition is trustworthy or not. The reliability of oral traditions cannot be proved unless there is some measure of agreement between various independent accounts and unless the facts conveyed correspond with those postulated by cultural historical studies.[34] Father Van Bulck is of the opinion that in Africa too little attention has been paid to oral traditions, and suggests that toponymical and genealogical data should be used as a means of checking them in addition to the other methods of control established by Graebner.[35]

4. Other ethnologists consider that every tradition conveys some information about past events, even if the kernel of historical truth is enveloped in fictitious material. Father R. Mortier states that while no reliance can be placed on the form of traditions, their content is reliable. By form, he means the names of ancestors, indications of time and place, and the manner in which the plot unfolds. As for the content, it includes the events themselves, the tribal names which are symbolized by the names of individuals, and the general situation as described by the narrative.[36]

For H. U. Beier, the factual information conveyed by a tradition is totally unreliable, and traditions are essentially sources of use 'for the history of thought or philosophy of a certain people'. Thus he infers from a Yoruba myth about an ancestor called Oduduwa that the name was once used for an earth goddess, and that a chthonic cult formerly existed. Traditions may also convey other kinds of historical information. For example, Beier infers from other myths that the Yoruba were formerly matrilineal, and did not practise agriculture.[37]

5. The majority of ethnologists have given their attention to

the various factors that affect the reliability of traditions, without however having committed themselves on the value of traditions as a source of information about the past, and without having made any systematic study of the essential character of tradition. That the length of time a tradition has lasted, the aims pursued by its propagators, and their attitude towards the events related, give rise to entirely different accounts of the same event, is something that is shown by P. Mercier in his study, based on several Yoruba and Bariba traditions, of the abortive attack made by these tribes against a Nigerian town called Ilorin.[38] He comes to the conclusion that, after a certain length of time has elapsed, a combination of circumstances leads to a selection being made among the various versions of a tradition, until the point is reached when only one, or at best two or three versions remain, which greatly complicates the task of finding out what actually happened. This is why it is so difficult to study the past in most parts of Africa. The emphasis laid by Mercier on the way the aim of a tradition interferes with it brings his position close to that of other ethnologists who emphasize the importance of the *function* fulfilled by a tradition in the society in which it is transmitted.

In this connection, the functionalist school is the first to spring to mind.[39] E. E. Evans-Pritchard summarizes their position well when he writes that the study of those traditions which are the collective representation of past events, which social anthropologists call myths, is part of the study of the society to which they belong.[40] The functionalists have spurned any attempt to reconstruct the past history of primitive tribes in the absence of written documents and archaeological evidence,[41] and lay so much stress on the function of oral tradition that they reach the stage of refusing to admit that it could contain any valid information concerning the past, regarding the content of traditions as being entirely determined by the functions performed by traditions within the social structure as a whole and as a means for maintaining that structure.[42]

Recently this position has again been very clearly expressed by I. Wilks, who finds that oral traditions have no historical content, but are simply myths invented to meet the demands of a particular—and usually political—situation. Their existence is thus entirely due to their function. The study of oral tradition has bearing in the field of customary law, not in that of history.[43]

These views are not held by Evans-Pritchard, who considers that oral traditions can be used as historical sources even if they are for the most part untrustworthy, since history always has a conjectural quality, and truthfulness in the reconstruction of the past is always a matter of degree. It is merely because nineteenth-century anthropologists were unable to adopt a critical attitude towards such reconstructions that all attempts in this direction have been worthless.[44] P. C. Lloyd also thinks that all traditions contain some truth. 'If the sociologist outlines the functions of these myths', he writes, '. . . the historian may be able to see in what directions distortion is most likely to have taken place and to assess better their value as historical evidence.'[45]

A. W. Southall maintains that traditions may contain historical information if there has been some motive for transmitting it. 'Societies with hereditary chiefs . . . usually have a positive vested interest in the transmission of historical information.' Oral traditions satisfy certain psychological needs, and in order to do so, they 'require only to emphasize particular qualitative aspects and details of events, not necessarily to distort the major historical sequences'. Thus a tradition need not be entirely without value as historical evidence. But it is 'still subject to countercheck of the versions of all the groups concerned in a particular event'. He is sceptical about the oral traditions of tribes without a chief, at least so far as the tribes subject to the Alur are concerned, whose traditions fell within his field of study.

With regard to migration, he observes that comparison of traditions often leads to confusion and contradictions, partly because of lapses of memory, partly because of possible motives for distortion. 'Also,' he writes, 'when large tribal movements are studied at close quarters there sometimes emerges such a welter of small individual groups moving apparently in all directions that any picture of a coherent general movement is obscured.' Southall finally insists that for the interpretation of traditions 'it is essential to know the general social structure of a people, the age, education and social status of informants, and the exact social groups and localities from which they come', and further, that some assessment must be made 'of a people's attitude towards time and history, and their possible motives for distortion'.[46]

Van Velsen holds that oral tradition becomes more meaningful if considered in the light of the present political and social structure. A tradition is inevitably biased, the bias being inherent in the political or social context. This means that there is no such thing as 'absolute truth' in oral traditions. Nevertheless, some traditions may be accurate on the whole. These views are shared by many members of the functionalist school.[47]

The view Nicholson expresses is that 'Inca interest in their past history was largely the result of the political and social advantage to be gained by the maintenance of careful genealogical records on the part of members of the royal *ayllus*, composed of descendants of each of the emperors, who kept up an elaborate cult to his memory'.[48] Linton and Luomala show how in Polynesia reasons of the same kind operated in favour of the preservation of carefully remembered traditions.[49]

Romero Moliner draws attention to certain factors which reduce the credibility of oral traditions. In his opinion, oral traditions have no value as historical evidence because the indigenous peoples of Africa have never elaborated any system of chronology, because facts are distorted in order to present the tale in an agreeable light, and because there is no causal connection between the events described, which simply follow one upon the other in a free and random manner.[50]

6. There are other ethnologists who maintain that it is the historians who must decide upon the reliability of oral traditions and that they must do so according to the rules of historical methodology. The authors of a standard handbook on anthropology state that 'where authoritative historical evidence is available, the investigator must evaluate it in accordance with the canons of the historian. Great care must be exercised in interpreting oral traditions historically. Frequently evidence about the past of a society can be derived from an analysis of present-day customs, from material culture, archaeological and linguistic data, and the physical anthropology of the people.'[51] It should be noted that although the methods are clearly enough laid down, little help is offered as to how to carry them out.

7. In practice, both ethnologists and historians have made

extensive use of oral traditions in order to reconstruct the past of the peoples they have studied. In most cases, they have not allowed their critical judgment to intervene beyond the point of omitting passages which seemed to go blatantly against the facts of nature, and interpreting what remained with the greatest possible latitude.

There is no better way of indicating the defects of this approach than by referring to a monograph which provides a typical example.

The monograph on the Akan by Mrs. E. Meyerowitz is one of the best works devoted to the past history of pre-literate peoples.[52] In a survey of the literature on this topic, von Fuehrer-Haimendorf extols it as a shining example of the results which can be obtained by studying oral traditions with a combination of scrupulous care and rich imagination.[53] It is, indeed, the case that in this book by Mrs. Meyerowitz there are several innovations which one would search for in vain in many other studies of this kind. She supplies information concerning her methods of work, together with a list of her sources of information and the name of the interpreter who collaborated with her.[54] Everywhere she questioned the chiefs and the tribal councils, and she visited the sacred sites of the country. Actually, this part of Ghana is full of sources of information, so that she experienced no great difficulty in her search for traditions. Another point in favour of this monograph is that it is one of the few to specify the character of the traditions used.[55] Its author notes that traditions are taught in schools by specialists, and that sanctions are brought to bear against those who fail to give an accurate account of the traditions entrusted to them. She also emphasizes the sacred nature of many traditions, notes the distortions which arise, and mentions instances of forgotten traditions. Finally, she mentions that traditions are not so well preserved in some places as in others, this being particularly the case in the small states, whose traditions are often fragmentary.

Nevertheless, she has not attempted to explore the reasons for this, nor has she exercised much critical judgment in her handling of her sources. Here are two examples of this lack of critical judgment. She tells the story of the civil war that destroyed Beeo-Nsoko. This town consisted of two parts, the one,

Beeo, being inhabited by pagans, and the other, Nsoko, by Moslems. A son of the king of Beeo and a son of the Moslem chief of Nsoko fell in love with the same girl. One day a quarrel broke out between them in the market-place, near a stone that still stands there, which ended by their making their way to the girl's house, where they cut the girl in half, each taking away a portion. This caused such bitterness between the two camps that civil war broke out and the town was destroyed. The writer introduces this story with the following remark: 'According to them, the occasion of the war was the following incident',[56] without making any enquiry into the truth of the tale. She has not thought of asking herself whether the cutting of the girl in half is not a stereotype theme, nor whether poetic licence may not have led to distortion of the tale as a whole. Lastly, she has not noticed that the tale must be to some extent a local legend about a stone and other ruined remains of the old town.[57]

She also tells how, during a war, the leader of one side succeeded in capturing the blade of the Sword of Rule and the leader of the other side held on to the handle, which was supposed by the natives to symbolize a division of power. But she has not troubled to find out whether the whole story may not be a stereotype, in spite of indications given by the informants themselves.[58]

Besides relying on oral traditions, Eva Meyerowitz also uses onomastics to trace the origins of various tribes, with lamentable results. She arrives at the idea that the tribal name *Guan* is related to the name of a place in the Sahara, *Ilagua*, the plural of which is *Laguantan*. These names do not actually exist, but are deduced from the Arabic forms: *Luvata* or *Lewata*, found in written documents.[59] But no argument is adduced, let alone any linguistic evidence supplied, to support this ready-made hypothesis.

In spite of its faults, the book was well received by some ethnologists because it gives information about sources, describes how they were discovered, and discusses their special features arising from the mode of transmission. All this shows a great advance on earlier monographs, where none of these things are found. But other ethnologists, including specialists in the area where Mrs. Meyerowitz carried out her fieldwork, stress the major defects of her work, particularly the lack of critical judgment it displays.[60]

8. This survey of the treatment of the problem in ethnographic literature reveals that many ethnologists are aware of the importance of oral traditions and of the need to apply methods of criticism to them. Of the six points of view adopted, the first two can simply be dismissed. The writers in the first group maintain that no oral traditions are trustworthy, whereas those of the second show that some have a certain amount of credibility; but it goes without saying that any discussion based on *a priori* views as to credibility which are unsupported by practical examples is not of any help in solving the problem.

The third point of view—that upheld by Graebner, Schmidt, and Van Bulck—is that the reliability of oral traditions cannot be established by internal evidence, but only by criteria taken from auxiliary disciplines, or by a correspondence between various independent accounts. This is a position which approaches that adopted by historians. It rests on the assumption that the inherent nature of oral tradition is such as to make it impossible to establish its reliability. I shall later have occasion to demonstrate that this is not the conclusion at which one arrives after studying the essential nature and characteristic features of oral tradition.

The fourth point of view does not admit the hypothesis that oral tradition completely falsifies events. Mortier and Beier even go so far as to maintain that all traditions have some factual basis. But they do not indicate what methods might be adopted for enabling a distinction to be made between those elements which do, and those which do not, contain factual information.

As for the fifth point of view, it is enough to say that all its upholders lay stress on certain particular features of oral tradition, or of certain types of oral tradition, which affect its reliability. What emerges from their discussions is that an examination of the true character of oral tradition is needed, and that an attempt must be made to describe the characteristic features of the various categories. Lastly, the writers who put forward the sixth point of view formulate the problem of the reliability of oral tradition without offering any solution.

From the monographs in which use is made of oral sources, it can clearly be seen that what is above all lacking is a theoretical study of the problem. Hardly any of the writers of these monographs apply any critical methods to their sources, nor do they take the special nature of oral tradition into account.

Ethnographical and historical studies on the subject show that the value of oral traditions as historical evidence is a problem that has to be solved, but although they have certainly raised important questions concerning it, none of them provides a general discussion on the special nature of oral traditions as a source of information about the past, nor attempts to apply the methods of historical criticism to these sources.

These are the two main aims of this study, and in the next chapter I shall deal with the whole phenomenon of oral tradition as it actually exists.

CHAPTER II

Tradition as a Chain
of Testimonies

INTRODUCTION

WHEN I outlined how I would set about describing the special nature of oral tradition as a historical source, the task assigned to this chapter was that of defining oral tradition and of examining the feature which this definition specifies as characteristic, namely, transmission by word of mouth—the natural consequence of which is that a tradition is a chain of testimonies. Then three problems are dealt with in greater detail in the sections which follow. These are: the relation between each testimony and the tradition as a whole, the methods of transmission, and finally the kind of distortions that may arise in the course of transmission.

I. DEFINITION AND CHARACTERISTICS

1. Definition

Oral traditions consist of all verbal testimonies which are reported statements concerning the past. This definition implies that nothing but *oral* traditions—that is to say, statements either spoken or sung—enter into consideration. These must not only be distinguished from written statements, but also from material objects that might be used as a source of knowledge about the past.

It further indicates that not all oral sources are oral traditions, but only those which are reported statements—that is, sources which have been transmitted from one person to another through the medium of language. Eyewitness accounts, even when given orally, do not come within the sphere of tradition because they are not *reported* statements. Oral traditions exclusively consist of hearsay accounts, that is, testimonies that narrate an event which has not been witnessed and remembered by the informant himself, but which he has learnt about through hearsay.[1]

The definition also excludes rumours from oral tradition, for although rumours are oral sources which are transmitted from one person to another, they do not concern the past. Indeed, it is their special function to give the latest information about the present. They are news. It is a well-known fact that rumours arise in situations of tension and social unrest, when the ordinary channels of communication are no longer functioning, or are regarded as suspect. This is proof enough that a rumour is a piece of 'news' that is only spread abroad by reason of its up-to-dateness, and that it is not a statement concerning the past. Obviously, however, rumours may remain in people's memory and may later give rise to oral traditions after having been transmitted as testimonies concerning the past. But that does not alter the fact that in themselves they are no such thing.

There are, therefore, three types of oral testimony: the eyewitness account, oral tradition, and rumour.

One final point should be made here, namely, that although the material we are concerned with consists of testimonies—that is, statements made by someone concerning certain specific facts or events—the informant does not have to have any conscious intent, when relating facts or events of the past, of doing so because of their historical importance. The aim of a testimony is not necessarily that of recording history. It follows from this that all traditions which communicate information about the past may be regarded as historical sources. Thus, for example, Aesop's fables are a source of knowledge about the past, because they give a certain point of view about a particular cultural aspect of a particular period of the past.

2. *Characteristics*

The relation between the fact or event observed and the final testimony describing it or, to go a step further, the first written record of it, may be described in the following manner. An observer reports whatever it is he has observed in a testimony which might be called the initial or proto-testimony. This testimony is heard by someone who repeats it to a second person, who in turn passes on the information by telling it to a third person, etc. Thus a chain of transmission comes into being, in which each successive informant forms a link and in which every testimony is a hearsay account. The final informant communicates the final testimony in the chain to someone who records it in writing. This sequence can be shown diagrammatically as follows:

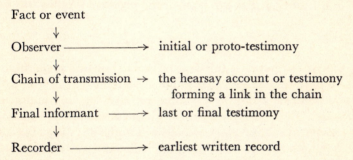

Fact or event
↓
Observer ⟶ initial or proto-testimony
↓
Chain of transmission → the hearsay account or testimony forming a link in the chain
↓
Final informant ⟶ last or final testimony
↓
Recorder ⟶ earliest written record

From the definition of oral tradition that has been proposed, and from the description of the above sequence, it can be seen that the truly distinctive feature of oral tradition is: transmission by word of mouth. But this very fact means that a tradition should be regarded as a series of historical documents, even if the documents are verbal ones.

The first thing to discuss is the relation that exists between any given testimony and the chain which precedes it. After that two further problems must be examined: the method of transmission, and the distortions that may occur in testimonies due to verbal transmission.

2. THE VERBAL TESTIMONY OF THE CHAIN OF TRANSMISSION

Verbality is a quality which the testimonies belonging to an oral tradition share with eyewitness accounts and rumours.

Thus the special character acquired by a testimony by reason of its verbality is not, properly speaking, peculiar to tradition. But, so far as I know, this particular aspect of oral tradition has never been emphasized. This has led me to devote the first sub-section below to it, so as to give it due emphasis.

The next sub-section deals with a problem that is peculiar to oral tradition: the relation that exists between any one testimony and the preceding testimonies forming the chain of transmission. A final sub-section deals with the text and variant versions of the verbal testimony. This is a problem that arises with all verbal accounts, but it has a special aspect in the case of oral tradition. For this reason, the problem is left to the last.

1. *The verbal testimony*

A verbal testimony is the sum of the statements made by any one informant concerning a single series of events, so long as all the statements relate to the same referent. An informant is a person or a group of persons who gives an account of a referent. A referent is that of which an account is given: in the case of an eyewitness account, it is the thing observed; in the case of a rumour, it is a piece of news that has been heard; in the case of oral tradition, it is a testimony that has been heard, about a series of past events, which may contain one or several traditions, for any one testimony of any one informant may be a combination of several traditions.

Thus the most characteristic form of the verbal testimony is the indirect account, which means that the informant who transmits it plays an important role. Indeed, it is the informant who determines the nature of a verbal testimony, and in traditional testimonies, the referent is comparatively unimportant. For it must be emphasized that a testimony consists of the sum of all the statements made by the informant. It thus includes not only the referent—the tradition or traditions that are being related—but also all the personal additions made to it by the informant. And there often are such personal additions. From the formal point of view, it is possible to distinguish between two types of traditions: those which have a fixed form and are learnt by heart and transmitted as they stand, and those which are free in form and not learnt by heart and which everyone transmits in his own way. An example of the fixed type of text is the poem, and of a free text, the narrative. The very words of the poem belong to the tradition, whereas in the case of the narrative, they are a contribution made by the narrator, and only the general outline of the narrative belongs to the tradition. Nevertheless a testimony consists of words spoken by the informant, whether it be a narrative or a poem.

That the nature of a verbal testimony really does depend upon the informant is not only shown by the additions to the referent contributed by the informant, but also by frequent failure to include all the traditions which have gone to the making of the referent. If the informant omits to relate certain points, then these points will not feature in his testimony, despite the fact that they did feature in the tradition or traditions from which the testimony derives. This may come about because the informant wishes to safeguard his own interests, or because he is unconsciously influenced by various factors in his social environment, and is thus led to omit certain facts either by mistake, or deliberate falsification. Moreover, as we shall see, the manner in which a testimony is given has a definite influence on the testimony itself. A testimony, in fact, is the tradition as interpreted through the personality of the informant, and is coloured by his personality.

It is this influence exerted by the personality of the informant on the testimony that enables one to postulate that a referent may consist of one or of several traditions. Ideally, a testimony might be thought of as deriving from one tradition only which the informant passes on, but in practice this is not always what happens. It can happen that an informant has heard only one tradition which he passes on. But an informant may, during the course of his life, have heard several traditions which become mixed up in his mind, so that he gives a single testimony embracing all of them. There is then no means of discovering which parts of his testimony belong to which of the various traditions that form the basis of his statements. He has merged them all together. One cannot speak of several testimonies. Everything is gathered together in a single statement.

On the other hand, it is best to treat the statements of different informants, even when they have the same referent and relate the same tradition or traditions, as separate testimonies. They cannot be regarded as belonging to one single tradition, because often each individual informant has contributed some touch of his own. One will accentuate such and such a point in the tradition he has heard, another some other point. One will have understood it in one way, another in another. Only in the case of a fixed text will all give the same version of it.

All this clearly shows how the informant colours the testimony. But the referent—the tradition—also colours the testimony to some extent.

2. *The verbal testimony and the chain of transmission*

It follows from the definition given of the verbal testimony that all the statements of one informant concerning a single series of events form one single testimony, but that this is only the case if the statements have the same referent. If A passes on something he has heard from B, it makes no difference how often he repeats it—what he says at various intervals of time still forms no more than one single testimony, since each time he is passing on what he heard from B. A remains the same person throughout, and the testimony, each time it is repeated, is influenced by the same personality; and each time, what is passed on is the tradition heard from B. Thus the tradition on which the testimony is based, and the informant, both remain the same, so that clearly the testimony in question remains the same throughout, irrespective of the intervals of time between the informant's repetitions of it. A man called Gakaanyiisha twice told a tale—once in 1954, and once in 1957—referring to the same events in the history of Rwanda. Between whiles he had not added to his fund of information. The two tales therefore constitute one single testimony, in spite of the interval of three years between them.

But if there is a change of referent in two separate statements made by an informant, there is no longer any question of their being the same testimony, despite the fact that the informant remains the same. An informant may first make a series of statements which include traditions A, B, and C, these being the traditions he knew at that time. He may then make a second series of statements including traditions A, B, C, D-N. He is not now giving an account of the same things, and his testimony cannot be regarded as the same as the previous one. An actual example makes this quite clear. A Bushongo called Anaclet Mikwepy first recited to me a list of kings containing only three names. Later he enumerated many more. He had meanwhile added to his fund of knowledge by information obtained from his uncle, Bope Louis. Thus the traditions on which his second statement rested were in part different from those of the first. It might, however, be argued that even so, both statements had traditions in common, for in the first, the informant may have used traditions A+B, and then later, having learnt about tradition C, he made further statements which rested upon traditions (A+B) +C. These statements still include the referent of the first statements, and it might be argued that since the old referent forms part of the new referent, the whole should be regarded as one single testimony. But this is not the only type of case that occurs. There may be two completely contradictory traditions concerning the same series of events, both of which are known to informants. In Rwanda there are two traditions explaining the coexistence of two different castes, the Tutsi and the Hutu, in the country. According to one tradition, an ancestor named Kanyarwanda had several sons, among whom Gatutsi and Gahutu were the eponymous ancestors of the Tutsi and the Hutu. According to the other tradition, Kigwa, the first Tutsi, fell from the skies on to land which had hitherto been occupied solely by the Hutu. Many informants know both traditions. But they never combine them. They choose either the one or the other, declaring that this one is true and the other false, or vice versa.[2] Yet here is a case of the same informant, dealing with the same events, but without mixing up his traditions.

It is therefore advisable to regard the statements of one informant as separate testimonies whenever the referents are different, even if the same referent occurs in the second series of statements as in the first, although this time with other traditions added. For it is important for the historian to know as precisely as possible exactly what the traditions are upon which a testimony is based. This is the underlying reason for postulating identity of referent as well as identity of informant in the definition of a verbal testimony.

3. *The text and variant versions of a testimony*

When an informant retells a tale he has told before, one must always ask oneself whether he has meanwhile learnt some further traditions. What has to be established is whether the two tales are merely variants of the same testimony, or whether they are two different testimonies. This can sometimes be done by direct questioning. The informant will either admit having incorporated further traditions in his tale, or will deny having done so. But often a more indirect approach is required. The two versions of the tale can be compared. If there is a wide degree of variation between them, it may be assumed with certainty that it is a question of two different testimonies. The case of Mikwepy Anaclet is a case in point. Frequently, however, the variations are very slight, being limited to a few details in a free narrative, or a few words in a fixed text. A type of variation that occurs fairly often in a free narrative is that the second version is simply an abridgment of the first. The informant knows that he has already recited this testimony for you, and now shortens it. In such a case one can assume that the informant's second statement is based on the same referent as the first, and that what has been produced are two variants of the same testimony. But in other cases where the variations are slight it is not so easy to determine whether it is a question of the same testimony or of two different ones. The second version may restore omissions contained in the first and be more complete, or it may be a distorted version of the first without there having been any additions to the tradition itself. But it may have been made more complete, or it may have been altered, because a knowledge of other traditions has been acquired. In either case, the research worker will have to form his own opinion, which will be guided by what he knows about the personality of the informant.

All this goes to show that a testimony is the sum of all the statements of an informant which relate to the same referent.

Thus the text provided by Gakaanyiisha consists both of the tale he told the first time, and of the shortened version he told the second time. No attempt should be made to reconstruct a so-called 'original' text, for, as I have said, a testimony consists not only of the tradition or traditions on which it is based, but also of the actual words of the informant; and in the case of the free forms of tradition, these words vary from one version to another. But even in the case of fixed forms of tradition, it is inadvisable to reconstruct an 'original'. For in both cases the variants are valuable because of the opportunity they provide for judging the informant's confidence in the reliability of his statements and his psychological attitude towards his testimony, and sometimes also for detecting errors and lies.

When, however, we come to the practical consideration of the publication of texts, the free and the fixed forms of tradition have to be handled differently. With a fixed text, one may give one version, and supply notes on the variants occurring in the other versions. With free texts, it is obviously impracticable to publish all the variant versions one after the other. One version must be chosen for publication, and variants must be indicated in notes which will either point to variations in formal structure in relation to the chosen version, or will cite the variant versions *verbatim* if the words used give rise to more than one interpretation.[3]

4. The manner of testifying

A testimony may be supplied by one or by several informants. If it is provided by one informant only, it will normally contain all that he knows of traditional lore, together with his own additions or, as the case may be, his omissions, made either deliberately or by mistake, and attributable either to the kind of person he is, or the interests he wishes to safeguard. But other ways of testifying occur. The testimony may be contributed by a group, or result from a dispute, or be given in reply to questioning. It is important to note these different ways of testifying, because each gives its own particular slant to the relation between the testimony and the tradition or traditions from which it derives.

(a) The group testimony

This type of testimony is contributed on behalf of a particular group of persons by a spokesman they have chosen, whose account they may correct or supplement. Thus when the king of the Kuba recites his testimony, he announces: 'You who are seated on the ground, if you have any accusations—such as: these are lies they are telling; they are not reporting the exact words; he goes on too long telling it this way—there is nothing to prevent you from scratching your back with your nail' (so as to interrupt and make the required emendation).[4]

At the *kuum* or secret conclave held by the Kuba in preparation for the recital of the group testimony, the spokesman is appointed and the testimony rehearsed, so that all are in agreement about it before it is recited in public. The group testimony is not peculiar to the Kuba, as is proved by examples cited by E. Meyerowitz.[5]

The fact that such a testimony is the concern of a group gives it a special character of its own. All those present must be in agreement about all the facts related, and nothing can be related that has not been agreed to unanimously. The testimony then acquires the character of an official statement, and at the same time it is a 'minimum' statement, for some of the members of the group may know fuller details about some of the facts which are not included in the account. In the Bushongo example already mentioned, it is said, with reference to the casting of the anvils, 'We were in agreement, we were in agreement with Mancu maShyaang, all this crowd came with the man of the Matoon clan'.[6] Almost everyone present knew much more about this matter, but no one interrupted because there had been no unanimity about the fuller details. So much for the characteristic features of the group testimony among the Kuba. Apparently elsewhere the vote for the spokesman must also be unanimous.

The group testimony, then, stems from one single tradition which is preserved by a whole group of persons, and its recital is under public control. Consequently the testimony adheres faithfully to the tradition, but provides a minimum version of it. A group testimony is always a minimum testimony.

(b) Dispute between informants

When two or more persons disagree about a tradition, the testimony produced, as a result of the dispute, by one of the parties to it must be attributed to all the parties to the dispute if it is found impossible to distinguish which parts of the testimony should be ascribed to which of the informants. When a dispute occurs, one or other of the following situations may arise: the parties to the dispute may adhere to their former testimonies, without introducing any changes; one party may adopt the whole or part of the other's testimony; the two parties may come to an arrangement whereby a new testimony is created which comes midway between the two former testimonies. Here is an example of a dispute among the Kuba that gave rise to a testimony which was a compromise. The chief of the Bokila had declared that when the Bokila arrived in the country they were its first inhabitants. During the course of a dispute with another group who also claimed to be the original inhabitants of the district, a declaration was made that the other chief had been the first to occupy the region, but that before his arrival the Bokila had set up a trading station for ivory, so that in a sense they were in effect the first occupants of the country.

Clearly a declaration resulting from a dispute must be attributed to the chains of transmission of the persons responsible for it. If one party has borrowed something from the other's testimony, then this part of his testimony derives from the chain of transmission of the other party. If a compromise is reached, then both chains of transmission have given rise to the statement. In such cases it is often impossible to determine which facts derive from which of the chains of transmission. This can only be established by comparison with other testimonies which derive exclusively from one or other of the chains.

(c) Interrogation of informants

A statement made in reply to a number of questions must be regarded as the work of two informants: the questioner and the person questioned. The testimony consists, in fact, not only of the replies, but also of the questions. Two kinds of questions may be distinguished: those which do and those which do not indicate the kind of reply expected. The latter are merely invitations to provide information, and cannot have any influence on the reply. They usually take the form of asking 'Tell me what you know about the past of your clan, your tribe, etc.', or simply 'What can you tell me about the past?' Clearly the replies are so little affected by questions of this kind that they must be regarded as testimonies that spring from the narrator alone. The questioner merely creates the occasion for giving the testimony.

It is a different matter when the question is put in a way that indicates the kind of reply expected. If one asks a Kuba: 'Who reigned before Mboong aleeng?' and he replies 'Shyaam', obviously the reply is not influenced by the question. But if the question is put in this way: 'Did Shyaam reign before Mboong aleeng?', then the reply is already suggested by the question. It stands to reason, then, that whenever a question can be answered by yes or by no, the testimony must be regarded as springing from both the questioner and the person questioned. Similarly if the question contains material which is repeated in the reply, there are grounds for attributing the testimony to both persons. Statements of this kind are only partially derived from the chain of transmission of the person questioned. For the rest, they simply consist of projections of information already in the possession of the questioner, and in this respect, should be attributed to the chains of transmission from which the information has been derived. In practice it is usually impossible to establish which part of the testimony is due to the influence of the questions and which stems from the tradition with which the person questioned is acquainted. Thus statements of this kind are generally unreliable.

5. Summary

In verbal testimonies, the informant stands in a very intimate relationship to his testimony, hence the nature of the testimony is primarily determined by the informant. But the relation between the testimony and the referent—the preceding testimony in the chain of transmission—is also important. Without it there would be no oral tradition. A further consequence of the verbality of a testimony is that it gives rise to variant versions. But in the case of oral tradition a special problem arises, which is that of distinguishing whether the various versions are variants of the same testimony, or whether they are in fact different testimonies because the referents are different.

The relation of the testimony to the tradition as a whole is also affected by the manner of testifying.

3. THE METHOD OF TRANSMISSION IN ORAL TRADITION

The transmission of oral traditions may follow certain definite rules, but it may also be a completely spontaneous affair, left entirely to chance. Where special methods and techniques exist, their purpose is to preserve the tradition as faithfully as possible and transmit it from one generation to the next. This may be done either by training people to whom the tradition is then entrusted, or by exercising some form of control over each recital of the tradition. Whatever the method may be, accurate transmission is more likely if a tradition is not public property, but forms the esoteric knowledge of a special group. The employment of mnemonic devices may also contribute towards ensuring accurate repetition of traditions.

1. Instruction

It has been found that among a large number of peoples without writing, and even among the Aztecs who did have writing, schools were set up for the purpose of giving systematic teaching of classical traditions. Here are some typical examples: in Africa, the schools of Bono-Mansu and of Rwanda;[7] in Polynesia, those of Hawaii, the Marquesas Islands, and New Zealand;[8] in America, those of the Incas and of the Aztecs.[9] It should, however, be noted that these examples all occur among peoples who had reached a considerable degree of state organization, and this would seem to be a prerequisite for scholarly institutions of this kind. As an example of how such institutions function, that of the Marquesas Islands might be mentioned. When a father desired to give his children special instruction, he built a large special house for the purpose, and hired the services of a bard who became the teacher. About thirty men and women, aged from twenty to thirty, would take advantage of the opportunity and participate in the lessons. All went to live in the newly constructed dwelling, and during the periods of instruction the pupils were taboo. The lessons lasted for a month and were then followed by a recess of about fifteen days, after which another period of instruction began. If the pupils did not make good progress, the bard would stop teaching and close the school. The lessons were given in two sessions each day, one in the morning and one in the afternoon. The outstanding feature of schools of this kind in Polynesia was that the instruction, and everything to do with it—down to the clothes worn by the pupils—was consecrated, and became taboo, because of the nature of what was taught.[10]

In the example quoted above, instruction was given by a specialist, as is the rule for schools of this kind. But other specialists in the preservation of traditions exist who are not in charge of a school, but who are employed as a sort of walking library. This type of specialist only transmits his knowledge to the man who will succeed him in office. This is an institution so widespread that the authors of *Notes and Queries* feel justified in saying that among those peoples who have a centralized form of government there is often found to be an official whose duty it is to recite their history at public ceremonies.[11]

Westermann states that officials of this kind are found at the courts of most African rulers.[12] It will be enough to mention here two examples of a highly developed and sophisticated form of specialization in the domain of history. In Rwanda, genealogists, memorialists, rhapsodists, and *abiiru* were each responsible for the faithful preservation of a certain category of traditions. The task of the genealogists, *abacurabwenge*, was to remember the lists of kings and queen-mothers; that of the memorialists, *abateekerezi*, to remember the most important events of the various reigns; the rhapsodists, *abasizi*, preserved the panegyrics on the kings; and lastly the *abiiru* preserved the secrets of the dynasty.[13] Specialization had reached such a point that an informant could declare to the Abbé Kagame, when questioned by him, that it was not his fault if he did not know

the answer to the question put to him, since he was not responsible for the preservation of these particular traditions. They
were the concern of other officials, whereas he had to remember
different traditions, of much greater importance.[14] With reference to the Akan States, Meyerowitz mentions the following
specialists: minstrels, masters of ceremony, royal drummers,
royal hornblowers, the king's spokesman, his grave priest, his
stool-carrier-chief, female soulbearers of the souls of deceased
queen-mothers, masters of ceremonies to the state gods, court
functionaries, and the administrator of the capital—each of
whom had to remember a particular part of the history of the
state and transmit it to his or her successor in office.[15]

2. *Control over recital of traditions*

An oral tradition may be accompanied by a system of sanctions
and rewards, which are meted out to those whose duty it is to know
the tradition according to whether they do or do not succeed in
reciting it without making any mistakes. This custom of meting
out sanctions and rewards was a direct outcome of the employment of specialists, and is an effective method of control for
ensuring accurate repetition of the testimony.

The Bushongo use only a mitigated form of sanctions. In
theory, no king could succeed to the throne if, during the
coronation ceremonies, he could not give a general description
of the history of the Kuba, and the candidate for an important
feminine role, the *mbaan*, could not be appointed if she could not
enumerate the names of her predecessors in office. In practice,
however, it would appear that the sanction had never been
applied. Nevertheless, the required results were achieved. The
actual successor to the throne applied himself to studying the
traditions in order to qualify for the succession.

In Polynesia it was usually ritual sanctions that were brought
to bear in cases of failure to be word-perfect when reciting a
tradition. As has been said above, in the Marquesas Islands
everything that was in any way connected with instruction in
such matters was regarded as sacred, so that it is not surprising
to find that when a mistake was made in reciting a tradition,
the ceremony sanctioned by the gods was abandoned.

In New Zealand, a single mistake in recital was enough to bring about the immediate death of the teacher who had made it.[16] Similar sanctions were found in Hawaii.[17] Elsewhere, and especially in Africa, the texts concerned with the worship of ancestors must be known thoroughly if the person who recites them does not wish to offend the ancestors and expose himself to their wrath.[18]

Ridicule also comes into play. Someone who does not know the traditions of his group is often the laughing-stock of the other members. This is what happens among the Kuba if someone does not know the clan slogan.

In Rwanda, the families of the rhapsodists provide an example of persons or groups entrusted with the guardianship of certain traditions who are granted certain privileges. They are exempted from corvées and are rewarded with small gifts when they recite short dynastic poems.[19]

3. Esoteric traditions

Some traditions may be a matter of esoteric knowledge, just as others may be known and recited by all ranks of the population. In the first case, they are only transmitted by certain persons attached to a particular institution, or are the property of a special group. No one else is allowed to transmit them, even if he should happen to be well informed about the tradition.

The Bushongo songs *ncyeem ingesh* are taught by a female specialist, the *shoong*, to the wives of the king. These songs are divided into two categories: the *ncyeem ibushepy*, which may be listened to by outsiders, and the *ncyeem ingesh* proper, which may never be performed in public, and which only the wives of the king may know. Whichever category they belong to, none of them may be performed or interpreted by outsiders. Similarly among the Kuba the tradition of the tribe is a secret and must not be known by outsiders who do not belong to the council that transmits it. Every esoteric tradition is of necessity preserved and transmitted through the medium of institutions. It could thus be said that all clan and family history comes under the heading of esoteric tradition, for, while it may be widely known by outsiders, it can never be transmitted by them. It is moreover obvious that traditions which are taught in schools are of an esoteric nature in virtue of the fact that they can only be taught in the school. In addition, such traditions are often exclusive to certain classes of the population, especially to the aristocracy and the priests. The only exception known to me is provided by the schools of the Aztecs.[20]

Thus esoteric traditions are in fact the property of certain special groups. Proprietorship in spoken legends is well attested in ethnological literature,[21] and a particular instance might be mentioned of ownership of historical tales, which occurs among the peoples on the Luapula. No sanctions are brought to bear against non-owners who recite the tales, but people would refrain from doing so for fear of spoiling it for the owner or because it would be bad manners.[22] The same is true of the Kuba.

In Rwanda, proprietary rights in traditions are taken more seriously. Kagame reports that, by a decision of the royal court, this or that poem was declared to be strictly hereditary in one family or another, and permission had to be obtained from a member of the family concerned before reciting it.[23]

Among the Trobriand Islanders of the Pacific a tradition could be bought. Thus it was that the chief Omarakana gave food and objects of value to the descendants of a certain Tomakam in exchange for the dance, the song, and the commentary on it, owned by them.[24]

The Inca kingdom provides an example of the use of several methods of transmission of traditions. It had four different kinds of history. The secret general history was taught in schools by specialists called *amauta*, who were housed and fed at the expense of the state and were exempt from taxes. Since this knowledge was esoteric, access to the schools was available only to the *élite*. History in a popularized form, expressed in poems, was given public performance, but the poets had no choice in the subject-matter, for after the death of each Inca, high state officials and *amauta* met together in council, decided upon the official history of the country, and chose the themes that could be popularized. Then the *quipumaoc* preserved all the traditions connected with figures, including chronological data. Was theirs an esoteric knowledge? There is no express statement about this, but it probably was, for the *quipumaoc* specialists also received specialized instruction. Finally, in each clan or *ayllus* which had a king as its founder, the genealogy of the king and the principal events of his reign became the subject of a tradition. It is also reported that certain historical lays could only be performed in the presence of the ruler, which indicates that they could be heard by outsiders. In the Inca kingdom all forms of history were strictly censored. On the death of a ruler who had led a disgraceful life, it was decided that his name alone should be preserved in the tradition and that all further facts concerning his reign should be omitted.

Thus, among the Inca, the state exercised total control over all traditions. Some historical episodes were diffused among the people for propaganda purposes, others kept secret but nevertheless preserved, while yet others were eliminated from the tradition as harmful precedents. Finally, those whose duty it was to know certain particular traditions were carefully selected, and specialists of this kind were encouraged to carry out their duties in a suitable manner by a system of privileges and sanctions. In these circumstances, it is not surprising to find that Rowe considered that all the traditions which have been recorded can be traced back to the official traditions of the capital. I am inclined to think that all the traditions were designed to present the Inca Empire in the light which would best preserve the existing regime.[25]

This examination of the instruction given concerning oral traditions, of the controls exercised, and of the existence of esoteric traditions, brings out the fact that traditions were often transmitted from one generation to the next by a method laid down for the purpose, and that in many societies without writing particular attention was paid to careful preservation and accurate transmission of these traditions. For this purpose, use was often made of mnemonic devices.

4. *Mnemonic devices*

For helping to remember traditions, use was sometimes made of material objects which were passed on from one generation to the next, which had certain memories attached to them that facilitated remembrance of the tradition. In other cases, a type of tradition which remained firmly engraved in people's memories was used in order to associate with it another tradition more easily forgotten. Both these are instances of mnemonic devices. It should be noted, however, with regard to material objects, that they are sometimes historical sources in themselves, but needless to say, any information they supply in this way, apart from the information conveyed when used as a mnemonic as device, does not form part of oral tradition.

Examples of mnemonic devices provided by objects are the use of the *quipu*, of carved sticks, of objects handed down traditionally, and of others connected with the land.

It was only in Peru that the *quipu* was used. It was a series of knotted cords of different colours and lengths which were tied together and attached to the head-dress in the form of a fringe. The colours, as well as the knots and the length of the string, all had mnemonic significance. The procedure was adopted in the Inca Empire for preserving oral traditions, particularly traditions concerned with figures, including chronological data. Apparently other non-arithmetical data were also transmitted by this method, according to Father Morua's account. He was astonished to find what a wide variety of things concerning the past these knotted cords could give information about—the length of each king's reign, whether he was good or bad, brave or cowardly—in short, the *quipu* could be read just as if they were books. He adds that a monk of his order had made experiments with an old Indian which were conclusive: the man understood his *quipu* just as if he were reading a book.[26]

After the native population was converted by Spanish missionaries, it often happened that penitents at confession read off their sins from *quipu* they had constructed for this purpose.[27]

The Incas went a stage further than this, and also used iconographic material for preserving their traditions. But here it must be admitted that the pictures give such clear information about the facts they represent that this is a technique that comes very close to writing. In a similar manner the marvellous bronze plaques of Benin were used not only to heighten the prestige of the ruler, but also as mnemonic material. They were stacked in a special room and consulted when required.[28] The paintings which decorated the royal palaces in Dahomey seem to have fulfilled a similar purpose.[29]

A mnemonic device much used in Polynesia is a stick on which incisions are made to which a meaning is attached.[30] The Kuba also employ this device, but only for keeping a record of financial transactions.

Another type of mnemonic device consists of objects which are traditionally handed down. In the Empire of Bono-Mansu, a pot called a *kuduo* was placed in a special temple at the death of each ruler. Every year, a nugget of gold was placed in the pot of the reigning king, so that when he died the number of years he had reigned could be established with precision.[31] In Rwanda a similar device is found, for every year at the time of the harvest festival the *abiiru* receive an object to be preserved.[32] Isolated cult objects of ancient origin often have a history attached to them. The Kuba say that the *mboombaam* knives which they still possess today are copies of the swords formerly used by the Whites.[33]

In Ashanti, the keeper of the king's stool must know the history of the 'stool'—that is, the past history of the kingdom.[34] In the Akan States objects were made as souvenirs of important events, and the keepers who saw to the preservation of these objects had to know the history attached to them.[35]

In Buganda, a ceremony was held at the new moon at which urns containing the umbilical cords of all the former kings, kings' sisters, and queen-mothers were brought to the court. As he passed before the reigning king, the bearer of each urn shouted out the name of the owner of the urn he carried. In this way all the names of the royal genealogy were remembered.[36]

The landscape, with its individual features, whether natural or man-made, can be used as a mnemonic device. It can give rise to well-known local legends. Cunnison reports that among the peoples on the Luapula, a number of traditions are only recited when passing the places mentioned in the tales.[37] A large part of their local history is contained in the prayers offered to the spirits of certain places.[38] Frobenius notes that in the Western Sudan, the site of the royal tombs is well known, and the tombs might be regarded as historical records carved into the landscape, because of the local legends connected with them.[39]

In other parts of Africa, the guardians of royal tombs know the history of the kings buried there, or at least know their names. This is so in the whole interlacustrine region, as well as among the Kuba, Lozi, Nyakusa, Xhosa, and probably many other peoples.[40]

Elsewhere tombs may not have specially appointed guardians, but the sites of those belonging to ancestors—chiefs who had founded villages, clans, or lineages, etc.—are always known by everyone. In fact, it could be said that wherever the cult of ancestors is practised, their tombs are known and memories of the past are connected with them.

Among mnemonic devices other than the use of material objects, songs and drum rhythms must be mentioned. In all traditions that are sung, mnemonic aid is found in the melody and rhythm of the song.[41] Throughout Africa drum rhythms are used as a mnemonic aid. Words and phrases can be transposed into the drum code in all languages in which the height of the tone plays a phonological role. It is easier to remember these rhythms than the phrases themselves from which the tonal melody derives. In West Africa, the history of the royal house of Dagomba, as well as that of the Akan States, is partially preserved by means of the drum code.[42] In other parts of Africa it is mainly eulogistic names and slogans that are preserved by the drum telephone.[43] Lastly, the actual form of a testimony may act as a mnemonic device.[44]

5. Summary

From what has been said, it can be seen that oral traditions are not always transmitted in the same way. A society may have certain institutions for regulating the method of transmission of certain traditions in such a way as to preserve the original testimony of the observer as faithfully as possible. Thus the historian can assess to what extent the method of transmission used for any particular tradition is likely to have provided favourable circumstances for an accurate handing-down of the proto-testimony upon which it is based. The next section studies the distortions that the proto-testimony may undergo due to the process of transmission.

39

4. DISTORTIONS DUE TO TRANSMISSION

Changes may occur to the initial testimony of a tradition as it gets handed down in the form of a hearsay account from one informant to the other until the last testimony in the chain of transmission is reached. Each informant may introduce changes of various kinds, but only omissions due to a failure of memory, and explanatory interpolations, are directly connected with the actual transmission of the tradition. Other changes introduced by informants into their accounts are of a more general nature and have no particular connection with the process of transmission. For this reason, discussion of them is postponed until later.[45]

1. Failure of memory

Failure of memory may bring about omissions and confusion—and indirectly, explanatory interpolations—in the successive testimonies of a chain of transmission. As this may occur in all kinds of oral tradition, it is necessary to find out the degree of distortion any particular tradition may have undergone through failure of memory.

A number of writers have expressed the opinion that peoples without writing possess exceptional powers of memory.[46] Others are of the opinion that only traditions concerning the not too distant past can be relied upon. For them, failure of memory is in direct ratio to the length of time a tradition has lasted.[47] Neither of these arguments will hold. So far there exists no proof that there is any inborn difference in cerebral faculties between the various races of man. Moreover, it is a well established fact that a decisive factor in the tremendous storage capacity of the human memory is the amount of attention given to the data that have to be memorized. Practice in the process of memorization is another factor that comes into play. Consequently failure of memory is directly related to the method of transmission, the degree of control exercised over recital of the testimony, and the frequency with which the testimony is repeated. These three factors together provide some means of estimating the amount of attention that has been given to the process of memorization and the amount of training undergone for the purpose. The length of time a tradition has lasted is in itself of quite secondary importance.[48]

(a) *The method of transmission*
Traditions which have been transmitted with the aid of mnemonic devices will be less susceptible of distortion through failure of memory than others. The same is true of traditions in fixed form taught by specialists in schools. If in addition to the operation of these two factors a tradition has rights of ownership or substantial privileges attached to it, the possibility of failure of memory may be entirely eliminated. In Hawaii a hymn of 618 lines was recorded which was identical with a version collected in the neighbouring island of Oahu.[49] In Rwanda, variant versions of the dynastic poems occur, but the divergences are 'of no moral significance in relation to the whole'.[50] Both are instances of texts taught by specialists and learnt by heart. But in the first case, a heavy ritual sanction is brought to bear if there is a faulty rendering of the texts, whereas in the second, no sanction is in practice brought to bear, although in theory it is potentially there. Hence arises a difference between the two. In Rwanda, there are occasional signs of a failure of memory, but not in Hawaii. It should be noted that texts learnt by heart are not necessarily less subject to failure of memory than free texts. A number of variant versions of Kuba clan slogans occur, despite the fact that these are fixed texts. But they are not learnt in any systematic way, and this is the essential prerequisite for accurate transmission. On the other hand, it would be possible to quote many instances of historical narratives in Rwanda which are very little affected by failure of memory, in spite of the fact that they are in free narrative form. But these tales were in part transmitted by people who had received a systematic training, and there is every reason to suppose that it was they who were responsible for handing down the tradition without any marked distortion, whereas versions handed down by 'amateurs' bore considerable signs of failure of memory.

(b) *Control over recital*
Controlled testimonies are less subject to distortion through failure of memory than others, because the precise purpose of

control is to point out omissions and clear up confusions due to the informant having a lapse of this kind. Group traditions are the standard form of controlled transmission. They are transmitted within a particular group, and no member of the group may recite the tradition unless the whole group is present to ratify unanimously the accuracy of the testimony. The traditions preserved by the councils of the Kuba chiefs are a case in point. Here a tradition is gradually handed down from one generation to the next, and not sporadically as is frequently the case when it is transmitted from one individual to another. What happens is that new members are accepted into the group who learn the traditions, and older members die; but since the older members do not all die simultaneously, nor do the new members all enter into the group simultaneously, so there is an overall continuity in the transmission of the traditions.

But testimonies which are not transmitted within an institution can also be controlled. A universal example is provided by legal precedents. These are invoked every time a particular situation calls for them, and are controlled by the party opposed to those who have invoked them, for an inaccurate precedent is immediately contested. Sanctions of various kinds provide another method of control which can be extremely effective, as is demonstrated by the example from Hawaii already quoted. As a general rule it may be said that the more a tradition is associated with a vested interest, and the more this interest is a concern of the public as a whole and is functionally important, the more exacting will be the control over its recital, and the better the guarantee against distortion through failure of memory. The religious traditions of Polynesia are very important for society, for they uphold the beliefs about the creation of the world, and it is thought that an inaccurate knowledge of them could give rise to natural cataclysms. In Rwanda the traditions of the *ubwiiru* are a code which regulates the powers of the ruler, guides his actions, and proclaims that his rule is justified by a divine right inherited from the past. These traditions are vital for the preservation of the monarchy in Rwanda, and that is why their transmission is rigorously controlled. On the other hand, the history of a family of Rwanda farmers or Polynesian fishermen will be transmitted in haphazard fashion and will soon be obliterated from human memory. It is the testimonies that have least to do with the public concerns of a society that are soonest forgotten.

(c) Frequency of repetition

Frequency of repetition is a factor which gives some indication of the extent to which a tradition may have suffered through failure of memory, because infrequent repetition makes this more likely. With many traditions, the frequency of repetition is laid down by custom. Among the Bushongo, the tribal tradition is only recited at the coronation of each new king. The dynastic songs, *ncyeem ingesh*, are sung once a month, at the new moon. Legal precedents are only cited in cases where they apply. Clan slogans are recited at the death of the member of a kinship group or in eulogy of the star dancers of the clan. Lastly, the *ncok* songs have no regular time laid down for their performance, which depends on the whim of the moment. In Burundi, all traditions are recited at irregular intervals, whereas in Rwanda, for instance, they are usually only recited at feasts held at the king's court or the courts of the great chiefs, or, in the case of the *bwiiru*, on occasions when a practical problem has to be solved—the *bwiiru* thus performing a similar function to that of legal precedents. Sometimes traditions are repeated very infrequently. Certain Mande traditions are only recited once every seven years.[51]

On the other hand, frequent repetition does not of itself preclude a possible lapse of memory. The frequent repetition of uncontrolled testimonies transmitted without special care can lead to a more rapid distortion of a tradition than infrequent recital. Indeed, every time a tradition is recited the testimony may be a variant version. Hence frequency by itself cannot enable any estimate to be made as to the distorting influence of failure of memory. Only when it is considered in conjunction with the methods and the control of transmission can it be a guide in this matter.

(d) How to evaluate the effects of failure of memory

It is usually easy to evaluate the effects of failure of memory if one has at one's disposal several testimonies belonging to the same tradition. It is enough to observe the extent of variation between the various versions recorded to arrive at an accurate assessment. This applies not only to fixed texts, in which a word-for-word comparison can be made, but also to free texts, in which the general contents can be compared. The technique of textual comparison can be equally precise for both kinds of text.[52]

If, however, one has only one or two testimonies at one's disposal, it is usually impossible to do more than make a rough check on the final informant's powers of memory. To do this, one must try to obtain further statements from him at longer or shorter intervals. The variants in his testimonies will then give some indication as to his powers of memory. Short of this, one has to make an estimate of the extent to which failure of memory may have distorted the tradition, based on the particular method of transmission employed.

2. *Explanatory interpolations*

It often happens that traditions become incomprehensible to the informants who relate them, either because the language has become archaic (which is often the case with fixed texts), or because the events spoken of bear reference to customs which no longer exist, and which are thus unfamiliar to the informants. In the *ncyeem ingesh* songs of the Kuba, many of the words have become incomprehensible. If one asks for an explanation, the only reply people will give will be to say: 'It is in *lambil*, the ancient language of the Bushongo. We no longer know what it means.' But in other cases they invent explanations to answer questions put to them by listeners. A case in point is the invention of popular etymologies. When it comes to incomprehensible events, the narrator almost invariably invents some explanation which he incorporates into the tradition itself. An example is furnished by a Kuba song about a war that was fought between the Kuba and the 'Whites' of the sixteenth century—the Portuguese. The tradition as it now exists tells that the two sides did not have any arms, but threw either sand or water at each other, according to which of the variant versions is being used. But this present form of the tradition derives entirely from the song itself, in which battle effects are rendered by an onomato-poeic *pu, pu, pu.* The present-day Kuba have inferred that this could only represent a noise made either by sand or water, but it seems highly probable that what it was originally intended to represent was the sound of the impact of cannon balls as they hit the earth. The original observers probably attempted to reproduce this sound of impact by *pu, pu, pu,* but the meaning of this has become completely lost to their descendants.

Interpolations of this kind are usually fairly easy to detect. They always tend to provide some explanation of the pheno-mena described, and amount to being an interpretation of the original tradition. By distinguishing carefully between the tradition and the interpretation given to it, it is possible to detect most interpolations of this kind. The only time when difficulty may be encountered in assessing the effects of in-comprehension is when unexplained archaic words occur. It often happens that as informants transmit these incomprehen-sible words one to another, the sound values change from one testimony to the next, and a word may become distorted after a certain number of hearsay accounts have been transmitted. But on the analogy of the transmission of proper names, such as clan names, it is unlikely that phonetic distortion will be of frequent occurrence. There is one type of passage which does not give rise to an explanatory interpolation but which is retained intact in the tradition because of its curiosity value for listeners. Thus the Kuba still talk of the Whites who wore garments of soft iron (coats of mail). The Portuguese ceased wearing coats of mail during the sixteenth century, but tradition still mentions them because it is a peculiar detail that strikes people's imagination.

3. Summary

The proto-testimony of a tradition may undergo certain distor-tions during the course of transmission which are specifically due to the very process of transmission. They all result from the fact that things become lost to memory, either through some lapse on the part of an informant, or because the circumstances which would explain the events described have been forgotten.

But the extent to which a tradition has become distorted can be very precisely estimated—sometimes even with complete accuracy. For assessing lapses of memory, the various versions of a tradition can be compared, and for detecting interpolations, a distinction can be made between the tradition and the interpretation of it which may be included in the tradition for aetiological purposes.

In this chapter I have stressed the special nature of oral tradition. It is differentiated from other kinds of historical source by being a chain of testimonies. Each testimony is an indirect account—as are all historical sources apart from archaeological evidence—which implies that it is strongly influenced by the informant; its verbality—a quality shared with rumours and eyewitness accounts, the latter of which may equally well form the basis of a written tradition—has as consequence that a tradition must be defined as including all the statements of an informant concerning a single determinant, which in this case consists of traditions. The special nature of oral tradition lies in the special way in which it is transmitted. Various methods of transmission may be used, some of which are capable of ensuring that the proto-testimony does not alter much in the course of transmission. If distortions occur through lapses of memory, it is comparatively easy to detect to what extent the final testimony has suffered from such distortions.

The final testimony is all that remains of an oral tradition, and in comparison with the testimonies forming preceding links in the chain, has a special value for the historian, because it is a testimony produced on request, the recital of which the historian can observe, and from which he can deduce most of the features of preceding testimonies. Hence the next chapter will be devoted to a study of the testimony itself. It is only through testimonies that historical research by means of oral tradition can be carried out, and in order to carry it out successfully, it is first of all necessary to know what a testimony is, and to be able to understand it. This is the problem to which the next chapter is devoted.

CHAPTER III

Understanding the Testimony

IF a historian wishes to understand the events of the past related by a testimony, the first thing he must do is to understand the testimony. He must first of all be able to recognize whether the testimony he is studying has a historical content or not, and estimate what effect this is likely to have. Next he must carefully examine its structure, for this may throw light on certain aspects of the testimony—perhaps on the reasons why it came into existence, and certainly on its meaning and the way it was transmitted. Finally he must make every effort to arrive at as complete an understanding as possible of its meaning, so that his interpretation will throw as much light as possible on the information it conveys. The historical content of a testimony, its structure, and its meaning, are the three topics discussed in this chapter.

I. CHARACTERISTIC FEATURES OF A TESTIMONY

It is possible to distinguish between various types of oral tradition and so of verbal testimonies. Each type has certain special features which affect the testimony and give each type of testimony a different kind of value as a historical source. These features are: the intentions or lack of intentions behind a testimony, the significance attached to it, its form and the literary category to which it belongs, the method of transmission used, and the manner in which the testimony is delivered. By making a survey of each and all of these features we can establish criteria of classification which will enable us to divide testimonies into various categories according to the features displayed. This will lead to the possibility of establishing a valid typology of oral traditions as historical sources, which will be elaborated when I come to discuss the question of the historical information that can be derived from oral testimonies.

1. *Intentional and unintentional testimonies*

The most important distinction to be established among the various types of oral tradition is that between testimonies which do, whether intentionally or unintentionally, produce a record of historical facts, and those which do not.[1] A testimony always has an aim of some kind, but it is not necessarily aimed at recording history. When a Bushongo song about an event which took place during the reign of King Kot aNce makes a passing reference to pearls, this is certainly not because there was any intention to convey the information that pearls had been introduced into the country in the eighteenth century. Nevertheless, the fact has been conveyed, even if the informant was unaware that he was conveying it. This can therefore be regarded as an unintentional testimony.

There is no such thing as a testimony that is exclusively aimed at recording history. A testimony could only be described as having this aim if it was exclusively intended to convey information about events of the past in order to enrich our knowledge of the past. But this is something one would search for in vain wherever writing is unknown. It follows therefore that testimonies which aim to record history have another aim as well, and they can be divided into those in which the main aim is historical and those in which it is not. If it is, the secondary aim is not likely to cause much distortion to the facts conveyed, but distortion will probably be more marked if the historical aim is secondary. Here are examples of each of these possibilities. When a chief gives a list of his ancestors in order to prove that he is the rightful chief, it is obvious that the historical aim is subordinate to the political one. But when the same chief —among the Kuba at any rate—recites the list of places at which his camp halted during the migrations of former times, in order to enhance his prestige in the minds of his listeners by displaying his knowledge, the main aim is clearly a historical one.[2] Although he relates past events in order to win respect, this concomitant purpose is scarcely likely to affect the historical facts thus reported. But as soon as a historical aim can be discerned, the testimony is an intentional one, even if the aim is secondary. And as soon as a testimony is intentional, it is influenced by the informant.

2. Significance

A varying degree of significance is attached to each tradition within the society in which it is handed down. Some traditions are imposed from above and ratified by those in power, in which case the facts they contain are accepted as the officially recognized truth about the past, and any other interpretation is excluded. These are official traditions. An example of this kind of tradition is the *ubwiiru*, the dynastic code of Rwanda. The official nature of the traditions contained in it is so marked, that the Abbé Kagame, who recorded them, had to be admitted as a guardian of the tradition by the king of Rwanda before he was allowed to set them down in writing. Moreover the guardians of the tradition still insist that they must not be published, particularly not in the Rwandese language, for these traditions are secret, and it is feared that readers might re-transmit them without official permission. The guardians are also afraid that they might lose the important privileges attached to their office once the tradition became public property. The official character of the *ubwiiru* is further emphasized by the fact that the king of Rwanda does not have control over the tradition. He may not have it recited whenever he pleases or to whomsoever he pleases. Only the guardians, formerly the highest officials in Rwanda, can decide this in council.[3]

Private traditions consist of those transmitted by individuals or groups which have no official ratification. In Burundi, for instance, there are no official traditions about any part of its history. History is told in proverbs and in songs, and above all in tales, which the Rundi do not distinguish from tales and fables with non-historical themes. The absence of any official dogma enables each informant to express himself in his own way. Those who like talking will produce a work of art, while those who are less communicative will tell their tales in a laconic, not to say telegraphic, style. Of course the idea of official as distinct from private traditions must not be taken too literally, but it must not be left out of account, since it has some bearing on the amount of social or political importance a tradition may have.

Thus, a testimony concerning clan history is private in so far as it contains information referring to the past of the tribe to which the clan belongs, for this information is not imposed from above for acceptance by all the members of the tribe as the official truth. Nevertheless, as regards events which only bear relation to the past of the clan, clan history is an official source.

It goes without saying that official history is more subject to distortions than private history, since the latter has few, if any, public interests to defend. On the other hand, the informant seems to put a more marked individual stamp on the testimony in the case of private testimonies.

But to find out the significance attached to a tradition, it is not enough to establish the extent to which it is official or private: it is also necessary to discover what the attitude of the guardians of tradition is in each instance. This is a psychological factor which cannot be used as a criterion of classification, because it does not permit of establishing clear-cut categories. Nevertheless it is obvious that their attitude will have an influence on the content of traditions, and traditions which are held to be sacred will be transmitted more faithfully than those which, while admittedly containing information about past events, are appreciated for their entertainment value rather than as historical documents.[4]

The significance attached to a tradition is also connected with its social role, or with the function which it fulfils. Traditions always serve some particular interest, and moreover provide those elements in the social system which together form the educational and recreational aspects of the culture of a society. The function of a tradition depends primarily on the significance attached to it, as is illustrated by the following example. Among the Bushongo, the purpose of certain magical songs is to reinforce the vital powers of the ruler. Their aim is not historical, but religious. Their function is political, because of the significance attached to them, for in the minds of the people, if they were to fall into neglect, this would mean that the political structure is no longer capable of survival.

There are numerous instances in which the function of a testimony influences its content. For example, a number of myths are exclusively aimed at providing an explanation of the creation of the world and of society as it exists, and their function is to justify the existing political structure. An eloquent proof of this is provided by the myths found in many parts of Africa explaining the arrival of a European administration.[5]

Many traditions are used to justify not only one, but several of the structures which form part of society. Thus the Polynesian genealogies have an important bearing on economic, social, political, and religious structures. Rights of landownership, social relations and the personal status of individuals in their relationship with one another, and rights of succession to hereditary political office, were regulated according to the genealogical position of each individual, and this was of religious importance as well, because the amount of *mana*—of sacred vital force—was similarly determined.[6] Clearly it is not easy, as this example shows, to establish any absolute classification of traditions according to their function. It is necessary to find out in each particular case what functions a tradition fulfilled.[7]

3. Structure and literary categories

Obviously the formal structure of a testimony will lend it a particular character, and here the most important distinction to be made is that between fixed texts and free texts. But formal distinctions can be carried still further, for in theory it would be equally possible to classify testimonies according to their internal structure, which provides a vehicle for the content of a tradition, as to do so according to their outward formal structure. But as far as I know, this has never been done, although it is a criterion that has been used in the establishment of literary categories.

Bernheim, Feder, and Bauer have all suggested a classification of traditions according to literary categories.[8] In a classification of this kind, account must be taken both of outward form and of internal structure, as well as of stylistic peculiarities and of the actual content of a testimony.[9] This means that the use of literary categories as a criterion of classification is often a complicated matter. But it is useful because of its importance for the interpretation of testimonies. It is, however, impossible to make a universally valid classification according to literary categories, because the same text may come under a different literary category in a different cultural context. An example will illustrate this. De La Fontaine's moral fable, *The Ant and the Grasshopper*, was transformed by the Shuswap Indians into a tale which explained why the grasshopper jumps and eats grass.[10] The content changed its meaning in the passage from one culture to another. The form may also change. The same tradition may appear in one place as a tale, and in another as a poem or even as a song. Within each culture, however, the traditions belonging to that culture can be classified into groups based on literary categories.[11]

4. *Method of transmission*

Here the fundamental distinction is that between traditions which are transmitted at random from one generation to the next, and those which are transmitted according to certain rules, and with the aid of special techniques. Thus one can distinguish between traditions that are transmitted with and without mnemonic aids, with and without special teaching, with and without controls, and between those preserved by special groups and those which form part of the common heritage.

5. *The manner of testifying*

The manner of testifying influences the contents of the testimony. If the informant is an individual, the testimony will reflect the tradition as it is interpreted by the informant. If the informant is a group and the testimony a group testimony, it will only be a minimum version, although a version that has been authenticated by the group as a whole, and thus a version which shows that control has been exercised on the transmission of the tradition. If the testimony results from a dispute or from questioning, it will have more than one source, and these must be distinguished from each other. Because of the influence which the manner of testifying has on the relation between the resulting testimony and the tradition which it relates, it is useful to distinguish between individual and group testimonies, those resulting from disputes, and those resulting from questioning.

6. Other criteria of classification

Bauer and Feder put forward other criteria for distinguishing between different kinds of testimony. Bauer makes a distinction between oral traditions which have been written down and those which have not.[12] This seems to me to be a secondary consideration, for in point of fact, a verbal testimony that has been recorded in writing is still just as much the outcome of an oral tradition as one which has not been committed to writing.

A criterion of classification used by Feder is whether the testimony is anonymous or not.[13] This is supposed to be a criterion of reliability. What immediately strikes me is that this supposition would not work in practice, and I find the criterion useless as a reliability test, for it often happens that there is no way of finding out whether testimonies which spring from a known source are reliable or not, whereas it is often possible to check the reliability of anonymous testimonies, particularly if one is sufficiently familiar with the cultural context.

Another criterion put forward by Feder is the length of time a tradition has lasted.[14] But this criterion does not permit of establishing clear-cut distinctions, and it is difficult to see why, for instance, he should have regarded proverbs as traditions which last a short period of time, and historical lays as traditions which last a long period of time. Furthermore, the classification implies that the reliability of a tradition is in direct ratio to the length of time it lasts, which does not accord with the facts. With regard to reliability, there is no doubt that the method of transmission is of far greater importance than the length of time a tradition has lasted.

7. *Summary*

The features I have described are the only ones worth considering when attempting to assess the reliability of a testimony, for they are the features which directly affect the testimony itself, and which account for its manner of composition, and for any distortions or statements without foundation which it may contain.

The survey made in this section would seem to be simply a résumé of various topics and features discussed elsewhere in this study. I have, indeed, already spoken of the distortions that arise from the methods of transmission and the manner of testifying, and in the following sections shall speak again of the structure and meaning of a testimony, and again in the next chapter of its aims, function, and significance.

The reason for this is that a historian, if he is to apply the methods of historical criticism, must assess what part each of these features has played in the formation of the testimony he is analysing. The study of how these features affect a testimony is a major part of his work as a historian, so that a survey of the characteristic features of a testimony amounts to being a survey of the problems with which he is faced.

2. THE STRUCTURE OF THE TESTIMONY

A testimony is always composed according to certain rules which restrict the informant's choice as to the way in which he expresses its content. So, in order to understand a testimony, it is important to know what these rules are. The structure of a text includes both its outward formal structure and its internal structure, and these are dealt with separately in the first two sub-sections of this section. Analysis of these leads to a discussion, in the third sub-section, of what we can learn from them about the testimony itself.

1. *The outward formal structure*

The categories in the outward form of a text are not literary, but linguistic. From the linguistic point of view a distinction can be made between formal and non-formal texts. In the latter, only the ordinary rules of grammar have to be obeyed, but in the former, certain linguistic regularities—phonological, morphological, or syntactical—also have to be observed. It would be possible to classify testimonies according to the particular laws to which they have to conform—laws of quantity or scansion, of rhyme, or tone, of morphology, or of syntax; but because of the special nature of oral tradition, I shall for extra-linguistic reasons divide the formal factors into two groups: a group containing the various factors which influence the construction of the testimony, and a group containing those syntactical factors which operate in the process of transmission. I shall call these groups: formal factors affecting the testimony, and formal factors affecting transmission.

(a) *Formal factors affecting the testimony*

Some time ago, Jousse, in an article that aroused a great deal of interest, maintained that the whole of oral literature was subjected to formal laws—mainly syntactical—which made it clearly distinguishable from written literature. Whatever the oral text might be, and from whatever culture it came from, it would be found to obey formal rules of some kind. His thesis, which was mainly based on biblical texts, is by no means convincing. The only marked difference between written and oral literature of fairly regular occurrence is that repetition is more frequently employed in oral literature.[15] But there is no special form belonging to oral literature alone.

Formal texts do occur in oral literature, but so far they have been very little studied. Whatever rules of versification are followed derive their linguistic features from the nature of the language in question. Thus the tones of syllables are used as formal elements in the proverbs of the Luba of the Kasai.[16] Oral literature uses quantity as a basis for verse scansion in a way that is analogous, in spite of differences, to the way it is used in Romance and French literature. There is one category of Rwanda verse that uses it, and a category of Rundi verse does the same; and the device plays a role in the poetry of the Nkundo, the Luba, and probably also of the Bushongo.[17]

(b) *Formal factors affecting transmission*

The formal distinction which particularly concerns the transmission of traditions is that between a fixed text learnt by heart, in which the form of the testimony is part of the tradition, and a free text, in which only the content belongs to the tradition. With fixed tests, the expectation is that the words and the order in which they come will be identical in all testimonies belonging to the same tradition. Every time the Rundi song *Remeera ryaa Nini, intaaho yabaami* ('Remeera of Nini, the place of the entry of the kings') is sung, one expects to hear a repetition of the same words in the same order. It does, however, sometimes happen that a tradition which an informant declares to be cast in a fixed form is found to have variants when other versions are recorded. But the intention is that it should have a fixed form, and the predominating tendency is to keep to the fixed form.

The formal distinction made here is valid enough, but it does not in practice apply to all testimonies. It is not difficult to imagine a case of a testimony that is not subjected to any formal rules, but which nevertheless is transmitted in a fixed form, and such cases are quite common. The dynastic poems of Rwanda, and prayers in many cultures, are examples in point. It is only with regard to the process of transmission that the distinction is operative, for if the tradition to be transmitted is a fixed text, the informant must reproduce every detail of the linguistic form, whereas he does not have to do so with a free text.

Attention should be drawn to the fact that while all formal testimonies are fixed testimonies, fixed testimonies can also include non-formal texts, as is shown by the examples mentioned. That is why I have coined the terms formal text, as opposed to non-formal text, and free text, as opposed to fixed text, so as to distinguish between formal criteria, and the criteria for the classification of traditions. The choice of these terms is not a very happy one, since it is because of certain formal characteristics that a text may be said to be a fixed one. The terms 'poetry' and 'prose' might have been used instead of formal and non-formal text. But in common parlance, poetry is a word which usually indicates a stylistic quality rather than something subjected to formal rules, so to avoid any misunderstanding I have refrained from using these terms here.

2. *The internal structure*

Most oral texts, although not all, have an internal pattern of arrangement. The content is not presented in random fashion, but is set forth in accordance with certain rules, and these rules enable a further classification of oral literature to be made, based on the kind of internal structure displayed.

It has already been realized that fixed texts, whether formal or not, have an internal structure. An example of the manner in which fixed texts are composed is provided by the *ibisigo*, the dynastic poems of Rwanda. These poems are composed in a style which distinguishes them from the two other main poetic categories in Rwanda: pastoral poetry, and warrior's poetry. Their purpose is to glorify the kings by telling of their mighty deeds. They form a category which can be further subdivided into three sub-categories, each with a different structure. The *impakanizi* consist of strophes separated by a refrain. Each strophe extols the reign of a king, from the first king of the dynasty to the one for whom the poem was composed. The *ibyanzu* has a similar construction, but deals only with events in the reigns of a few kings. Lastly, the *ikobyo* does not consist of strophes and only sings the praises of the king to whom the poem is offered. All these form part of a whole which falls into three quite distinctive parts: the introduction (*interuro*), the main body of the work which goes through all the names (*impakanizi, ibyanzu,* and *ikobyo*), and the peroration (*umusaayuuko*), which contains the traditional prayer of the poet to the king. A further feature of this literary category is that the poems are composed in a special style, in which use is made of symbolic statements, archaic words, words specially coined for this type of poetry, and words without meaning for filling in gaps in the line.[18]

But it is of even greater importance to realize that nonformal, free texts also always have an internal structure. I shall illustrate this by means of a Burundi tale.

THE STORY OF MITIMIGAMBA[19]

(a) 1. The story of Mitimigamba: then they depart; they take provisions saying 'Let us go and make war against Ruganguuza so that I may be king. As for Ruganguuza, we shall kill him.' They take provisions, they set off.

2. When Mitimigamba is on his way, the king with whom he has set out feels hungry and says 'Mitimigamba'—and Mitimigamba replies: 'Calm yourself, king of Burundi, I know what it is'—'Since you knew', he says to him, 'what is it I was going to say?'—'You were going to say', he replies, 'that we should lay down the provisions beside that bush, that you should eat, and that then we should continue on our way to make war against Ruganguuza.' It was so. So he lays them down. He eats.

3. He says to himself that they must take up their load again. He says: 'Mitimigamba.'—'Calm yourself, I know, my friend.' —'Since you know, what was I going to say?'—'You were going to say', he replies, 'that I should place the provisions on my head again and we should depart.'

4. They go a little further, they begin again. He says: 'Mitimigamba?'—And Mitimigamba replies: 'Calm yourself, my friend, I know.'—'Since you know, what was I going to say?'— He replies: 'You were going to say that we should take off these fine clothes we are wearing and then we should go and pay court to the king.'—They arrive there. 'We are going to pay court to the king, we shall clothe ourselves like those who pay court.'—They agree to do this. They take off their clothes. They re-dress in servants' clothes.

(b) 5. They arrive at the king's and pay him court. They say: 'Take us under your protection, guard us.'—'Very well', he replies, 'let each state the work he wishes to do.' The one says: 'Let me milk the cows.' The other says: 'Let me be your servant.' The one goes among the servants: this is Mitimigamba; the king goes among the milkers.

6. During the night, they counted up the days their journey had taken. Then he comes and says: 'Well, since you are awake, I am a servant, I know what goes on around the king.

58

You are a milker we are going to send a message.' Then they thought about whom to send to warn the army which had stayed behind in the rear. Thus they conspired together while everyone was asleep.

7. The king, this king war is being made against,[20] is asleep. Ah, eh, he wakes up, saying: 'What is that that is rumbling?' The king[21] replies: 'Hm, O king of Burundi, it is the rain. It rumbles over Muguruka of Muhunde,[22] who bellows whenever someone is about to throw a lance at him and howls whenever someone is about to throw a stone at him. There are eight hens looked after by eight girls. When it rains, the rains will destroy the *inyaambo* cows.[23] They will not be milked any more.'—'Is it true?' he asks.—'Yes,' replies the other. He leaves it at that, day breaks, he departs.

8. They are told: 'Go and look for firewood which you will set alight when it is time to go to bed.' He tells the servant. He goes to look for it in the forest. There he goes to Muguruka, Muguruka of Muhunde. He splits firewood. When he brings it back it crackles.

9. 'Hm' he wakes up.[24] 'This firewood should not be set alight, the fire which crackles in this way.' The other replies: 'Let it be set alight, let it be set alight.' The first says: 'It must not be set alight.'

(c) 10. The army is still in the rear. After a short while, the army of which it was said that it would destroy the cows, so that they would be milked no more, arrives. He enters his room.[25] 'We have got you', they say. He enters his room and cuts his throat. Then the king who set out with Mitimigamba is enthroned. Ruganguuza dies.

An episode is a sequence in the action which can be regarded as a functional unit of the narrative,[26] each episode providing a new development in the plot. If the narrative were to be compared to a game of chess, the plot is the equivalent of the entire series of moves, and each episode the equivalent of a single move. I have numbered the episodes in the example given. They run as follows:

1. A claimant to the throne and his diviner set off to kill King Ruganguuza.

2. Mitimigamba displays his powers by guessing his companion's thoughts.

3. Repetition of motif 2.

4. Repetition of motif 3.

5. They become servants.

6. They plot the downfall of Ruganguuza.

7. Ruganguuza has some suspicions. They are confirmed in a veiled way which he does not understand.

8. Mitimigamba cuts firewood from a sacred wood. He commits a sacrilege. Repetition of motif 6.

9. Repetition of motif 7.

10. The claimant to the throne kills Ruganguuza.

The term 'motif' simply means the stylized contents of an episode. The general idea behind the use of the term is to bring out the functional significance of the episode, whereas the use of the term 'episode' brings out the placing of the motif within a series, and within the structure as a whole.

The plot is the ordered unfolding of the narrative. In the example I have given it runs as follows:

(a) Exordium: 1. Presentation of the situation.
    2, 4. Presentation of the way of solving it.
(b) Action: 5. Engagement of the servants.
    6, 7. Danger for Ruganguuza, suspicion, warning not understood.
    8, 9. Repetition of 7, 8.
(c) Conclusion: 10. Death of Ruganguuza.

For the purpose of analysing this tale, I have made use of the following concepts: episode, plot, motif, setting, and theme. Some or all of these concepts can be applied to any and every kind of oral text in order to discover its internal structure.

The functional elements of a tale can be used to make a graph of the internal structure of a text. This is done by placing the episodes along one axis in the order in which the narrator has told them (the plot), and along the other axis according to the degree of tension conveyed by each episode. The chief artistic requirement of all tales is that they should be able to hold the interest of the listener and keep him waiting with bated breath for the denouement. Hence the construction of a tale pivots on the attempt to attain this end. Now the ability to hold the listener's attention can be gauged for each episode, for it depends mainly on the extent to which the listener can foresee what is going to happen next. An episode ends with a given situation, which can develop in a number of different ways leading to a number of possible new situations. In the next episode, the narrator has already made his choice between these possible situations, and again places his listener in front of another series of possibilities. It can therefore readily be seen that the kind of episode least able to hold the listener's interest is one that can lead to one outcome only. The listener realizes this and knows in advance what is going to happen, so that the unexpected is ruled out and there is a complete lack of excitement. Next in order of low degree of tension comes the kind of episode which leaves the door open for a large, or even an infinite, number of possible outcomes. The listener cannot foresee anything, and although interested to know what will happen, is not roused to excitement at all. The tension increases to the extent to which the number of possible outcomes is reduced from an infinite number down to two. When there are only two possible outcomes, the listener can foresee this, and is anxious to know which of them will take place. Or he may see that one of these is bound to be what happens, yet feels that it does not fit in with the rest of the story, and is left wondering if there may be some other solution. All other possibilities are ruled out, yet he feels there must be a solution. This is a favourite situation in tales of heroes who are supposed to be invulnerable, but who find themselves in a desperate situation. The listener knows the hero is invulnerable, and also knows the situation is desperate, but he cannot see what the solution of the problem will be. He is impatient to see how the situation will develop. From this argument it follows that, in theory, tension is measurable; but, in practice, one usually has to content oneself with making a rough estimate, if complicated calculations of probability are to be avoided. The graph of the above example is shown on the following page.

By means of graphs of this kind, texts can be classified into various structural groups. The graph given here shows that the narrative is well constructed. The tension rises, and reaches a

Graph of the structure of the tale 'The story of Mitimigamba'

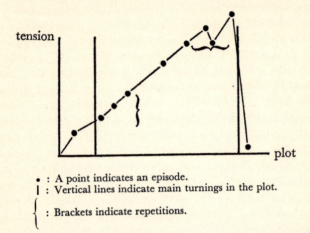

• : A point indicates an episode.
| : Vertical lines indicate main turnings in the plot.

{ : Brackets indicate repetitions.

climax just before the denouement. Moreover, the use of repetition in the episodes is a sign of artistic refinement. In other, less artistic, narratives, there may be no climax, or it may come much earlier, and there may be fewer devices for heightening the tension. In others, there will be more, etc. A classification of this kind is particularly useful when analysing free texts.

Besides the functional elements, there are other aspects of a text which the historian must take into account. These are: the setting, and the theme of the narrative. The setting includes the time and the place in which the tale unfolds, and the names of the persons who appear in it. In the narrative quoted, these are: Burundi in former times, the claimant to the throne, Mitimigamba, and King Ruganguuza. The theme is simply the title, or the general subject of the plot. In this case, the story is about the murder of a king, and might be called 'The kingdom won by a trick'. The theme must be distinguished from the plot, for in some cases the same theme may give rise to two entirely different, or partially different, plots. For instance, there is a series of Burundi tales on the theme of 'the rise of kings in Burundi', but despite the common theme, there are three main types of plot, each quite different from the other.

3. *The light thrown on the testimony by its structure*

The historian will find that analysis of the outward formal structure and of the internal structure of a testimony is extremely useful. It throws light on the problem of how the testimony was transmitted, is a guide for purposes of comparison of testimonies, makes it possible to discover the sources of error and falsification, and clarifies the question of interpretation of the testimony.

As regards the transmission of a tradition and the comparison of testimonies, clearly the distinction between fixed and free texts is of paramount importance, for since in fixed texts the words themselves belong to the tradition, it should be possible by comparing different versions, to reconstruct an archetype of the proto-testimony; and it should be equally possible to establish an archetype of the proto-testimony in the case of free texts, for the internal structure belongs to the tradition just as much as do the words of a fixed text. A comparison of the episodes, the plot, the theme, and the setting of the various versions of a free text enables one to reconstruct a model of the structure of the original source from which the versions that have been compared derive. A distinction should be made here between the functional elements of the original source and the secondary elements. The latter, which include the theme and the setting, are more subject to variation than the former, because they can be altered during the course of transmission without the essential structure of the original text being in any way affected. It is difficult to make alterations to the episodes or plot of a text without destroying its intelligibility, whereas other alterations, particularly of the setting, need scarcely make any difference to the subsequent understanding of the text. As for the form of the testimony itself, this can also be of the utmost value in the reconstruction of the archetype, for if various versions are compared and a passage in one of them is found not to conform to the formal laws regulating the rest, one must assume that this passage has suffered distortion, and a reconstruction of an earlier form of the testimony can be based on the formal laws obtaining in general.

I shall mention only two of the ways in which the internal

structure of a testimony can help in detecting sources of error or falsification. We have just seen that it is fairly easy to falsify elements in a free text which are not functional, especially so far as the setting is concerned. Yet it is precisely the details of the setting that are of the greatest historical interest, because they identify the events recounted with a definite place, and associate them with definite historical figures.

Now it is precisely points such as these that informants may find it advantageous to falsify, because details of this kind can provide the required historical slant and fulfil the sociological functions of a tradition. If, for example, a free text proves legal rights of ownership, all that need be done is to change the family name of the hero of the tale in order to enable another family to use the text as vindication of its claim to these rights. And this is easily done, because the informant can leave the functional elements of the narrative entirely unchanged. Comparison of versions does indeed show that this is something which frequently occurs, sometimes by mistake, sometimes for deliberate purposes of falsification. It is then that the outward form and the internal structure of a testimony can give us some indication as to the amount of artistry put into the testimony by its author. If we find we are dealing with a perfect work of art, we can assume that the original testimony has been embellished in the course of transmission, or that perhaps the original testimony itself was not entirely in accord with the actual facts of the case. The facts have either been inadvertently distorted, or deliberately falsified by informants who wanted to make the testimony more lively and exciting.[27] The more perfect the structure of a text, the more likely it is that it has been altered for artistic reasons.

Lastly, the structure of a testimony helps greatly in interpreting its meaning, for the structure imposes certain rules of composition. The outward formal structure of a testimony is of particular importance in this respect. The form of a poem, for instance, can have a marked effect on the content. Grammatical and syntactical features, such as the use of poetic licence, of repetition, of unusual syntactical constructions, of 'stop-gap' words which are meaningless in themselves and which simply serve to fill in the lines of a text to meet the demands of the form, are cases in point. The internal structure can also influence the meaning. The material of the testimony is arranged according to its laws, and repetition, deliberate exaggeration, anticipation of later events in the plot, etc., are often the outcome of the rules imposed.

4. Summary

Every testimony has a structure. Its outer structure may be formal or non-formal, it may be a fixed or a free text, and it has an internal structure which regulates the arrangement of its content. The historian must study the structure of a testimony because it enables him to discover certain facts concerning the transmission of the tradition, because it also enables him to reconstruct various archetypes according to different structures, because it discloses the various possible sources of distortions and falsifications made by the informant, and lastly, because it is important for interpreting the testimony. Indeed, to say the least, it is imprudent to interpret a testimony without first knowing its structure. That is why this section precedes the section on interpreting the meaning of a testimony, which is what the study of an oral document finally aims to achieve.

3. THE MEANING OF THE TESTIMONY

One of the most essential tasks for the historian is to find out the exact meaning of a testimony. To do this, he must not only discover the literal meaning of the text, but he must also see whether this tallies with the meaning the informant intended to convey. The literal meaning is obtained by examining the language in which it is expressed. The intentions of the informant can be deduced from the literary qualities of the testimony, including both its structure and its style. As regards the latter, particular attention will be paid to symbolic expressions and stereotypes.

1. The literal meaning of a testimony

When one comes to study a testimony composed in the language of a people without writing, it often happens that no description of the language exists, or that, if there are any, they are not to be relied upon. In that case, the research worker's first task will be to study the structure of the language before he can even begin to collect testimonies. This amounts to saying that a historian must either have had a fairly thorough linguistic training, or must only work among peoples whose language has been studied by a competent linguist. In any case, the historian must always indicate the linguistic studies on which the interpretation of his documents is based.

A second problem arises here, that of knowing the exact meaning of the words used in a testimony. This is never a simple matter when dealing with unfamiliar cultures. The meaning of a word only becomes intelligible when the total context in which it has been uttered is taken into account.[28] The words which express cultural values—the 'key-words' of a culture—cannot be understood unless one is thoroughly acquainted with the society in question. They are untranslatable, except by lengthy descriptive explanations. The Polynesian word *tabu* and the Indian word *totem* are two examples in point. Both have been adopted into European languages for lack of any equivalents. Another example is the word for 'force' in the language of the Luba of Katanga, around which one writer has built up a whole system of Bantu philosophy.[29] Among such key-words must be included complicated technical terms, particularly those concerning the social, political, or religious organization of the people who use them. The Rwandese often use the term *ubuhake*, which is a kind of clientage contract. A description of the whole political system of the country would be needed in order to convey its exact meaning. A book had to be written to give an exact and complete description of the idea conveyed by the word *buloji*, 'witchcraft', often used by the Luba of the Kasai.[30]

Some of the words in a testimony may be archaic, or may belong to a foreign or a secret language, and may be unintelligible to the informant himself. This most often occurs with fixed texts. The slogans of the Kuba include many words of this kind, and people simply say they are *lambil* words. *Lambil* is thought to be a secret language of ancient origin. Further investigation showed that it consists of words of which the semantic content had changed, words borrowed from foreign languages, archaic words, circumlocutions, and a number of words of which neither the origin nor the meaning could be discovered. Similar features are found in the secret languages of Rwanda, notably that of the *abiiru*, the guardians of the country's esoteric traditions.[31]

It is often impossible to discover the meaning of many words of this kind, and when that happens, then a testimony remains partially unintelligible. Outside the Kuba and Rwanda areas, J. A. Barnes reports coming across the same difficulties among the Ngoni of Nyasaland,[32] as does P. C. Lloyd for the Yoruba,[33] and G. Van Bulck for the Congo.[34]

2. *The purport of a testimony*

The literal meaning of a testimony is not always the meaning the informant intends to convey. When discrepancies occur between the literal meaning and the purport of a testimony, this is because the testimony belongs to a literary category in which either an internal or an outer formal structure must be conformed to in a way that hampers the free expression of ideas, and imposes a style which affects the way thoughts are expressed, particularly if the style requires the use of symbolic expressions and poetic allusions, or of stereotypes. The way the structure of a testimony affects its interpretation has been outlined in the foregoing section, and I shall say no more about it here, but shall confine myself to discussing literary categories, symbolism, allusion, and stereotypes.

(a) *Literary categories*

The concept of the literary category covers the sum of all the literary qualities of a work. Classification of categories can never be based exclusively on form; the content must also be taken into account. But the word 'content' is a complex and somewhat vague expression, and it is better to classify oral texts into literary categories according to their internal structure, the style used, and sometimes the subject dealt with. The style is the particular manner of expression. It is therefore largely a matter of the semantic usage chosen by the author, who may indulge in symbolism, convey his meaning by allusions, make use of stock phrases and of every kind of rhetorical device—in short, who may clothe his ideas in all sorts of seductive and fancy fashions. Or he may scorn the use of literary devices and express himself in everyday language, or may cultivate a compressed, abrupt, laconic style. All this comes under the head of the literary, or rather, the stylistic qualities of a work. By extending the concept of style, one might include within it the way in which a work is performed—whether it is sung or not, and if so, whether sung as a solo or in chorus or partly one and partly the other; whether it is recited collectively or individually; whether it is recited in a particular manner or in the same way as ordinary speech, etc. As for the subject treated, this often plays a part in the classification of categories. One category may have a bucolic character, another an epic touch, others again may have a didactic purpose, or be full of dramatic suspense, or deal with historical themes, and so on.

Thus the criteria for classifying literary categories are very complex, and vary from one category to another. Consequently, from the historian's point of view at least, it is dangerous to simplify matters and present the criteria as simply being those of form and content, as has been done by De Rop.[35] Nevertheless, despite its complexity, the concept of literary categories is a useful one as an aid to the classification of texts. Once one has realized what literary category a text belongs to, one then has a general idea as to the mode of expression likely to be found in the testimony, and one is thus made aware of the type of difficulty in understanding it one is likely to come across. Hence it is important for the historian to find out exactly what place the work he is studying occupies within the various categories of the oral literature as a whole, and within the culture to which it belongs.

A classification of this kind must take into account the distinctions between categories made within the culture itself. Categories thus distinguished will each have a special name, and it should be possible to discover the criteria of classification used. The Bushongo regard the *shoosh* (slogans) as a separate category characterized by a form which is fixed though not formal and in which archaic features occur, and by the way in which they express some salient characteristic of whatever it is to which they refer, which may be the name of a person, a group, a place, a function, or an object. Thus the category includes poems in praise of individuals, allusions to the cultural characteristics of groups (such as descriptions of clan food taboos or of tribal costumes), picturesque descriptions of places, indications of the administrative functions of certain official positions, and poetic or ironic statements about the essential nature of certain material objects. The category is distinguished from the songs known as *ncyeem*, and from the proverbs known as *mikwoon*, although these are very similar in form to the *shoosh*, for the *shoosh* can be sung, and the proverb has the same structure as the slogan. The only difference between them is the subject matter. From all this, one can infer the requirements that must be fulfilled by a *shoosh* and the effect this has on the text of the testimony. If an examination of the various categories has not previously been made, it would be impossible to differentiate the *shoosh* from the *mikwoon* and the *ncyeem*. The adoption of a different form of classification would lead to a failure to recognize the characteristic features of this category, and these could not be taken into account as a means of estimating how much the characteristics of the category are likely to have influenced the composition of the testimony one is studying.

(b) Symbolism and poetic allusions

Among illiterate peoples, one of the most highly appreciated stylistic features is the symbolic statement.[36] In the dynastic poetry of Rwanda there are three kinds of symbolic statement. In the first type, a synonym is used instead of the word which would express directly the idea to be conveyed. For instance, a poet might speak of 'the rower' when referring to the name of one of the Burundi kings which means 'to make a river pass by'. The second type of symbolic statement depends upon the use of homophones. Reference is made to qualities appertaining to a word which is homophenous with the word to which reference is actually being made. Thus, one of the titles of the kings of Burundi is homophenous with the Rwandese word for 'lion'. A poet will describe the king of Burundi as 'the hunter of zebras'. The listener will translate: 'hunter of zebras' = 'lion' = the homophenous word for the royal title. In the third type of symbolic statement, use is made of metonymy. The name Burundi resembles, though it is not homophenous with, the word which means the lesser tibia, so a poet will be referring to the name of the country when he speaks of 'the country of legs'.[37]

Obviously symbolic statements are unintelligible to foreign listeners without accompanying explanations, because they often arise from free association. Among the Bushongo, the word for 'abyss' is sometimes used to convey the meaning 'king'. The explanation for this is that 'abyss' is the antinome for 'hill', and the king's highest title is 'God of the Hills'. Clearly a stranger would be unable to find any connection between the two words without having it explained to him.

Symbolism exists in every culture. Among the Luba of the Kasai the name 'Nkole' appears at the head of every genealogy. P. Denolf regarded it as a proper name, but R. van Caeneghem has shown that it is an honorific title, with the literal meaning 'the essentially powerful', given to the three most distant patriarchs, and that it is inserted symbolically in all genealogies.[38] The use of veiled expressions is, in many cultures, a highly admired stylistic device. Here the symbolism is basically simply a technique whereby circumlocutions are used to express an idea which one does not want to state bluntly. But as well as the uses of symbolism which are intelligible to everyone belonging to the culture concerned, there is another type of device—poetic allusion—which remains unintelligible to all those who do not already know some or all of the facts of which a testimony gives an account.

I have called these devices poetic allusions because they most often occur in what are usually regarded as poetic categories of literature. In the dynastic poems of Rwanda, the names of the kings are not usually mentioned, the names of their capitals being used instead. No direct reference is made to historic events, but merely the name of the place where they occurred is mentioned, etc. Thus mention of Kiganda alludes to the place where King Ndahiro of Rwanda was killed. The phrase: 'The cows given in marriage payment to Gisanze increased the numbers in your households' means that the queen-mother

Nyiramavugo had many children. She was born in Gisanze, where the marriage payment was made to her parents, which in Rwanda consists of cattle. 'Sovereign of Ruganda' indicates King Ruganzu II, who inaugurated this capital. All these examples are taken from the same poem, in which they follow closely upon each other.[39] They indicate clearly that the poem cannot be understood without a thorough knowledge of the events to which they refer. These instances from Rwanda are by no means exceptional; similar examples could be quoted from almost every culture. It follows that, in order to understand poetic allusions, one must have at one's disposal other traditions concerning the historical events mentioned in the poem, which provide an explanatory commentary. Thus a poem can only be interpreted by means of a different, but parallel, tradition to that which is transmitted by the poem. This parallel tradition will have neither the same characteristics nor the same historical value as the tradition it explains, and the historian must distinguish between the two. Thus for instance there is a Rwandese proverb which says: 'There is a cracking up at Nkoondo', and there are several explanations of this proverb. Everyone agrees that Nkoondo was a battlefield, and that the proverb refers to the loser of the battle. But some think that the reference is to the battle between the regent of the country of the Ndivyaariye and the rebels who rallied round Twaarereye, while others hold that it refers to a war between the kings of Mweezi and Ndivyaariye, while yet others think that another battle is referred to. The proverb itself does not seem to have undergone any distortion, but there seems to have been some carelessness in the handing down of explanations of it, and they seem to have suffered from frequent distortions.

The examples quoted give some indication of the added complexities of interpretation that arise when a historical document contains symbolic statements and poetic allusions. Symbolic statements can soon be explained by someone who has a good knowledge of the culture concerned, but the same cannot be said of poetic allusions, for these can only be explained by means of a parallel tradition, and in cases where a parallel tradition is inexistent, or cannot be relied upon, the text will remain unintelligible.

(c) Stereotypes

Stereotypes are found in most oral traditions. There are two kinds of stereotype: the stock phrase, and the 'Wandersage', a more complex form of stereotype.

(i) *The stock phrase.* Stock phrases appear in texts which express the commonly accepted ideals of the culture concerned. When the same ideas recur in different texts, this often leads to the same expressions being used. Typical examples are provided by the slogans known as *kasala* applied to the various lineages of the Lulua. The ideal of many Lulua is to have a pale skin-colour, and this accounts for resemblances between the following slogans:

> (a) Bena Ntumba, the chosen ones,
> No grass grows on their bodies
> All of them are pale
> Not one of them is black; if you see a black
> He is a stranger on a visit.

> (b) They are handsome
> They are pale
> They are blacks
> With big, long fingers
> For eating palm-nuts.

> (c) Ciyago of Lita Ngoyi
> Who gives birth to pale children
> No blacks
> If you see a black
> He is a stranger who has come to look after
>   the child.
> He who sent him was Kabongo.[40]

It is to be noted that the resemblance between (a) and (c) amounts to identity of expression in the statement 'if you see a black, he is a stranger'. It is essential for the historian to recognize these stock phrases, in the first place so that he may avoid interpreting literally, and also so that he can discover what the cultural ideals were during the period concerned. The Bena Ntumba probably have black-skinned as well as pale-skinned people among their numbers, and the text about them does not

enable one to postulate any racial differences between them and
the rest of the Lulua. But one can infer from the texts as a whole
that a pale skin has been an ideal of beauty among the Lulua
since the nineteenth century at least—that is to say, since before
the arrival of the Europeans.

(ii) *The Wandersagen or the complex stereotype*. There are some
stereotypes which do not consist merely in an idea and the stock
phrase used to express it, but which form the motif of an episode,
or even take the form of a complete narrative. They frequently
occur in European oral traditions as well as in written texts, and
they have been given the name of *Wandersagen*.[41] They are found
just as often among illiterate peoples. In Africa, for instance, the
motif of 'the tower of Babel' is found over a very wide area.
Another motif is found among the Luba of the Kasai, the Kuba,
the Yaka of Kwango, the Luapula tribes, and probably among
others as well.[42] This is the tale of the chief who invites his
enemy to sit down on a mat under which a ditch has been dug.
The enemy, in good faith, sits down, falls into the ditch, and is
assassinated. The trick usually leads to a war or a migration.

These complex stereotypes in the form of tales are the result
of diffusion. Linguistic barriers do not put a stop to the diffusion
of tales, and they can have a very widespread distribution.[43]
But does this mean that they still retain some historical significance? Most writers think that they do.

In the opinion of Crazzolara, the various versions of a complex stereotype may refer to different events which are, however,
psychologically related to each other. Thus a tale which tells
about a dispute over a lost lance probably indicates that a split
occurred in the Lwoo tribes, the lance being the emblem of the
Lwoo ancestors.[44] Father Mortier distinguishes between the
form and the content of the complex stereotype, and considers
that only the content is of historical significance. A tale which
describes how a bridge of twisted fibres broke as a tribe was
passing across it, so that the tribe was then divided into two,
records, in his opinion, one historical fact only—namely, that
two tribes which are today distinct from each other were
originally one and the same—and for the rest the tale simply
follows the pattern of the stereotype.[45] On the other hand,

Cunnison thinks that in the case of the Luapula tribes, stereotype tales are told in order to justify changes in landownership, and for providing plausible reasons for their departure from their original territory, and that all are aetiological myths without any factual foundation.[46]

It would appear that complex stereotypes of this kind are no more than a literary device for explaining a historical fact that is already known, for adding colour to a narrative, or for describing a disagreeable past event without upsetting existing cultural values. The story, found in the Bible, of the river or sea that is crossed by dividing the waters crops up in many parts of Africa.[47] It is a motif which seems to serve no other purpose than that of explaining how a large group of people succeeded in crossing a wide river. A motif known throughout the Great Lakes district which describes how a young prince had to flee from his country and take refuge with his paternal aunt, and how, after growing into manhood there, he reconquered his country from his enemies, seems to be simply a veiled way of saying that a new dynasty conquered the country.[48] There may therefore, be a kernel of historical truth in these Wandersagen, but again there may not. Clearly the invention of explanations for contemporary situations, or for events arising from a known historical situation, is without any kernel of historical truth. Thus, for instance, the motif of Noah's vine is used by the Kuba to explain why they are at a disadvantage compared with the Whites, and also to explain why they have matrilinear descent.

Thus when one comes across a complex stereotype offered as explanation of an event, the event need not *a priori* be rejected as unhistorical, but on the other hand, it cannot be accepted as historical simply on the grounds that it has been explained by a stereotype. The historian must in every case make a careful study of the Wandersage he is dealing with and weigh up the probabilities before accepting or rejecting any statement made in the narrative. Since stereotypes of all kinds are of frequent occurence in historical texts, particularly in free forms of tradition, the student of oral traditions must be aware of their existence and endeavour to track down as many as he can. This is not always an easy task, for very little has been published on the subject, particularly so far as Africa is concerned.

3. Summary

A knowledge of both the literal meaning and the purport of the text of a testimony makes it possible to arrive at an accurate understanding of its overall meaning. But it is impossible to carry out this work of interpretation without a thorough knowledge of the language in which the text is composed, because otherwise the literal meaning of the text will be unintelligible. The purport cannot be understood without a thorough knowledge of the society which has produced the testimony. Thus it is absolutely essential for the historian to be acquainted with the language and with the culture of the people he is studying. He must either be himself trained in linguistics and social anthropology, or must confine his studies to areas already explored by anthropologists and linguists.

In this chapter, all the problems involved in arriving at a thorough understanding of a testimony have been examined. The next chapter will be devoted to the distortions which may occur in the account of past events given by a testimony, to an analysis of the factors accounting for such distortions, and finally to the method the historian should adopt for assessing the extent to which these factors operate and for forming an estimate of the amount of distortion the facts recorded by the testimony are likely to have suffered.

CHAPTER IV

The Testimony as a Mirage of Reality

A TESTIMONY is no more than a mirage of the reality it describes. The initial informant in an oral tradition gives, either consciously or unconsciously, a distorted account of what has really happened, because he sees only some aspects of it, and places his own interpretation on what he has seen. His testimony is stamped by his personality, coloured by his private interests, and set within the framework of reference provided by the cultural values of the society he belongs to. This initial testimony then undergoes alterations and distortions at the hands of all the other informants in the chain of transmission, down to and including the very last one, all of them being influenced by the same factors as the first: their private interests and the interests of the society they belong to, the cultural values of that society, and their own individual personalities.

Obviously one of the historian's tasks is to find out to what extent a testimony is affected by these social, cultural, and personal factors. He will try to assess how much of the testimony relates to observed facts, but will also be interested in possible deviations in the account of the facts and in the reasons for their presence, because the way distortions come about can throw a great deal of light on the existing social and cultural background of the informants who introduce them, and may in some cases provide information about the past. For instance, poems in praise of the kings have been composed among the Kuba since the days of King Mishe mi Shyaang, and in Rwanda since the time of Ruganzu Ndoori. The purpose of these poems is to extol the kings, therefore they distort the events of the past in the sense that they exaggerate the valorous deeds of the kings, and pass over their defeats in silence. But the fact that it was from the time of a certain king onwards that these poems appeared does not in itself enable us to conclude that the attitude towards the sovereign reached a state of enthusiasm at the time of their appearance which had not been felt before. This example underlines how important it is that the historian should not regard himself as a detective who is out to find out the right answer from a large number of false clues, but simply as someone who is trying to disentangle which aspects of reality relate to the various elements of which a testimony is composed; and the distortions a testimony contains can be just as revealing about past situations and events as an undistorted account.

It is usually impossible to provide absolute proof that distortion has taken place. One can only hazard guesses as to the probabilities, lesser or greater, of the text being distorted. And in order to assess these probabilities it is advisable in every case to find out what the reasons for distortion may have been. As I have already said, they belong to three main categories: distortions made in defence of private interests, which are ultimately accounted for by the social structure; distortions made under the influence of cultural values, which relate to the culture and the social structure concerned; and lastly, distortions due to the individual psychology of the informant. Analysis of these three factors which give rise to distortions is the subject of the three sections of this chapter.

1. THE SOCIAL SIGNIFICANCE OF A TESTIMONY

Every testimony and every tradition has a purpose and fulfils a function. It is because of this that they exist at all. For if a testimony had no purpose, and did not fulfil any function, it would be meaningless for anyone to pass it on, and no one would pass it on. It is usually the interests of the informant that give purpose and function to a testimony. He wants to please, to earn money, to gain prestige, etc. But the interests of the informant are almost entirely conditioned by what might be called the interests of the society of which he is a member. If, for instance, he wants to gain prestige, this is only because the idea of prestige already exists in that society, and it is an accepted assumption that some measure of prestige can be won, and won by doing certain things. Whatever the private interests may be which one is analyzing, it has to be remembered that they are always socially conditioned. Furthermore, some kinds of testimony may be of more direct service to community interests than others. A tradition of rebellion, for example, is important to the community as a whole, for it provides its members with concrete proof that they are no longer dependent upon another community to which they used to pay tribute in the distant past. Those who preserve a tradition of this kind often do so by order of the community. Most group testimonies are official testimonies that reflect the basic interests of the society concerned.

It cannot be sufficiently stressed that, in a last analysis, every tradition exists as such only in virtue of the fact that it serves the interests of the society in which it is preserved, whether it does so directly, or indirectly by serving the interests of an informant. Its significance in relation to society is what I call its function. A royal genealogy, for example, signifies that a certain family may occupy a certain status, that it enjoys certain privileges and is under certain obligations, and that it is thereby distinguished from the rest of society. It signifies that a certain social structure—that of royal power—depends upon a hereditary mechanism, and that this ensures social stability. Its function, therefore, is to provide a rule of succession and to support the institution of kingship. Let me add as a general remark that all social functions can be reduced to two main functions: that of adaptation of the society to its environment, and that of permanently maintaining the social structure.[1]

As for the informant who recites a tradition, he has purposes of his own. The tradition has, for him, a more limited significance—that of serving his own private purposes. Even if he is entrusted with the preservation of an official tradition that is of great importance to society, he will still be serving his private purposes and interests in doing so. The task of the *abiiru* of Rwanda is to preserve the official dynastic traditions of the country, and they have a personal interest in the task, because their status as *abiiru* gives them great prestige, political power, and exceptional privileges. All these advantages are dependent on their office, and they enjoy them solely in virtue of the fact that they know the traditions.

A tradition is affected by the purposes and functions which it fulfils. An informant may alter the content of a testimony in order to make it correspond better with his own private purposes; social influences may force a tradition to follow a certain direction because in this way its social function is more adequately fulfilled. It is, therefore, essential to discuss the purposes and functions of traditions, so that one may know just what they consist of. It should further be noted that when an informant alters his testimony for the attainment of his own ends, he usually does so intentionally, whereas alterations made so that the tradition should fulfil its social function are usually unintentional. The private purposes of the informant lead to falsification, the fulfilment of social function to error.

In oral tradition as a whole, three kinds of informant can be distinguished: the initial informant, the informant who forms a link in the chain of transmission of hearsay accounts, and the final informant. Private purposes and social functions affect all their testimonies, but not in precisely the same way. The testimonies in the chain of transmission are affected most, because the tradition has become an institution in the society concerned. The initial and the final testimony both add something to society, introduce something new—in the first case, a new tradition, and in the second, the first written record of a tradition. So I shall first examine the way in which purposes and functions affect the testimonies of the chain, next, how they affect the initial testimony, and lastly, how they affect the final testimony.

I must add that it is very difficult to show—that is, to provide positive proof—that a testimony contains distortions which are almost certainly due to the way it has been affected by purposes or functions. But it can be proved in some cases.

In accordance, therefore, with the foregoing remarks, this section will be divided as follows: I shall first deal with the testimonies of the chain, and shall examine the possible effects on them, first of the purposes pursued, and then of the functions fulfilled, and what proofs or indications of such effects can be traced; I shall then carry out the same examination for proto-testimonies and for final testimonies.

1. *The testimonies of the chain*

(*a*) *Purpose*. To return to a useful distinction made earlier, we can classify texts into testimonies not aimed at recording history, testimonies mainly aimed at recording history, and testimonies in which the recording of history is only a secondary aim; for the possible occurrence of distortion in a testimony depends very much on the extent to which informants give a historical content to their testimonies.

Testimonies which are not aimed at recording history are the most reliable, because the informant has no reasons for falsification. Set phrases of all kinds, whether ritual or not, are examples of this kind of tradition. A proverb or a ritual phrase is not designed to give historical information, hence there is no reason why any such information it may contain should be intentionally altered. The same applies to all poetry that is not on a historical subject. And even tales may include passages which unintentionally provide historical information. The Pueblo Indians have stories in which the characters go in and out of rooms by the use of ladders when this was no longer the custom. The stories go back to the times when the houses had neither doors nor windows, and, for reasons of security, access to the communal structure was only by means of ladders.[2]

Those testimonies which are aimed mainly at recording history are unlikely to be falsified, for their secondary aim, which is often that of enhancing the informant's prestige, or which may be of an artistic or didactic nature, is not likely to lead to intentional distortion of any historical facts contained in them. Sometimes one part of a testimony is designed to prove the informant's reliability, so that the rest of the testimony may go unchallenged. In the first part, the main aim is historical, but the secondary aim is not. It may then ensue that the secondary aim of the first part becomes the main aim of the second part, so that the main aim is no longer a historical one. A typical example is the list of place-names of the Kuba tribal migrations. This list usually precedes recital of the tribal history, and it is designed to convince listeners of the excellence, accuracy, and reliability of the informant. But in the account of tribal history which follows, it can be assumed that the main aim is now a political one. It is hoped that the reliability of the account of the tribal history will not be questioned, because the reliability of the informant has already been established by means of the preceding text. Obviously there is little likelihood of the list of place-names being falsified, since its accuracy is in the nature of a guarantee for the accuracy of that part of the testimony where the secondary aim comes into play. It is equally obvious that falsifications are to be expected in the recital of tribal history which follows.

Texts in which the main aim is not a historical one are likely to be falsified, for, with some definite aim in view, they tend to attempt to prove their case by supplying historical evidence of legal precedents. It is absolutely essential to find out what purpose a tradition is used for, so as to be able to judge the kind of falsification it may have undergone. When the inhabitants of the Kuba village of Mboong Bushepy say that the iron mine at Nshaanc Spring used to belong to them, and tell how the collector of the tribute payable in iron used to come regularly to their village, and not to the neighbouring villages, all they are trying to do is to vindicate their claim to ownership of the iron mine by means of a historical precedent. The people of the next village, who also lay claim to the iron mine in question, may also try to supply historical precedents, and may, for instance, say that it was only to their village that the collector of tribute came, or that the former sites of their villages were near the spring in question, whereas those of the Mboong Bushepy were situated elsewhere, etc. In this example, any falsification that may have occurred is likely to have been that the collector of tribute, for instance, was an invention, while the name of the place he is supposed to have visited, the sites of the old villages and their names and the slogans attached to them— all of which may be used to substantiate the tradition—will probably be correct. There are any number of cases of this kind, particularly as regards traditions bearing on political, legal, or economic matters.

A testimony always has some purpose, whether it be historical

81

or otherwise, and this purpose always has some effect on the testimony. Thus, in a tale which is intended simply as a work of art, the denouement may be altered to make it more satisfactory. A Rundi tale tells how Macoonco, who rebelled against King Gisaabo, was captured by the Europeans and held in prison at Usumbura. One day he saw two messengers from the king coming down from the mountains. Certain that they had been sent to ask that he should be condemned to death, he committed suicide. But in fact, the messengers had come to ask the Germans for a reprieve for Macoonco. The real story was quite different. Instead of committing suicide as the story had it, what Macoonco had done was to attack a German officer with a lance while attempting to escape. There does not seem to have been any question of messengers coming from Gisaabo. But someone, in telling the tale, must have thought up this new twist so as to give the story a more satisfactory ending.

It is impossible to draw up a list of all the possible purposes an informant may have in mind. The most common are those of a legal, economic, political, didactic, or artistic nature, but there is a whole host of other possible purposes. In order to discover what an informant's purpose is, it is of course necessary to be acquainted with—indeed, to have a thorough knowledge of—the society to which he belongs. One must know what its main interests are, and what the aims of the majority of its members are. That may help the investigator to discover exactly what purpose the informant has. It is also often possible to deduce the purpose a certain type of tradition is likely to be used for. Lists of place-names may be used for claims on land. Lists of persons always have social or political connotations— the informant is attempting to obtain political office, or suceed to an inheritance, or vindicate some privilege, etc. Historical tales are generally used to protect the interests of a group, didactic tales are intended to teach, tales of artistic merit to please, etc. Through a knowledge of the society, and examination of the type of tradition to which a testimony belongs, it is comparatively easy in most cases to discover what the underlying purpose is.

But even if the purpose is known, an assessment must still be made as to the effect it is likely to have on the testimony itself.

Sometimes a number of factors operate together to provide definite proof that this or that falsification has occurred for one reason or another. But a case of this kind, of which the story of Macoonco quoted above provides an example, is rare. Most of the time one can suspect an influence without being able to prove it. For instance, a story may be artistically told, and one may suspect that it has been touched up, but there is no way of providing positive proof.

On the other hand, sometimes it is possible to provide proof that a given tradition is unlikely to have been falsified. A case in point is where a tradition contains features which are not in accord with the purpose for which it is used, such as the Bushongo tale about a battle which they lost and at which one of their kings was killed; or another which tells of the death of a king called Mboong aLeeng, who was ambushed by the enemy, and killed by a poisoned arrow. In neither of these tales are the facts likely to have been falsified. They are part of the tribal tradition, but are only transmitted in secret, precisely because they go against the purpose of the tradition, which is the enhancement of national prestige. A Kuba tradition tells how the mother of King Shyaam was a slave, which means (since the Kuba are matrilineal) that there is a break in the dynastic line of succession. It is, however, possible to argue that tales of this kind do not, after all, run so very much counter to the purposes for which they are used. The lost battle was a supernatural punishment, and the death of Mboong aLeeng fits in well with the account given of his life, just as does King Shyaam's ancestry with the account given of his. Mboong aLeeng is the prototype of the warrior, and Shyaam that of the magician. Nevertheless, the events recorded are intrinsically incompatible with the interests the traditions in question are supposed to defend. Similar examples abound. In Rwanda, for instance, the loss of the royal drum—symbol of the country's unity—is remembered, and the death of several kings. In Burundi, it is admitted that a battle was lost and a king killed, etc. Here, too, the events described are diametrically counter to the purposes the tales are meant to fulfil, and a certain amount of embarrassment is noticeable whenever events of this kind are recalled. One may take it that traditions such as these can be relied upon, and fortunately they are to be met with, it would appear, in a large number of societies.

(b) *Significance*. All traditions can be divided into official and private traditions. This distinction corresponds fairly well with that which could be made between traditions in which the social functions are of primary importance, and those in which these functions are secondary, which is sufficient justification for the use of this distinction when examining the effect of the functions of oral traditions on their content. Official traditions convey information of public importance, and for this very reason are controlled by social or political groups of people in authority. Hence facts which do not help to maintain the institution which transmits the tradition are often omitted or falsified. Among the Bushongo, the official tradition maintains that the reigning dynasty is the first the country ever had, although this is almost certainly not the case. In the Akan States, the official version of historical facts is that the ruling dynasty is indigenous, although the members of the royal clan know very well that they were immigrants.[3] Examples of this kind could be multiplied indefinitely. With private traditions, there is no point in distorting the events of the past, because they only defend private interests, and the fulfilment of a social function is of secondary importance. Information conveyed by a private tradition about events that concern social groups other than the group in which the tradition is transmitted is of secondary importance from their point of view, has no social significance, and can thus be relied upon. For example, the members of a Kuba clan, the Kweemy, say that they are descended from a female dignitary of the Bieng tribe, and in the course of their account, they declare that the Bieng chiefs formed an earlier royal dynasty which was eliminated by the reigning Bushongo dynasty. There is no doubt that this version of the facts is to be preferred to the official Bushongo version, because the tale fulfils no function that might affect the testimony, whereas one is led *a priori* to suppose that falsification will occur in the official testimony, one of the functions of which is to preserve the royal power and the reigning dynasty.

One must not, however, discredit all official traditions just because they are official. In Uganda, for instance, the Ganda occupy a privileged position in the present-day state. Yet they have not falsified their traditions in order to explain the present situation or to serve current political purposes.[4] Here again one might counter-argue that the functions fulfilled by these traditions relate to the state of Buganda which is now included in present-day Uganda, and that they are only relevant to the maintenance of the political system of that state as it was formerly, so that they are on a different level, sociologically, from the modern political myths which do have a bearing on the modern state of Uganda. That is partly true, yet it must be realized that these traditions also play their part in the modern political myths, and that in spite of that, their content has remained unchanged. Similarly it could be argued that some traditions, although private, are nevertheless influenced by official traditions, and hence by the functions these fulfil. This is especially liable to happen whenever any danger is attached to providing an interpretation of facts which differs from that offered by the official traditions. In the Akan States, for example, transmission of traditions which contradicted the official version of history was expressly forbidden.[5] Fear is a factor that must be taken into account when one studies private traditions and finds that they conform in every detail with the official traditions.

A last point worth mentioning with regard to the relative reliability of official and private traditions is that the former are usually transmitted with great regard for accuracy, precisely because of their functional importance, whereas the latter are often transmitted at random, free from any form of control, and open to alteration according to individual fancy. One of the consequences of this state of affairs is that official traditions often go back much further into the past than private traditions. Thus an official tradition is less trustworthy as a historical source than a private one in so far as it is official, but more trustworthy in so far as it is much more carefully transmitted. For example, the *ubwiiru*, the code of Rwanda, is the dynastic tradition, and fulfils a number of functions of vital importance for the state. Yet it is probably falsified from start to finish. On the other hand, it is the best preserved of all the country's traditions, because it is taught by specialists, learnt by heart, its recital is controlled, etc. It probably goes further back into the past than any other Rwandese tradition. In comparison, the memories handed down to the grandson of a warrior about a battle in which his grandfather had taken part will no doubt have suffered less from distortion, but they will be one-sided, strongly coloured by the imagination of the grandfather, the father, and the informant himself, and will all in all be a source of secondary interest for the general history of Rwanda; whereas the *ubwiiru* is of much wider interest, because it is connected with the central social structures of the country, and because these are reflected in it, even if only through the very distortions which it contains. It must, therefore, be remembered that an official source is not of any less interest than a private source simply because it is probably more distorted. Each type of source has its own kind of value for the historian.

Traditions may have many different kinds of function, and one tradition may combine several functions, so the possible effect of the functions of a tradition on its content is not always easy to assess. For instance, the characteristic feature of the historical tales of the Ngoni of Nyasaland is the stress they lay on the tribal characteristics which distinguish them from the neighbouring tribes among whom the Ngoni live in diaspora. Many tales make special mention of former Ngoni customs and emphasize their unique nature: none of the other tribes in the neighbourhood have them. Some of these tales are certainly not factual, but they continue to circulate because they succeed in fulfilling the function expected of them—the upholding of national prestige. But from another point of view, these tales fulfil another special function: each one might be regarded as an aetiological myth which explains a custom and stresses its importance. The tales belong both to official and private traditions, etc.[6]

This example is a good illustration of how difficult it may sometimes be to discover what the functions of a tradition are. The only way to do so is to make a sociological analysis of the society in which the traditions are found, and that is why a historian must also be a social anthropologist, or must at least only work in areas where an analysis of this kind has been carried out by an anthropologist. Studying the various versions of a tradition may be of help in discovering what its special functions are. It often happens that each version is the special property of a particular social group, and that the differences between the various versions reflect conflicting group interests. The commonest example of this sort of thing is the use of genealogies for justifying existing forms of stratification of various social groups. In Africa, it often happens that each of the groups concerned claims descent from the eldest of a group of brothers, and regards the other groups as being descended from the younger brothers, thus implying that it has moral, and sometimes political, superiority over the other groups. Here the function of the tradition is easily seen. It rationalizes inter-group relationships, emphasizes the individuality of each group as against the others, and expresses the power-relations between them, either as these relations actually are, or as the fancy paints them. The technique of comparing the different versions of a tradition may also enable the anthropologist to make a more thorough analysis of the social structure than would be possible otherwise.

2. *The initial testimony*

In most cases, the circumstances surrounding the initial testimony are no longer known, and if no obvious inferences about them can be drawn from the tradition itself, clearly the only obtainable information would be whatever could be derived from a parallel but independent tradition which referred to the same events as the first, but was of a different nature, and had quite separate claims to trustworthiness. Thus it is usually impossible to know what the purpose and the function of the initial testimony were. But it can be assumed *a priori* that with regard to the relationship between the testimony and the facts observed, or invented, which have given rise to it, the purpose of the initial informant is likely to have been more important than the function of his testimony. The testimony may indeed later acquire a social function, and does in fact do so in virtue of the fact that it starts a tradition, but in itself it may very well have been communicated without being in any way affected by the function it later acquires. If an initial informant announces the death of a king, he does so in order to announce the news, not in order to record history. His purpose is to supply information, and in most cases he does so because he occupies an official position which he holds for the purpose of making announcements of this kind. The immediate function of his testimony is simply to set in motion the institutional procedures for governing the chiefdom during the interregnum and for nominating a new chief. Afterwards, when the death he has announced becomes part of a tradition—a genealogy, for example—the function of the genealogy will be much more complex, and will be of an entirely different nature from the simple function fulfilled by the initial testimony. In many other cases it will be found that a first-hand account does not give rise to a tradition, precisely because it does not fulfil any recognizable social function. If an informant narrates the life of his father, he does so because it is of interest to him and to the extended family of the deceased. But his son or grandson will not transmit his testimony, because the deceased no longer belongs to their social group, and he is of no account to other social groups which are larger and more permanent than theirs. This presupposes, of course, that the deceased was an ordinary villager. If he had occupied an important position within the society, his son's testimony might give rise to a tradition, because there would then be a social group for whom the deceased was of some account.

I only know of a few cases in which information concerning the initial informant, and about the purpose and function of his testimony, has been transmitted. The Trobriand Islanders, for instance, have a song in which the heroic deeds of a certain Tomakam are sung. A traditional commentary was handed down side by side with the song, in which it is said that Tomakam himself invented the song. It is therefore not improbable that he considerably exaggerated the events recorded, for obviously his aim was to acquire prestige. After his death the song was handed down, partly because of its artistic merits, and partly because of the prestige it conferred on the group which held exclusive proprietary rights in it.[7] In the case of some of the dynastic poems of Rwanda, a traditional commentary gives precise information about the circumstances that gave rise to the poem. One of the poems was composed by Ngogane, the son of a famous poet, on the occasion of a murder committed by a member of his family. The murderer went into hiding at the home of Bigeyo, a friend of the family. But Bigeyo set intrigues afoot at the court in order to blacken the name of Ngogane's family, and finally handed over the murderer to the family of his victim. Thereupon Ngogane composed the poem, which he dedicated to the king, and in which he stigmatized the hypocrisy of Bigeyo and advised the king to be on his guard against duplicity of this kind. The poet's aim is obvious: he wanted to refute the attacks made against his family.[8] In the case of some of the other poems, it is known that the king commanded them to be composed to commemorate a victory.[9] This is a purpose very much in line with the true function of the dynastic poems as a whole, which was to perpetuate and extol the idea of kingship.

It is sometimes possible to draw conclusions about the purpose and function of an initial testimony by making a literary analysis of the text concerned, or by taking note of the type of tradition to which it belongs. Obviously the eulogies of the Kuba kings in the *ncyeem ingesh* songs cannot be taken literally, for the songs belong to the category of poems of praise. The same argument applies to the dynastic and warrior poems of Rwanda. A concrete example will show the latitude towards facts a poem may display. One day a young Rundi, about fifteen years of age, recited to me the *amazina* verses he had composed in praise of himself. Included in the poem were the names of the enemies he had killed with his lance or his bow. When questioned, he freely admitted that he had not killed anyone, but said that the *amazina* was a type of poem in which one must boast of mighty deeds, and it did not matter if the boasts were about entirely imaginary deeds. With a category of this kind, therefore, the historian may well be led to entertain reasonable doubts as to the truth of the statements contained in a testimony. On the other hand, the category may be of a kind which rules out assumptions that falsification has occurred. The spells used by the Kuba when they apply the poison oracle describe what the results of the oracle will be. The man who has composed the spell, or, if it is one that has gradually acquired its final form, the men who have composed it, have put into it their feelings towards a person accused of witchcraft. There is certainly no likelihood of falsification here, and the function of the spell at the moment when it was invented was to provide a prayer to the powers of the poison, beseeching that justice should be done. The text is in line with the function it fulfils, but the fulfilment of the function was brought about by means of a truthful description of the feelings expressed in the text. There are other categories as well as this one in which no falsification occurs. The names of the list of the Kuba kings are not falsified by the first informant, who is simply the man whose duty it is, at the death of a king, to add his name to the list. Nevertheless, one must be on one's guard against assuming that an informant has not falsified his testimony simply on the grounds that the category to which the text belongs does not lend itself to falsification. Westermann gives examples of lists of chiefs which investigators found to be falsified. The names of chiefs who had been a shame to the chiefdom were not included in the genealogical lists after their death. Their reigns were regarded as null.[10] In Rwanda, the reign of Ruaaka, Karemera I, was never included in the official list of kings, because, after a long reign, he abdicated in favour of his brother. It then became the official theory that he had not reigned, but had simply officiated in the capacity of regent.

In most cases, however, there are no available facts to inform us about the purpose of the informant or the function fulfilled by a testimony at the moment when it was first created. One can only suppose that the function was of minor, and the purpose of major, importance. In the absence of any information, one must not, however, proceed to the assumption that the factual accuracy of the testimony is open to doubt because there is nothing concrete to go on that would justify distrust. To distrust all traditions *a priori* on the grounds that they might have been distorted to suit the purposes of the first informant would be a hypercritical attitude to adopt.

The Kuba—to make a further point—are afraid of arousing the jealousy of superiors, who, they feel, might be offended if their inferiors show that they know something of which they themselves are ignorant. The idea of prestige stands high in Kuba society, and is a frequent cause of falsification. An informant will not communicate what he knows for fear of harming the prestige of his superiors, but on the other hand, he sometimes tells more than he knows in order to enhance his own. Thus one of my Bushongo informants had always refused to testify, until one day he learnt that another specialist in traditions had told me everything he knew; whereupon he came to ask me to record all the traditions he had so far withheld from me, so as to defend his reputation as an expert.

3. The final testimony

The final testimony is a hearsay account like all the other testimonies in the chain of transmission, and everything that has been said about them applies to it in the same way. But there is one important difference between them, and that is, that the final testimony arises from a new social situation: that in which someone wants to commit something to writing which has hitherto never been written down. The final informant has various reasons for making his testimony, one of which is that someone has asked him to do so in order to write down what he says. Thus the testimony acquires a special character due to the fact that it is an act of acculturation. The informant must take into consideration what the reactions of his fellow countrymen are likely to be, and he knows that they will be critical of how he behaves; and since he finds himself in a novel situation, he is never quite certain what he should do. In addition, he also must take into account what the reactions of the person who is recording the testimony are likely to be. The latter, for his part, can perceive exactly what motives the informant may have for distorting his testimony, since he himself is taking part in the situation. Any distortions which occur will therefore result from the influence both of the informant's fellow countrymen, and of the investigator.

(a) The informant and his fellow countrymen

It often happens that an informant will try to avoid testifying for fear of unfavourable reactions on the part of his superiors. When I first began my researches among the Kuba, no one knew to what extent the king was prepared to give his permission to the recording of traditions, and everyone kept quiet for fear of possible sanctions. But after the king himself had testified, they were much more co-operative. Nevertheless, some topics, such as the murder of kings, still remained taboo, and tales about them were only told in some out-of-the-way spot, or at night, away from prying eyes.

As soon as an informant performs for an audience, and particularly if the testimony is a group one, some subjects will be glossed over, and mention will only be made of things which would have the approval of everyone present.

It sometimes happens that when a dispute about testimonies arises, one of the informants abandons the position he had taken up and adopts that of his opponent, because he is persuaded that the other knows the tradition better than he does. For instance, the Lulua are under the impression that they originated from a place called Nsangu Lubangu, although this is not in fact the case. They have arrived at this belief because the old men, who know the genuine traditions, have, on this point, accepted the testimony of the teachers in a school situated in another area, on the grounds that, since they were teachers, they must know better than ignorant people.[11] It is of more frequent occurrence, however, that an informant adopts the opinion of his opponent in a dispute because the opponent enjoys a higher social status than he, and he wants to safeguard the prestige of a superior.

There may be other reasons for altering the content of a testimony. The examples I have given all come from Kuba society, but the same sort of thing is found in Rwanda and Burundi. The reason for this is that all three societies have a hierarchical structure in which the prestige of status is the dominant feature. No doubt in other types of society distortion of testimonies will occur for other reasons than those I have mentioned. Each society will have its own reasons.

(b) *The informant and the investigator*
The behaviour of the informant will depend very largely on the impression he has formed of the fieldworker. Has he been in the area for long? Do people trust him or fear him? What is his status in the society? What motives does

the informant impute to him? What does the informant stand to gain by testifying? The fieldworker must know the answer to all these questions if he is to tell what the reasons might be that would lead the informant to falsify his testimony. He must therefore know in advance what attitude the people in the informant's environment have towards him. The Kuba, for instance, are acquainted with four categories of Europeans: state officials, missionaries, business men, and the railway personnel. The state officials hold power and are therefore always dangerous, and it is only to be expected that they will want to know all traditions of a political nature, and each political group will make every effort to present them in such a way as to convince the agents of government that the group in question is important and possesses the maximum number of rights. The missionaries want to convert people and to introduce Christian habits into the country. They too are expected to be interested in traditions. But they must not be told traditions that go against their teaching, because then they will criticize them, which will harm the prestige of the narrators, and will fight against them, which will harm the whole community. The business men are thought to be only interested in trade. No one expects them to be interested in traditions. But if business men and railway officials were to take an interest in traditions, the people would be worried and suspicious, uncertain as to what motives would make persons of this kind take an interest in matters that had nothing to do with their professional interests. I, as a fieldworker, was regarded as being in a class of my own, because my behaviour made it impossible to place me in any of the existing categories. Nevertheless it was some time before it was accepted that I was collecting traditions simply because I was interested in the past history of the country. In Rwanda and Burundi the classifications are slightly different. Here too, though, I became accepted as a fieldworker who was collecting traditions solely in order to document myself about the country's history. In Rwanda it was at first thought that I was collecting them for political purposes, since many traditions are used as a basis for modern political myths, or that one way or another I was hoping to raise my status by the knowledge I was acquiring. In Burundi people refrained from telling me the more recent traditions, since they are still relevant in present-day national politics. As for the old traditions, no one could understand why I should be interested in them, and I was usually regarded as a friendly, harmless lunatic. But yet other classifications may enter into the picture. For instance, in some parts of Africa it is believed that Europeans are harmful because they are eaters of souls, or because they practise witchcraft. In that case, all attitudes towards them are dictated by fear.

After the fieldworker has made contact with his informants, the situation generally develops as follows: each informant tries to find out exactly what the fieldworker's motives are, and then makes a rapid calculation as to what benefits he is likely to gain by making a testimony, and what the disadvantages might be, and whether he ought to distort his testimony, and if so, how. Meanwhile the fieldworker tries to guess what the informant is thinking. And this is the atmosphere in which the testimony is made. It is important that the fieldworker should not show his reactions to the testimony, in case this might lead the informant to distort it; for if he were to express either satisfaction or dissatisfaction, the informant would immediately respond by adapting his testimony to suit what he thinks are the fieldworker's wishes. The fieldworker must keep the informant, and any other people who may be present, under careful observation, so as to be on the alert for the slightest sign that the testimony is being distorted and for any indications as to why. Thus the atmosphere in which these final testimonies are made is inclined to be somewhat tense. But if the fieldworker becomes well known in the area and contacts the same informant several times, the tension slackens, and sometimes disappears completely.

Most informants hope to gain financially from testifying, and expect that the longer their testimony is, the greater the reward will be. For this reason one must make it a rule to pay the same amount each time, thus removing the motive for any falsifications of this kind. Again, an informant will often try to win the friendship of the fieldworker if the latter seems to him to belong to a privileged class, hoping thus to get any help from him he may require—whether economic aid in money or in kind, or help in legal or even in political matters—and this is an attitude which is also likely to lead to falsification of testimonies. For instance, in 1907 a certain Shaam aShaam recited a list of Kuba kings containing more than a hundred names, solely in order to gain the support of the European who was questioning him.

4. Summary

A major source of error and falsification is the influence exerted on the contents of a testimony by the functions of the testimony and the purposes of the informant. Functions and purposes ultimately derive from the social structure of the society being studied. The distortions caused by them can be detected by the historian. They occur both in the testimonies of the chain of transmission, which are more directly conditioned by society, and in initial and final testimonies, where personal motives have the greater influence. There may be more than one reason for the occurrence of distortions, and the cases I have quoted are only a few examples among many. In practice, the collection of traditions must be preceded by a thorough analysis of the society and culture in which the traditions have arisen and developed and are finally recorded. This will enable the historian to conclude with some degree of certainty that some testimonies have been distorted, and with others there will be sufficient indication of distortion as to throw doubt on the accuracy of some of the statements. Sometimes, however, he may be unable to find any definite indications of distortion, in which case he must apply a methodological rule that is valid for all historical sources: In the absence of any indications of distortion, he must accept the text as being reliable. In point of fact, a historian can never arrive at a full knowledge of the past, but only at an approximation to the facts, and this approximation can only be based on whatever data are available. Therefore, in the absence of any indication of falsification, he must not postulate it *a priori*, or he will falsify his whole approach to his work.

2. CULTURAL VALUES AND THE TESTIMONY

The cultural values of a society are those ideas and feelings which are accepted by the majority of its members as unquestioned assumptions. They are the 'prejudices' of a society.

To its members, they give life its meaning, laying down the ideals to be striven for, the relative importance of things in relation to these strivings, etc. They are seldom formulated overtly, usually remaining unconscious for most members of a society, whose behaviour, however, is governed by them to a marked degree. Obviously the aims pursued by each individual are closely linked with these values, which, however, also play a major role in the society as a whole, since they are the ultimate guarantee of its functioning and perpetuation.

Informants have been impregnated with these cultural values from earliest childhood, and the traditions they know have also come under their influence. Traditions are altered, more or less consciously, to fit in with the cultural values of the time. There are three main types of cultural values which give rise to distortions of this kind. In the first place, there are those which determine what historical significance should be read into the events described. Next come certain basic concepts concerning history which influence those traditions that have to conform to certain cultural assumptions about history. Lastly, there are the cultural values which determine the ideals to be striven for, and since in almost every society the guardian of tradition is the *laudator temporis acti* and the *magister rerum*, he is expected to draw lessons from past experience and to idealize the past according to the norms laid down by such cultural values.

The connection between cultural values and the purposes and functions of traditions is so close that these two aspects could have been discussed in the same section. But the distortions of tradition which each bring about are on quite a different level, so that the historian must treat them separately. The influence exerted by cultural values is an underlying one, less obvious than that of the purposes or even the functions of a tradition. It is an unconscious influence which does not affect details or parts of a testimony, but which permeates the tradition as a whole. There is no question here of error or falsification, but rather of a certain bias or tendency. That is why the search for distortions brought about by cultural values can only be carried out by examination of the content of a testimony. That alone will indicate what the values in operation may be, although this is by no means the case when attempting to find out the purposes pursued and the functions fulfilled by a tradition.

All testimonies manifest the influence of cultural values, but not all do so in the same way. The initial testimony, for instance, cannot yet have been influenced by the need to adapt the testimony to current concepts about history, nor will it contain any idealization of the past—or at least, not to any marked degree—because there is usually very little lapse of time between the event and the first account given of it, and these factors require time to produce their effects. On the other hand, it is the initial testimony that chooses what events to record and what significance should be attached to them. In contradistinction, the testimonies of the chain of transmission, right down to the final testimony, are more and more affected by cultural values in two of the ways in which these operate: adaptation of a tradition to current concepts, and idealization of the past. So I shall first deal with the influence of cultural values on the initial informant, next with cultural concepts concerning history, and lastly with the idealization of the past.

1. Cultural values and the initial informant

An observer never gives a complete and accurate description of the events he has observed; and in order to describe them at all, he has to give them some meaning. Since no one can describe everything he has seen, a choice has to be made between the various events observed, and only those which are regarded as important or interesting will be recounted. The importance ascribed to an event depends to some extent on the personality of the informant, but much more on the general concensus of opinion in the society of which the informant is a member. It is society which is the operative factor in deciding upon the significance of events. A testimony is always a communication of some kind, and an informant only communicates something which he thinks will be of interest to his listeners. He knows what will be of interest to his listeners because he knows where their centres of interest lie, since they are those of the society as a whole. The spirit of the times and the cultural values of that society will determine what things are regarded as important.

An initial informant is therefore bound to be influenced by cultural values, although not always by the same cultural values. It is facts he relates in his testimony, but he colours them by giving them a certain significance; and it is by trying to distinguish between what is factual and what is interpretative in his testimony that one can estimate the influence of cultural values. For instance, several Bushongo testimonies mention that King Kot aNce stipulated that members of the royal clan should reside at the capital so as to be under surveillance, but none of them draws attention to the remarkable political foresight displayed by this decision, the result of which was that from the time of this king onwards, successors to the throne were strictly under the control of the king and his council, and it became impossible to make any attempt at secession or revolt. The state of the traditions shows that contemporary observers did not foresee the political effects of the measure. The tradition was preserved merely in order to explain why all the members of the royal clan resided in a quarter of the capital specially set aside for them, and the event recorded might never have been preserved by tradition at all if at some later time the members of the royal clan had once again been dispersed about the country.

Some important events do not get recorded in a tradition because those who witnessed them did not realize that they were important. The Kuba remember who the first European was who visited their country, but do not remember the second, although the first was a merchant who simply happened to travel through it, while the second came to take it over on behalf of the newly formed state. Lowie notes that the Assiniboine Indians have not preserved any traditions concerning the introduction of the horse into the plains where they live, although this was an event of capital importance for them, since their whole mode of life was later changed by it. The Nez Percé do have a tradition about the introduction of the horse, but it gives no indication of the importance of the event.[12] It was of course impossible for observers of the event to know in advance that the newly introduced quadruped was going to change the whole course of their lives, and one can easily imagine a hypothetical case of an Indian tribe having no record of the introduction of the horse, and, some ten generations after the event, seeking an 'origin' for this animal that had become such an important part of their lives, ranging it along with fire and iron as things provided by a celestial demiurge.

The question may be asked here whether the history of peoples without writing can be reconstructed with any degree of accuracy at all, since many events of importance are not recorded by tradition, others have their significance reduced, and others of lesser importance have a significance attached to them that seems exaggerated, so that the whole historical perspective becomes distorted. The reply to such objections is that in every testimony one must try to distinguish between the facts recorded and the significance attached to them. It is the historian's task to attempt to discover the real importance of the events of the past. Furthermore, the examples quoted concern the introduction of something new into a culture, the importance of which cannot be assessed at the time. Distortions of this kind will be found to be much less pronounced in the many other cases where the events recorded have taken place within the cultural environment of the observers concerned, and where all the features are familiar ones. The general outlines of the unfolding of history are not then greatly distorted. A further reply to such objections is that the historian cannot do more than reassemble those fragments of the past made available to him by the documents at his disposal, and his reconstruction of the past will always be fragmentary.

2. *Cultural concepts concerning history*

There are some cultural concepts which impose a certain attitude towards the past on the members of a society, and those in vogue at the time influence and distort traditions, because historical facts have to be brought into line with the attitude imposed. Among these concepts, the historiographical ones are those which most affect traditions. They can be classified into three categories: those concerning the measurement of time, those which relate to the idea of historical truth, and those concerned with the nature of historical development.

(a) *The measurement of time*

Peoples without writing do not have any units of time based on the concepts of mathematical physics.[13] They divide time according to standards of measurement based on ecological or sociological data. Ecological time is measured by natural phenomena which appear at certain given moments and which regulate human activity. This kind of time is cyclical, and the largest unit seldom exceeds a year or a season.[14] In the Congo, for instance, the year is divided into seasons. There are two main seasons, the rainy season and the dry season. Each is sub-divided into periods which, in the rainy season, are determined by differences in the amount of rainfall, and in the dry season, by differences in temperature. The names of these periods refer either to the rain itself, or to the flourishing of certain plants or the behaviour of certain animals. The day is divided up accord-ing to the positions of the sun, or to the crowing of the cock, or to work done at various given times. Thus they speak of 'the first cock crow', 'the sun is low', 'the palm-wine gatherers are coming down from the trees', or 'the time for chatter', etc. They have special terms for indicating the day, the night, the morning, and the evening. The week has four days, which gave their names to the localities where markets were held on each of these days. The month is lunar, and is subdivided according to the phases of the moon into five parts. There is no correlation between the week and the month, the month and the seasons.[15] This kind of ecological time measurement is typical for most central African tribes, and the techniques used, as well as the lack of any co-ordination between the various separate systems of time-reckoning, are found among tribal peoples in most parts of the world.

Calculations of past periods of time longer than a year or a season are made according to a calendar based on sociological data. A recurrent feature in the social system serves as a point of reference for time-reckoning. Hence arise customs such as dating events in relation to the years of a reign, the lapse of time between markets, by age-grades, by the length of time since the foundation of a village at a certain site, etc. Finally, the whole of the past can be conceived in terms of social structure.[16] Time is then divided into periods corresponding to the splitting up of human beings into various social or political groups since the time of the first man. Consequently time is measured by, and in relation to, the structural relations actually obtaining between groups. These relations are expressed by a genealogy which also serves as a measurement of time. The measurement of time therefore depends on the actual facts of the social system, and the past is simply a reflection of the political and social conditions that have actually existed. But it often happens that this calendar based on social structure does not stretch back very far into the past. The chronology of historical events in the distant past is then indicated by reckoning time by historical periods, and the calendar based on the social structure only applies to the last period. Thus, for the Kuba, the past consists of three periods: a period of origin, a period of migrations, and a static period during which no fundamental changes have occurred. The first period is not divided up in any way; in the second, the list of the names of places halted at during the migrations serves as a chronology; and the third has a calendar based on the social structure. The Alur[17] have two periods, the dividing line between them being the crossing of the Nile during the tribal migration. The pre-Nile period is one of mythical time, while the post-Nile period has a chronology based on the social structure. In both these examples, the mythical period precedes the historical one. That is not the case with the Lugbara, nor with the Trobriand Islanders, for whom the two periods coexist side by side.[18]

Calculations based on ecological data, those based on sociological data, and those based on periods, are three systems of time measurement which can coexist, and which normally do coexist, within the same society. Only the first of these systems is based on natural phenomena, the others being entirely determined by the social system or by cultural values. This is particularly marked when time is divided into periods, for these represent the stages of development which the members of a society think their society has gone through: chaos, the beginnings of social organization, and the final establishment of the social system. Clearly concepts of this kind will cause distortion of traditions. In cases where a mythical period is contrasted with a historical one, the duration of the former is reduced to a single moment in time, and chronological calculations become impossible. For instance, the events of the mythical period of the Kuba—their inhabitation of a coastal area and their wars in Kwango against the Poom and the Imbangala—are described in the tradition as having happened simultaneously and not in sequence. Time measured by sociological data also often distorts chronology. Whenever it is based on an aetiological genealogy, which includes the birth of mankind and its division into existing social groups, not only is time foreshortened the farther back the genealogy stretches, but other telescopings also occur. Ancestors who are not founders of lineages are omitted because they are of no importance in explaining the relations obtaining between the various existing social groups, and although this occurs most commonly with distant ancestors, it can occur anywhere in the genealogy. It should further be noted that the units of time measured by sociological data are not constant. The duration of a reign, or of a generation in a genealogy, are striking illustrations of this fact. One of the biggest handicaps in the study of peoples without writing is the absence of any ecological measurement of long periods of time. As Westermann has remarked, in a discussion on the historical value of African traditions, this has resulted in many false chronological estimates, and in much confusion.[19]

(b) The idea of historical truth

Not all societies have the same idea as to what historical truth is. It is an idea which influences traditions, because they must be 'true', and everything which is not true must be kept out of the hearsay testimonies of the chain of transmission. So it is the operative criterion in social or individual control of transmission. For the Kuba, historical truth is whatever is accepted by the majority as worthy of belief. In the Trobriand Islands, the decisive argument for establishing the 'truth' of a tradition is that the ancestors have declared it to be true. Their conception of truth does not exclude regarding certain events of the past, which they know could not possibly have happened in reality, as 'true'. Such events belong to myth. Whether an event could or could not have happened does, however, influence their belief in it to the extent that they have to have their belief confirmed by some trace left in the landscape. Here the testimony of the ancestors is not sufficient guarantee.[20] In the Congo, 'truth' is what has been transmitted by the ancestors as having really happened. So long as a testimony corresponds with the testimony that preceded it, it is true.[21] The Rundi have the same idea of historical truth, and as soon as something is accepted as a historical truth, they do not trouble to think whether it could have happened or not, or whether it really happened in the way the tradition describes. In their eyes, analysis of a testimony is meaningless. Sometimes there is a touch of ironical humour in the way they relate certain traditions, being aware that curious things are being told such as could not happen nowadays. But they say that perhaps they could have happened in former times, and their amusement is due to the unusualness of the tale, and is not at all a sign of scepticism. It is a similar kind of amusement to what would be felt by a Westerner if, today, he happened to look at fashion engravings from the times of his grandparents. All the attitudes towards 'historical truth' which I have been describing are very similar. But since no serious study has been devoted to the problem as it affects other illiterate societies, there is no way of knowing whether the similarities are accidental, or whether, as I suspect, they are to be found everywhere.

As a consequence of this attitude towards historical truth, informants will sometimes give several contradictory testimonies, all of which they declare to be 'true'.[22] Thus for a Kuba it does not make sense to compare different traditions in order to find out the truth. Another consequence of the attitude is that traditions are seldom, if ever, examined with any kind of critical judgment. The capacity for critical judgment does exist among peoples without writing, but it is not applied to traditions.[23] All that people do is to try not to change anything in the traditions handed down by the ancestors. But if changes are inadvertently introduced into a tradition, they in turn become 'true', for one or two generations at least. It should, however, be noted that this concept of historical truth tends to prevent the distortion of tradition rather than add to it, and it would seem, therefore, to have little effect on the content of a testimony.

(c) Historical development

For all societies history has a meaning and is thought to have followed a certain pattern, but in none of the societies of the kind I have been dealing with is any attempt made to establish relations of causality between historical events, and most certainly no idea of 'progress' exists in any of them. For the Kuba, every existing material object, institution, or custom was 'invented' at a given moment in the past, and has remained unchanged from the moment it was invented until the present. There thus exists a direct causal link between everything which now exists and something which has happened in the past, but this causal link is not thought of in terms of development. In addition it is believed that all the basic institutions of the social system go back to mythical times, when they were created by the demiurge Woot exactly as they are now. The Trobriand Islanders similarly lack any conception of evolutionary development.[24] For the Lugbara, the mythical period was one of chaos. Some of the things which still exist today were to be found there, but in inverted form. The historical period began with the appearance of a series of culture heroes who made order out of what then existed and introduced further inventions.[25] In Burundi, history is cyclical. The names of the kings form a cycle, and as one king succeeds the other, history runs its course and begins again. After a Mwaambutsa comes a Ntare, then a Mweezi, and finally a Mutaaga who precedes a new Mwaambutsa. Each king in the cycle has an ideal character, and every fourth generation each ideal type reappears. Ntare is the conqueror who founds a dynasty, Mweezi the ruler who has to maintain his power in the face of rebels, but who is very long-lived; Mutaaga is the good but unlucky king, and Mwaambutsa the king who prepares the way for a new Ntare. This idea of cyclical return has so much force that insurrections have been known to occur for the purpose of enthroning a new Ntare, because the reign of the Mwaambutsa actually in power has lasted too long. The concept of eternal recurrence implies the idea of predestination or fate. There is a Rundi tale in which a mother, whose child had, when playing his childish games, brought about the downfall and death of the king, his father, is asked: 'What were you doing when these things happened?'

She says, 'They happened, just as I was instructing the child in the way he should go; they had to happen.' And this story is no isolated example. In many tales diviners predict the future, and nothing can prevent their predictions from coming true. Another feature of Rundi history is that it is static. It consists of a series of tableaux, of unconnected events, in which no development takes place, and no consideration is given to causes and effects. Thus for instance under the reign of Mweezi II there occurred a series of risings on the part of various members of the same family of *abatare*. Each rising is described as a separate happening, but no mention is made of the obvious interconnections.

The belief that the world as it was first created is the same as the world as it is now is a belief that is well attested in the relevant literature. Creation took place in a time which is regarded as sacred, and which is distinct from, and placed alongside, time regarded from the profane point of view. The only access to it is effected by means of certain rites.[26]

Thus the inhabitants of Tikopia carry out 'the work of the gods'. The ceremonial consists mainly in the carrying out of ordinary everyday activities which are made sacred by the ritual, because they take place in sacred time and thus acquire creative value.[27] This is the only point on the subject of the concept of historical development that is made in the material that has been published. The examples quoted above, however, particularly the one from Burundi, indicate that fruitful research could still be carried out in this field. But there are already a large enough number of examples to enable the conclusion to be drawn that the particular conception of historical development arrived at by each society has a very great influence on its traditions, which are only preserved to the extent to which they conform to the conceptions current at the time. The distortions thus brought about permeate all the traditions of a given society, all of which are systematically biased in the same way. Fortunately for the historian, this means that a close study of the texts enables him to discover distortions of this kind fairly easily.

3. *Idealization of the past*

In every society, each role or status is modelled after an ideal to which every holder must conform, and the behaviour of each individual is judged according to certain value judgments. Approval is accorded the closer an individual approaches to the ideal norm, and disapproval the more he deviates therefrom. But since history performs an exemplary function for many societies, traditions become distorted into providing examples of ideal types. In fixed forms of tradition, this occurs according to ideals which were current at the time the text was formulated. Free forms, on the other hand, are more likely to reflect the ideals held at the time. Distortion of testimonies through adaptation to new ideals is thus something which occurs unconsciously from one generation to another. Moreover, changes in the conception of ideal types occur slowly and unconsciously. Nevertheless, the distortion of a testimony in order to make it conform to a new ideal is something which happens suddenly. Thus, fifty years after his death, the Kuba king Mbop aMabiinc maMbul had become the type of tyrant who kills and tortures out of sheer sadism. 'But God finally killed him', said a Bushongo who had spoken of him and who wanted to draw a moral from history. Yet this king reigned for a longer time than most of the other kings.

The process of idealization is very well illustrated by the Kuba tale which describes how one day a woman stole an anvil, thereby stealing the royal power from her brother. The Bieng chief who told it said: 'Men, all of you, do not forget the spitefulness, the importance of what has now been told. It happened in the house of Kotokoto, sister of Samba Ngolo.'[28] And later, he spoke of her as 'the woman who kills her children' (that is, the children of her clan). She is the prototype of the wicked woman who sets her husband's interests above those of her brother, in spite of the fact that in this matrilineal society she ought to have favoured the interests of her brother.

Distortions brought about by idealization are very common, and sometimes striking. For instance, among the Kuba, King Shyaam is the prototype of the magician, and Mboong aLeeng of the warrior. Every time a past event is to be attributed to a certain king, the tendency is to attribute it to Shyaam if it has a magical character, and to Mboong aLeeng if it has to do with a military campaign. The same thing applies to Burundi. Every conquest is attributed to a Ntare, and almost every revolt to a Mweezi, etc.

There is yet another way in which value judgments influence traditions. Among the Kuba, and in both Rwanda and Burundi, it is thought that the only history that exists is that of the dynasty, because the kingship is the expression of the whole country, and the past of the royal house is that of the entire nation.[29] Consequently the historical traditions of clans or lineages usually only preserve episodes in which one or other of the kings figures alongside one of the ancestors of the group. Thus the whole historical perspective is distorted owing to this value judgment about royal status.

The historian must always be on the lookout for distortions caused by idealization of the past. His suspicions must at once be aroused if a character in a testimony conforms too closely to an ideal type. And this happens so often, that the best way to study ideal types is to use material supplied by historical traditions. I have myself made an analysis of ideal types in Rwanda based mainly on the historical tales of the country.

While it is true that traditions are frequently distorted by idealization and that these distortions can be detected, it is also possible to establish that some parts of a testimony, or in some cases an entire testimony, have not been affected by the tendency towards idealization. When features which do not correspond to those commonly attributed to an ideal type nevertheless persist in a tradition, they may usually be regarded as trustworthy. Thus for instance, among the Kuba, when wars are attributed to King Shyaam and not to Mboong aLeeng, and in Burundi, when victories are attributed to Mweezi and not to Ntare, the account of the facts can be regarded as reliable. Finally, the fieldworker must find out what the current value judgments about traditions are. If a tradition is highly valued, that immediately explains why it has been transmitted, but also indicates that it probably conforms to cultural ideals and hence is likely to be distorted, whereas the content of sacred traditions or of those endowed with great prestige—particularly myths, or fixed ritual texts—is much less likely to be distorted, and so on. The attitude of the informant and of his listeners is a far from negligible factor in helping the fieldworker to assess the value of the testimony as a historical source.

4. Summary

Cultural values colour testimonies in three main ways. Through the medium of the first informant, they determine the choice of what events to record and the significance attached to them. Through the medium of certain cultural concepts, chiefly those concerning time and historical development, they distort chronology and the historical perspective. Lastly, they make testimonies conform to cultural ideals, thus turning them into examples to be followed. All these are unconscious processes. The historian can, however, gauge the effects produced by examining the traditions themselves, except in so far as the choice of events is concerned. But he must exercise the most careful judgment when doing so, for this is the most potent of all the influences which tend to make testimonies into a mirage far removed from reality.

3. THE PERSONALITY OF THE INFORMANT AND THE TESTIMONY

The distortions I have been speaking of so far are those which are caused by sociological factors. These factors affect all testimonies of the same nature, and especially all the testimonies of a particular chain, in more or less the same way. Now we come to a distorting factor which operates differently for each separate testimony of a chain, or for each testimony contributed by a different person. It is a factor which is of less importance than those I have already discussed, and which has more limited effects, but it is sometimes more difficult to detect. The factor in question is the influence of the individual characteristics of each informant.

In the case of the initial informant, it is not only cultural values, but also his individual characteristics that determine his choice of what to put into his testimony and his interpretation of events. That is obvious. And what has already been said about the difficulty of detecting cultural values equally applies to this second factor. It should, however, be noted that information about the character and personality of an informant who is no longer alive is still harder to come by than information about his purposes in testifying and the circumstances in which he testified. In practice, I have not come across any information of this kind whatsoever.

In the transmission of traditions, the main effort is to repeat exactly what has been heard. If the text is a fixed one, it cannot be affected by the personality of the informant, nor is there much likelihood of this being a distorting factor if transmission is controlled. In fact the only kind of hearsay testimonies that lend themselves to distortions of this kind are personal recollections, tales of artistic merit, and certain kinds of didactic tales. Van Gennep has given a very good account of how such distortions occur. The texts he refers to are of the kind that are transmitted freely. Only persons interested in doing so transmit them, and since they are texts designed to teach, entertain, or edify the listener, those interested in transmitting them are persons of outstanding intelligence and full of artistic talent. A person of this kind has a strong personality. Moreover the amount of interest he can arouse in his audience largely depends on the way he tells the story and on the individual twist he gives it. In such circumstances, the tradition inevitably becomes distorted. Each informant who forms a link in the chain of transmission creates new variants, and changes are made every time the tale is told. It is therefore not surprising to find that very often the original testimony has disappeared altogether.[30]

Another kind of distortion due to the personality of the informant in a chain of transmission is the following. Traditions often become unintelligible to the informants who recite them because they contain archaic features. Changes take place in societies, and when traditions refer to certain social situations of the past which no longer exist, the knowledge about them which is necessary for a full understanding of a testimony gets lost. If archaisms of this kind occur in a fixed text, they are seldom omitted or altered. The only distortions likely to occur are changes in the pronunciation of words that are no longer understood, and it very seldom happens that the whole testimony is falsified in an attempt to reinterpret its meaning. Free forms of tradition, however, are extremely prone to distortion whenever archaisms occur. Often the archaistic features are simply eliminated from the tradition. The Kuba, for instance, have quite forgotten that they once worshipped two superior beings called Mboom and Ngaan, and the only traces of this cult are those found in genealogical accounts of creation, in which the names Mboom and Ngaan have been preserved in the names of animals they are supposed to have created. Downright distortion arises only if one of the informants happens to be a man of marked intelligence. He then tries to reinterpret the unintelligible features, and invents a traditional commentary which is handed down alongside the original tradition. In this way the archaisms are preserved, but the commentary must be regarded as unreliable, since, as a critical examination of the content will show, it is a pure invention. The story mentioned above,[31] of the war between the Whites and the Blacks, is a typical example. There the archaism is preserved, but is explained as the sound of water or of sand. A tradition will continue to preserve archaic features if they have a touch of the marvellous. Thus the Kuba still speak of the Portuguese wearing garments of soft iron (that is, coats of mail). These were no longer used after the first part of the sixteenth century, but the traditions have retained this detail ever since that time, because informants were fascinated by its unusualness.

Informants show little interest in the traditions they know. The testimony of a final informant will be unconsciously distorted because of his individual characteristics in the way already described. In addition, his testimony will be affected by certain aspects of acculturation, which can be detected when note is taken of the informant's attitude towards the traditions he knows. In some cases, informants will ascribe no importance to them. In the Congo, especially, it is usual to find nowadays that those who have had traditions handed down to them are strongly influenced by European civilization, and are ashamed to recite the traditions they know because they find them childish. This is also the case with the majority of those who have been uprooted from their original environment. When a fieldworker asks one of them to testify, he will try to carry out the task as speedily as possible, and will omit all details he regards as 'childish', and abbreviate his account as much as he can.

An attitude quite the reverse of this is also to be found. An informant may be deeply interested in the traditions of his people. He may, on his own initiative, collect a number of traditions, combine them, and draw from them his own view of the past history of his tribe. His testimony will then be coloured throughout by the view he has arrived at. Moreover, since he himself does not distinguish between his sources of information, which may be numerous and varied, his testimony is apt to be less a reflection of tradition than a historical study in which none of the sources are mentioned. Indeed a few informants of this kind give a written account of the results of their investigations.

Yet another type of final informant experiences a kind of stage-fright about testifying. He feels uncomfortable about reciting traditions to an unknown stranger, and, unaware that he is doing so, he will abbreviate his account, omitting some parts and combining different episodes.

Here, as in other instances of distortion caused by the individual characteristics of the informant, it is only free texts that get regularly distorted. The only effect stage-fright has on the recital of fixed texts is that it gives rise to hesitations, repetitions, and a certain incoherence in the actual recitation.

It is fairly easy to test the trustworthiness of a final informant, all that is required being to get him to testify several times and then compare the various versions. This will not only indicate the points he is uncertain about, but may sometimes throw light on what effect his individual characteristics have had on the text.

Summary

This chapter has shown that a testimony is always a mirage. The social significance of a testimony influences various parts of a tradition. In order to achieve certain definite purposes, an informant may intentionally falsify this or that point in a tradition. The function fulfilled by a tradition will also influence it on certain given points. Hence, if one succeeds in finding definite indications of the existence of given purposes pursued or functions fulfilled, one can infer which parts of the testimony are likely to have been distorted and what kind of distortions are likely to have occurred.

Cultural values affect the testimony as a whole rather than affecting separate parts of it. Some distortions, such as those resulting from an arbitrary choice of events to record, cannot be detected. Others can be discovered through examining the text itself, from the contents of which deductions can be made about the cultural values held at the time and the effect that idealization of the past may have had on the testimony. Similar deductions about cultural values can be made from other types of existing non-historical texts.

Finally, the personality of the informant may cause distortion of the entire testimony or of parts of it only, and such distortions can be discovered, in the case of a final informant, by comparing the various versions he has recited, or, in the case of a chain, by comparing the various testimonies which are all descended from the same proto-testimony, since variations are due to the personal influence of informants. Direct observation of a final informant also helps to provide clues.

Since a testimony is never an unbiased description of what actually happened, one must always try to check on as many sources of error and falsification as possible, while at the same time avoiding a hypercritical attitude which would end in rejecting *a priori* all testimonies whatsoever. This is an attitude which could be adopted towards any kind of document— including written documents—which gives an indirect account of events. It is based on the hypothesis that it is possible to discover 'the truth' about history and the exact sequence of past events. But this is impossible. One can only arrive at an approximation of the truth. Another error to be avoided is that of hunting out distortions in a testimony like a detective on the trail. Every distortion is in itself a piece of documentary evidence, either about the past, or about present-day society, and should be treated as such.

Following upon this discussion of the relation of testimonies to the actual events they are supposed to describe, the next chapter is devoted to studying the evaluation of testimonies according to the amount of historical information that may be gleaned from them, and the extent to which they provide reliable evidence of the facts they are supposed to describe.

And that is the aim of all historical research.

CHAPTER V

The Evaluation of Testimonies

THE value of a testimony is always a relative matter, depending upon the extent to which the account it gives of a historical event, or a series of historical events, is reliable or not. It may be of very little value with regard to one event, but useful with regard to another. A falsification, for instance, is of no value as evidence, but of considerable importance for anyone studying falsifications as a sociological phenomenon during a period of the past.

The way to decide what weight should be attached to a testimony is to find out what connection there is between the initial testimony of a tradition and the facts it describes. If this testimony is a falsification, then the facts described must have been invented, and the testimony is not based on fact at all. But the falsification to which the testimony has given rise is in itself a fact which is of relevance to the testimony. Examination of the information on which a testimony is based is therefore the first step towards evaluating its reliability.

The next step is to compare it with all the other testimonies which describe the same facts. The comparative method is the one which enables the historian to arrive at an overall estimate of the relative reliability of the various testimonies. Therefore the first section of this chapter is devoted to the origin, and the second to the comparison, of testimonies.

I. THE ORIGIN OF TESTIMONIES

In assessing the amount of weight to be attached to a testimony, the degree of distortion it has undergone during the process of transmission, and the inaccuracies of the initial testimony due to the initial informant's choice of events to describe and the interpretation he put upon them, are not the only factors that must be taken into account. The opportunities open to the initial informant for acquiring knowledge of the events described must also be considered. Obviously if he himself has not witnessed these events, his testimony will be valueless as evidence.

But one can search for the origin, not only of the initial informant's testimony, but of the testimonies which have been handed down as hearsay accounts in the chain of transmission. Each of them is supposed to have repeated the previous one, and one must endeavour to make sure, in so far as this is possible, whether this has really been the case, or whether a testimony is not simply an invention. I shall therefore discuss this question after devoting the first sub-section to the initial testimony.

1. *The initial testimony*

It is possible to gauge the value of the information supplied by the initial informant if something is known about the circumstances in which he made his testimony. In a number of cases it can be assumed that he could have known about the events described, because he was in close contact with the persons involved. Thus a certain Mweemy Bulaam composed a song on the death of one of the sons of the Kuba king Mbop aMabiinc maMbul, to whom he offered it in condolence. The information supplied by the poet about the death of the king's son is correct, although he himself may not have witnessed it, and may have described it in his testimony according to accounts of people who had.

This is a case in which the circumstances in which the testimony was made were preserved in a traditional commentary. Such cases are, however, rare. Usually the circumstances surrounding the making of initial testimonies are only known indirectly. Among the Bushongo, the poems in praise of the kings are composed upon the death of each king by his wives. It can be assumed that this happened in the past as well, and on this assumption, the information upon which the songs are based can be regarded as reliable, since it was supplied by the wives of the persons concerned. Similar conclusions can be drawn for other traditions in this society and in others.

Most of the events transmitted by traditions are public events in which a large number, or all, of the initial informant's contemporaries were involved. This holds true of migrations, the death of kings, wars, cultural borrowings of traits that became integrated into the life of the community, and other events of the kind that are known to every member of society. Traditions describing such events are based on reliable information if they have been transmitted by the groups involved. If, as frequently happens, the first observer remains anonymous, but can be shown to have belonged to a group that was involved in the events described, this amounts to proof that his information was reliable. And if the tradition is one which has been transmitted within such a group, it is almost certain that the first observer belonged to the group.

Sometimes the text itself provides internal evidence that the tradition cannot have been founded on observed fact. Myths of origin are cases in point. The Kuba, for example, tell of the disputes that broke out between Mboom and Ngaan, the gods of creation. But since, after their disputes, one of them became the heavens and the other took on the nature of water, no one can have been present at the disputes, and the tale cannot rest upon observed fact. The creation of the first man is a similar example. Mbo-Maloom, a Bushongo wise man, once replied, when asked to tell about the demiurge Woot: 'Woot was the first man. There was no one present to witness his creation, and he himself has given no account of it. How then can we know about it?'

The possibility that there may be some foundation in observed fact must not, however, be ruled out too hastily. For instance, there is a Bushongo tradition which tells how the Kuba king, Mbo Pelyeeng aNce, wiped out nine tribal spirits. This could be explained away by saying that, as spirits do not exist, no one would have witnessed their extermination. But it would be wrong to do so, for there is a ritual for killing spirits, and it was probably a ritual act of this kind that was performed by the king and witnessed by the initial informant. As I have said above, a clear distinction must be made between the facts observed and the interpretation put upon them. The foregoing example is a good illustration, as is also the following one. There is a tale which tells how a Kuba king died of remorse, shortly after he had been enthroned, because of having had all the sons of his maternal uncle assassinated. Here the cause of death—the king's remorse—must be regarded as mere supposition, while it can be accepted as fact that the assassinations took place, and that the king died an early death. In every case one must distinguish between the two levels of discourse: the events described, and the significance attributed to them or the interconnection established between them by the observer. His interpretation is also a historical event, but of another kind. It provides evidence of how the initial informant, and perhaps his contemporaries as well, interpreted or reacted to certain events.

The question might be raised as to the number of ways a tradition can originate. There would seem to be no more than three possible ways. Either it has been entirely invented by the initial informant, or it springs from an eyewitness account given by the initial informant, or else it springs, not from direct observation, but from a rumour, a piece of 'news' that the initial informant heard and made use of in his testimony. This last process is well illustrated by a Rundi example. A tradition from eastern Burundi tells how a certain Kilima, who had been a rival claimant to the throne, was killed by King Mweezi II, his head being subsequently displayed in the royal kraal. Nothing of the kind in fact occurred. Mweezi died in 1908, and Kilima died later. The first thing to strike one about the tradition is that it was found in a district at some distance from the places where the events occurred, and further research showed that the chain of transmission was short enough to allow the conclusion to be drawn that the tradition must have originated in the district where it was told. This meant that it must almost certainly have been based on a rumour. At some moment during the course of events Mweezi must have got the upper hand in the struggle for the throne, and it must have been spread abroad that Kilima was dead. The initial informant must have heard this false rumour, which may perhaps already have had the romantic details of the traditional narrative woven into it, or else he himself may have elaborated the information conveyed to him by the false rumour. A large number of traditions which show signs of being tales remembered by private individuals, perhaps handed down within a family, or circulating at random in a locality, may be suspected of having originated in a similar way. If they are found in a district other than that where the events are supposed to have occurred, it is more than likely that the information on which they are based was supplied by a false rumour which seemed to convey an exciting piece of 'news'. For it must not be forgotten that rumours arise automatically at times of tension and in the absence of regular sources of information. These are circumstances which almost always occur at times of social crisis; and it is, on the whole, the critical moments of a society's history that get handed down to posterity as historical events. In addition, there is in some countries, such as Rwanda and Burundi, a traditional technique for discouraging the enemy and for rallying faithful followers, which consists in spreading false rumours for this purpose. This gives rise to the supposition that false rumours may, and probably do, form the basis of a large number of traditions, which, needless to say, thereby become devoid of value as historical evidence. The only value which such a tradition has for the historian is that the false rumour that has given rise to it gives a picture of contemporary reactions to the events concerned.

2. *Hearsay testimonies*

In order to assess the value of the testimonies of the informants in the chain of transmission, one must make sure that each has had the opportunity of hearing the testimony of the preceding link in the chain which he is supposed to have repeated. It is usually impossible to know by name all the informants included in a chain, or even to know how many links there have been in it. There are, however, cases where this is possible, as when the tradition is the property of one family and is transmitted from one generation to the next of a known genealogy. This is true of the poets of Rwanda. Here the names of the informants forming the links of the chain are known, and it is known how many of them there have been, and that the tradition was passed down from father to son, so that one can conclude that the sons really did have the opportunity of learning the tradition.

In other cases, the circumstances in which the tradition has been transmitted must be studied. When transmission is in the hands of a social institution designed for this purpose, one can be confident that the chain is an unbroken one, for the members of the institution are known to each other, and opportunity is provided for the younger ones to learn the tradition from their elders. But only those traditions concerning the group to which the institution for transmission belongs—whether it be a tribal or a lineage group, or even a group formed by the people of a district—can be vouched for. Any traditions concerning other tribes, for instance, are usually based on hearsay only, and may contain information that is unreliable. But it is characteristic of many peoples without writing that groups only narrate their own history, and refuse to recite traditions belonging to neighbouring groups, even when they know them well—or at least this is so when the alien tradition has no connection with their own past history. Certainly this applies to traditions which are protected by rights of ownership. A Kuba example illustrates the point. In the Ngongo tribal council in Matumba, a speaker was reprimanded by his listeners because he recited traditions which did not belong to his own tribe, but to the Ngeende. He had to break off his recital and restrict himself to speaking of Ngongo matters. Yet the information contained in the Ngeende tradition he had recited was afterwards found to be correct. The members of the council had merely considered it incorrect to recite traditions belonging to another tribe.

As far as traditions which are not connected with an institution are concerned, one has to distinguish between those which are common knowledge and those which are not. With the former, the circumstances in which the traditions are currently transmitted must be examined. The *ncok* songs of the Bushongo, for instance, are not connected with an institution, but are freely transmitted when masked dances are held. The character of the songs makes it clear that they are transmitted because of their artistic merits. From the content of the poems it would appear that they were composed by members of the royal court, who customarily lived at the capital. Thus the poems arose in the same environment as that in which they are still transmitted, and this continuity enables one to conclude that there has been no break in the chain of transmission. Traditions which are not connected with an institution and which are not widely known are usually simply something which individuals happen to remember. Here it is essential to trace the links in the chain of transmission, so as to make sure that each preceding link was indeed the person quoted. Since the chain of transmission in traditions of this kind is usually a short one, this can be done in a large number of cases.

3. Summary

By careful examination of all available indications, the historian can often arrive at an assessment of the reliability of the information supplied by the initial informant and of the continuity or discontinuity of the chain of transmission.

Once a testimony has been understood, and, after examination for possible distortions, has been found to contain reliable information, one can then proceed to the final stage of critical analysis—the comparison of testimonies, which will lead to a better assessment of the weight to be attached to each testimony as evidence of the events described.

2. COMPARISON OF TESTIMONIES

The aim, in comparing testimonies, is to get a better idea of the relation each testimony bears to the events of which it preserves a record. One therefore only compares testimonies which record the same event or series of events.

Comparison of testimonies will establish their degree of reliability. If the texts of two versions bear a close enough resemblance to each other as to warrant explaining the resemblance between them by mutual borrowing or by common derivation from an earlier text, then the testimonies may be said to be dependent. The same holds true of different chains of a tradition, if analysis shows that at some time in the past they formed the same chain.

By means of the various dependent testimonies, one can reconstruct the text of the archetype from which they probably all derive. In turn, analysis of the variants of the archetype makes it possible to assess the quality of the transmission and the kind of distortions the tradition may have undergone.

If the testimonies are independent, comparison of them will lead to a higher degree of certainty as to the reliability of the account of events given by the various traditions, some of which may agree, some of which may differ, while others supply supplementary information.

Reliability can be tested either by textual comparison, or by comparison of circumstantial details. Both techniques should be used in combination, although either one of them can suffice to show a link of dependence between texts, or the absence of one. But the combined probabilities which both techniques together provide form a bundle of probabilities which will be more convincing than the indications provided by the use of one or other of the techniques on its own.

The results obtained by the comparative method finally enable us to judge the relative value of the texts, and to draw the maximum amount of information from them. This section will therefore deal in turn with textual comparison, comparison of circumstantial details, and lastly with the results to be obtained from using the comparative method.

1. Textual comparison

(a) *Fixed texts*

Textual comparison of testimonies will have to be carried out in a different manner according to whether the testimony we are dealing with is a fixed or a free text. With fixed texts, the words themselves form part of the tradition, and a word-for-word comparison can be made, following the usages established for the comparison of written texts. Similarities can be judged to be accidental or not according to the degree of correspondence between the two texts as a whole. They may correspond completely, in which case they may be regarded as being entirely dependent; or only parts of the texts may correspond, and in this case there have probably been interpolations which one of the texts may have borrowed from the other, or which both may have borrowed from a third.

It is not enough simply to establish the fact that there is a relationship between the two texts; in addition, one must try to find out which text has borrowed from the other, or show that both derive from a common parent. The possibilities can be represented by the following diagrams:

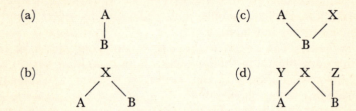

The first two diagrams represent total dependence. A and B are the texts being compared. In the first diagram, B derives from A; in the second, both derive from a common source X. The next two diagrams represent cases of interpolation. In diagram (c), B has an interpolation which is a partial borrowing from A, whereas in (d), A and B have made a partial borrowing from a source X which is different from their respective sources Y and Z.

The following examples illustrate the sort of difficulties one is likely to encounter.

Among the Kuba, various sections of the Ndoong clan have the following slogans:

A. *Makum aLabaam amiin mel aNdoong.*

B. *Makum aLabaam amiin mel aNdoong.*

C. *Makum aLabaam amiin mel aNdoong. Mbul aNdoong yashyaam bwiiky.*

D. *Makum aLabaam amiin mel aNdoong. Ibul yashyaam bwiiky.*

E. *Makum aLabaam amiin mel aNdoong. Ibul inyaamk imitetl.*

The slogan for rain:

F. *Yooncdy inyaacdy mateem ikaangl byeenc yaan a dik di maan. Makum aLabaam amiin mel aNdoong. Kweemy acik mimbyeem bwil abwil.*

The slogan for the Bieng:

G. *Yooncdy anaacdy mateem ikaangl bakidy adik di maan . . .*
Nshamwook ntyeem, mwaady aNdoong, ilooncy yaady Pwaaloom . . .

All the testimonies from A to F have in common: *Makum aLabaam amiin mel aNdoong* ('Makum of Labaam among the names of Ndoong').

A and B are obviously completely dependent, and in view of C-F, descend from the same parent text.

The testimonies C to E have a common structure: the first part corresponds to A and B; the second part is different in each case, but there are correspondences between them. C and D have *bul . . . yashyaam bwiiky*, D and E *ibul . . .* in common. Probably C and D have a common parent text that is less remote than the parent text common to A and B (or, in fact, A-F), and E has an interpolation from an unknown source, which covers the whole of the second part of the slogan. But E has borrowed a further interpolation from D which has resulted in the introduction of *ibul* instead of *Mbul aNdoong*. Comparison shows that A-E, F and G are good examples of interpolation, and that F borrows interpolations both from A-E and from G. In comparing F and G, one finds that G is nearer to the original than F, and that G', the direct parent of G, is the source for F', the parent of F. For the genealogies confirm that *Yooncdy* is the ancestor of the Bieng clan. A curious point, however, is that the phrase: *Yooncdy . . . byeenc yaan adik di maan*, in F ('Yooncdy, his litter above the ground'), is nearer the parent text G' than it is to G, which has: *Yooncdy . . . bakidy adik di maan* ('Yooncdy, his friends above the ground'). In fact, the Bieng clan slogan describes all the insignia of the great chiefs of Yooncdy, of which the mat (*ikaangl*) and the litter are examples. G is a corruption of G'.

The only thing common to all these slogans is the name Ndoong, which is the name of a clan, and also of villages founded by the clan. In G, Ndoong indicates a village, and in A-E it indicates the clan. F probably derives entirely from a parent text of G, and includes the slogan for the Ndoong clan as it appears in A-E. In a recent parent text of F there must have been some confusion over the use of Ndoong as the name of a village in G, so that the slogan for the Ndoong clan got added. This sort of thing often happens. Among the Kuba, when a clan gives its name to a village, it often confers its slogan on the village. One might therefore postulate that F' was something like the G text which we have, as far as *Ndoong*, this being followed by the slogan, thus: *Nshamwook ntyeem, mwaady aNdoong, Makum aLabaam amiin mel aNdoong, ilooncy yaady Pwaaloom*. Later, the tradition in the course of transmission between F' and G must have lost the intervening parts.

A further curious point to note is that the end of F, *Kweemy . . .*, is part of the Kweemy clan slogan, and must therefore be an interpolation. F is therefore composed of three parts: (1) an interpolation from G'; (2) an interpolation from the parent text of A-E; (3) an interpolation from the Kweemy clan slogan. The relationship between the contents is that (1) is the Bieng clan slogan, (2) is the slogan for a clan which owns a well-known village in Bieng territory, some of whose members live there, and (3) is the slogan for a clan descended from the Bieng. The slogan as a whole is said to refer to the rain because of (3), which means 'the net (the word for this being a homonym of the name of the Kweemy clan) is stretched all round the darkess' (i.e., the rainclouds). Analysis of F indicates that the slogan probably originates from the Bieng.

A diagram of the *stemma codicum* could be constructed as follows:

Stemma codicum of various Kuba clan slogans

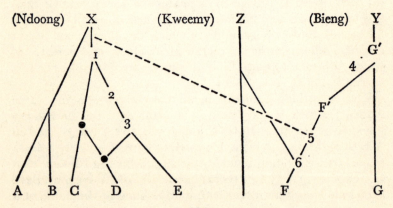

The interpretation of the figures is as follows:

1. One branch retains *Makum aLabaam amiin mel aNdoong*, the other adds something.
2. One branch adds: *Mbul aNdoong yashyaam bwiiky*, the other *Ibul inyaamk imitetl*.
3. A parent text of D repeats *Ibul* from the parent text of E.
4. One branch retains *byeency yaan adik di maan*, the other has *badiky adik di maan*.
5. A parent text of F repeats the Ndoong clan slogan.
6. A parent text of F repeats the Kweemy clan slogan.

The example quoted shows how the *stemma codicum* can be more complicated than it is for written texts—and it is a simplified version I have given here. It also shows how one can reconstruct a number of archetypes belonging to different periods of the past. The *stemma* gives depth to a tradition.

In this particular case it was easy to trace authentic links between the traditions, but sometimes this requires more ingenuity, and account must be taken of the type of tradition with which one is dealing. For instance, a Kuba slogan is found among the Lulua, not now in the Bushongo language, but in that of the Luba of the Kasai. Its meaning is: 'It is not his own house, but other people's houses he sets fire to'. Among the Kuba the slogan applies to the king, while among the Lulua it applies to the name *Losho aNtande*.[1] The Kuba version derives from the Lulua version, which is an explanatory commentary on the name. The Bushongo version has no narrow explanatory function of this kind, but is simply used proverbially to describe the sovereign.

While in the examples quoted above it was possible to provide proof of the probable relations of dependence between the various testimonies, this is not always the case. For instance, there is a Rundi proverb which is found in two versions:

Gira Ntare naRuhinda. 'Long live Ntare and Ruhinda'.
Gira Ntare naRuhaga. 'Long live Ntare and Ruhaga'.

Comparison of the versions does not reveal which is the authentic one. It is only by careful examination of other sources in which Ruhinda and Ruhaga are mentioned that one is led to assume that *Gira Ntare naRuhinda* is the original version.

(b) Free texts

Textual comparison is more complicated with free texts than it is with fixed texts, for here the words do not form part of the tradition. But what can be compared are the features which do belong to the tradition, namely, plot, theme, episodes, and setting.

The plot may be identical, partially the same, or different. If it is identical or partially the same, the theme will also be the same, if it is different, the theme may or may not be the same. Again, if the plot is identical, the episodes may be so also; but they may be partly different, in which case the setting may be identical, or else partly or entirely different. When the plot is entirely different, certain episodes or parts of the setting may nevertheless be identical. The various degrees of similarity are shown in tabular form as follows. I have found it necessary to invent a technical term for each type of comparative relation, the term being an adjective describing the type of text.

TABLE I

Degrees of similarity between free texts

Plot	Theme	Episodes	Setting	Technical terms
+	+	+	+	Identical
+	+	±	± and −	Divergent
+	+	+	± and −	Parallel
+	+	±	+	Variant
±	+	±	+, ±, and −	Hybrid
1 > 2	+	±	+, ±, and −	Combined
−	+	−	+, ±, and −	Similar
−	+	±	+, ±, and −	Aberrant
−	−	±	+, ±, and −	Contaminated
−	−	−	−	Alien

+: identical; ±: partly different; −: different; 1>2: the plot of one includes the plot of the other but goes beyond it.

Comparison of free texts makes it possible to draw certain conclusions about the relationship between testimonies. These conclusions are based on the degree to which common features are or are not to be found in the various authenticated versions of a testimony.

Identical texts are almost certainly related. The correspondence is too close for it to have been brought about by chance. It is unlikely that two informants should describe the same event in the same way, unless the event described is of very brief duration —and even then it is unlikely, and it is something which hardly ever occurs in a free text.

We know, from what we learn from psychology and from everyday experience, that each individual observer has his own way of seeing and describing things, and that a complete correspondence of this kind can only come from borrowing.

Parallel texts may be assumed to be related, for the same reasons. It would be a coincidence if the same things had happened, in the same way, in two different settings.

Variant texts are not any more likely to be independent. Almost all the events which occur are the same, and they occur in the same setting, with the same persons taking part.

Divergent texts may be either related or independent. Here, events which differ to some extent take place in a setting which is either partly, or entirely, different. The greater the divergence between the traditions, the more likely it is that they are independent. But experience has shown that in actual fact, divergent texts are usually dependent.

Hybrid texts indicate hybrid testimonies. They share in common part of the hearsay testimony from which both have stemmed, and for the rest they are different. If A and B are hybrids, this means that they have a common parent X, but also other parents, Y and Z. This is as much as to say that there has been interpolation.

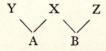

Combined texts are an extreme case of hybrid texts. One of the testimonies shares a common parent with the other, but the other has other parent texts from which the first is not descended, thus:

Similar texts are always independent, but there has been diffusion as regards the theme or possibly part of the setting, or both.

Aberrant texts are also independent, although here there are more features in common than in the preceding type, because the episodes have in part been repeated.

Contaminated texts are independent, but here diffusion is limited to the episodes, and/or to parts of the setting. Wandersagen usually belong to this type.

Alien texts are completely independent.

All this can be summarized in the following table:

TABLE II

Degree of independence of the various types of free texts

Related texts:	without alterations	identical
	with alterations	parallel variant divergent
Partially related texts:		hybrid combined
Unrelated texts:	with diffusion	similar aberrant contaminated
	without diffusion	alien

It is impossible within the scope of this book to give detailed examples of each of the possible types. I shall therefore confine myself to giving one diagram showing the relationship between a number of not entirely unrelated Bushongo texts. More detailed examples will be given in a later publication.

The Bushongo testimonies recorded at the capital are for the most part connected with three main chains of transmission: that of the royal clan, that of a branch of the royal clan, the members of which are excluded from succession to the throne, and lastly, that preserved by a tribal council called the *ishyaaml*. The three chains have, however, always been in contact with each other, to such an extent that they might almost be regarded as one chain. The result of a situation of this kind is that a number of testimonies that give the appearance of belonging to a private tradition in fact belong to the official traditions. Moreover, proof is hereby provided that all informants living in the same place, or rather, all testimonies belonging to chains that derive from the same place, are found to be related to each other. Nor is this peculiar to the Kuba. Rowe states that all the Inca traditions that have come to hand stem from the court at Cuzco, and all are interdependent.[2] This need not surprise us, since it is a well-known fact that oral traditions of a non-historical character rapidly become widespread, and their diffusion can sometimes be traced over whole continents.[3] The Wandersagen provide a striking example.

It is even more difficult to follow the intricacies of relationship between dependent free texts than it is with fixed texts. Usually it cannot be done through textual analysis alone, which at best only gives vague indications, whereas circumstantial proof is often conclusive.

2. Comparison of the circumstances of transmission

Comparison of the circumstances in which testimonies were composed or transmitted often reveals connections between them which enable the historian to postulate their inter-dependence. Proof of such interdependence can be based on indications bearing relation either to the informants, or to the method of transmission, or to the type of testimony.

(a) The informant

Different testimonies may be communicated by the same informant, in which case they are definitely related. One must carefully distinguish between a case of this kind and that in

DIAGRAM I: *Relationship of Busho*

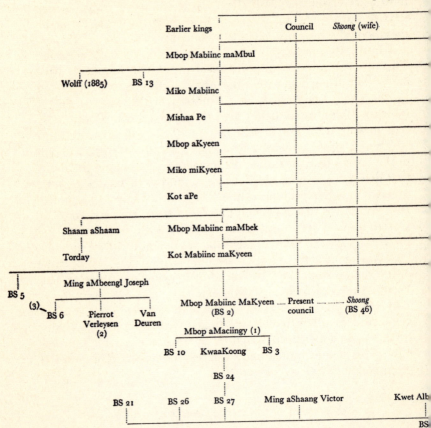

which the same informant gives different versions of the same testimony, for in the second instance, the difference between the versions is entirely due to the personality of the last informant of the chain, since it is this which accounts for the changes he makes each time he recites the tradition. He may hesitate, forget passages, add embellishments, abbreviate, etc., but it is not difficult, by comparing the texts of the various versions he has given, to discover what the testimony was that was handed down to him and on which his versions were based. In the contrary case, the informant bases his first version on one chain

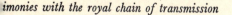

imonies with the royal chain of transmission

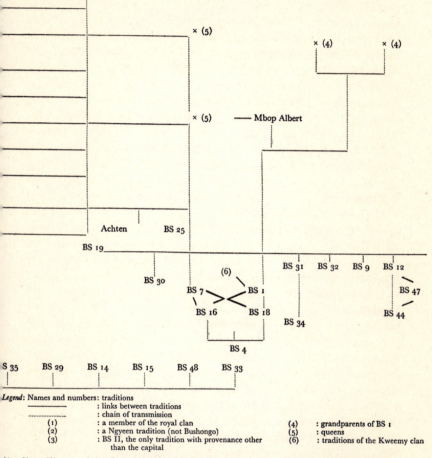

Royal clan II (*Cikl*)

× (5)

× (4)   × (4)

× (5)   —— Mbop Albert

Achten   BS 25

BS 19

BS 31   BS 32   BS 9   BS 12

BS 30

(6)

BS 7   >< BS 1   BS 47

BS 16   BS 18   BS 44

BS 34

BS 4

S 35   BS 29   BS 14   BS 15   BS 48   BS 33

Legend: Names and numbers: traditions
    ——————— : links between traditions
    .... : chain of transmission
    (1)   : a member of the royal clan
    (2)   : a Ngyeen tradition (not Bushongo)
    (3)   : BS II, the only tradition with provenance other
                 than the capital

    (4)   : grandparents of BS 1
    (5)   : queens
    (6)   : traditions of the Kweemy clan

Note: Six traditions recorded at the capital could not be linked directly to any others, but they probably are related.

of transmission, and his second on another, or perhaps on the
first with another added to it. This often happens if the informant is telling about something about which several oral
traditions exist. He chooses one or other of the traditions he
knows according to his own personal preference. Thus the
brother of the village headman of Loon, a Kwa village in Kuba

territory, stated at first that the Kwa were indigenous there. When the village headman heard this he was annoyed, for the official Bushongo tradition states that the Kwa were 'brought' from the West by the Kuba, and have always been subjected to them. The village headman was afraid he might get into trouble with the Bushongo authorities, and sent his brother along to make a second statement that would correspond with the Bushongo tradition—which he did. Obviously the second statement was a different testimony, even although it was made by the same informant. Nevertheless there is a definite connection between the two testimonies, consequent upon the narrator being the same for both. Cases where the second testimony contains more information than the first are of frequent occurrence, the informant having acquired fresh information during the lapse of time between the two testimonies. Thus a Bushongo informant at first only mentioned three kings for the period 1885–1954. Later he added many more. He had meanwhile added to his store of knowledge by information obtained from an uncle. Hence the second testimony was partially based on different traditions from those of the first; but clearly the second is partly dependent on the first, even though it is more complete.

It also sometimes happens that contradictory traditions get transmitted, not only in haphazard fashion by an individual informant, but along one and the same chain—in which case the relationship between them is more significant than that between contradictory traditions transmitted by an individual informant. The chief of Takyiman, a state in the Ashanti Confederacy, stated in one testimony that his clan was of native origin. Later he made another testimony, from which it appeared that the clan were immigrants. The first statement was directed towards all those who were not members of the clan, and the second towards the members themselves.[4] The circumstances clearly indicate that the second testimony was simply a falsification of the first. This will usually be found to hold good for all cases of this kind.

Sometimes the chains of transmission of two testimonies can be proved to go back to one informant belonging to a certain period of the past. This often happens when a tradition belongs to a family or a recognized lineage. It then becomes possible, in many cases, to reconstruct an archetype which can be regarded as the parent text of a group of existing testimonies. This applies notably to a number of testimonies of the dynastic poems of Rwanda. Circumstances of this kind enable one not only to show that the texts are related, but also exactly how they are related with reference to a common parent text. Moreover, an analysis of this kind can run parallel to a textual analysis, and each should arrive independently at the same conclusions.

(b) *The locality of transmission*

Attention has already been drawn to the fact that oral traditions often undergo diffusion and can be found to have a wide area of distribution. This explains, particularly so far as free texts are concerned, why a tradition comes under so many different influences. Since diffusion is known to be of such common occurrence, one is prone to suspect that testimonies will be related when it can be proved that they come from the same locality. Conversely, when textual analysis shows that two testimonies are not related, this can be confirmed by circumstantial proof that they have not been transmitted within the same locality, and that there has been no contact between the informants of the two chains of transmission. To supply the necessary proof, it has to be shown that there have been no economic, social, political, or religious contacts between the two localities—but this is very difficult to prove. It seldom happens that no trade or barter of any kind exists between two localities, or that there has been no intermarriage on the confines of two neighbouring tribes. Religious ties also exist oftener than has been supposed. They come about through the diffusion of rites and of myths, and through proselytizing or pilgrimages. In practice, the best way of proving that no contact exists between two localities is to show that their oral traditions have no common features—an argument which gains strength from the well-known fact that oral literature spreads more rapidly than anything else; and historical traditions are part of oral literature. Another argument that can be used in this connection, although with a certain amount of circumspection, is that of the existence of barriers to diffusion. The inhabitants of the Easter Islands, for instance, are isolated from other Polynesians, as are a few groups of Eskimos from other groups in the north of Greenland.

If textual analysis discloses no common features in two traditions, one can only assume that they are independent, and circumstantial proof can do no more than reinforce that provided by the texts themselves. The circumstantial argument is much more useful in those cases where textual analysis shows a certain affinity between two traditions, without however leading to any clear proof as to whether the texts are partly independent or wholly dependent. Here it is useful to combine all the evidence at one's disposal, either to show that the chains of transmission derive from the same locality, so that the texts are probably dependent, or to show that they do not derive from the same locality, so that there may have been some degree of diffusion from one locality to another, but very little likelihood of there having been any direct transplantation of a tradition from one locality to another. Happily evidence is much easier to come by for this last type of research.

(c) *The type of testimony*

Sometimes the type of tradition to which the testimonies being compared belong gives some indication as to how independent they are. For instance, esoteric traditions cannot be recited to uninitiated members of a group, and so cannot influence exoteric traditions, although they can be influenced by them. If, therefore, two such traditions are related, it is the exoteric one that is genuine. One must bear in mind here, however, that instances occur such as the one already mentioned, when a falsified version of a tradition is manufactured by the members of an esoteric group for the consumption of those outside this group. Such is the example from Takyiman already quoted, and it would seem that similar examples occur in Rwanda among the traditions of the *ubwiiru*. Another example is the tradition about the ruling house in Ashanti. The official version states that the dynasty was autochthonous and 'came from a hole in the ground', whereas the esoteric version said that it was of foreign origin. But no member of the royal lineage, which formed the esoteric group in question, might divulge the secret, on pain of death, and the second version was invented solely in order to keep the secret of the first.[5] When esoteric traditions from two different groups are compared one can be quite certain that they are independent of each other, but otherwise one can only assume that either the exoteric version is genuine and has influenced the esoteric one, or that the exoteric version is a falsification of the other.

The type of tradition to which the testimonies one is comparing belong can also give indications that they are related. For instance, if a Bushongo slogan is found among the Lulua, it is highly probable that the two are related, even if—since they are in different languages—they do not consist of exactly the same words, for experience shows that slogans lend themselves to borrowing, either whole, or in part as interpolations, so that the slightest degree of similarity between slogans immediately leads one to suspect that they are related. The type to which testimonies belong is also often a guide as to whether diffusion, partial borrowing, or some link of relationship has occurred between one testimony and another. In the examples of Bushongo slogans used to illustrate the discussion on the textual comparison of fixed texts, we have seen how the meaning of the word Ndoong was changed from the name of the clan to the name of the village, and I observed that this was by no means a rare occurrence. The same sort of thing is found in Rwanda, where, in historical tales, it is common to find a personal name followed by the warrior's slogan given to that person. The same slogans are also found in tales belonging to completely independent traditions, the only point in common being that in each a person who happens to have the same name appears, or the same person appears in both tales.

In addition, the purposes and functions of a tradition may help to establish which of two testimonies is the genuine one. Among the tribes on the Luapula there exist two kinds of history which are often similar; universal history, applying to the whole of society, and the history of local groups, clans, and lineages, from which the universal history is made up. If, therefore, a similar passage is found in the history of a lineage and in the universal history, one can be certain that the genuine tradition is the lineage history.[6] The explanatory function of the slogan for the Lulua name *Losho aNtande* proves that it is genuine in relation to the similar Bushongo slogan which does not have the normal function of slogans in such societies.

Lastly it should be noted that sometimes appeal must be made to the whole body of a people's traditions, or a major part of them, in order to decide which of two variant versions of a text is the genuine one. An example of this is provided by the Rundi proverb: *Gira Ntare na Ruhinda* and *Gira Ntare na Ruhaga*. There is a tale about the coming to the throne of the first king of Burundi, in one version of which the protagonist is called Ruhaga, while in another he is called Ruhinda, this being the only difference between the two versions. But in other tales about a later event in Rundi history a Ntare is opposed by one Ruhaga, and in various versions of these tales the names Ruhaga and Ruhinda are again confused. Tales from other regions, Rwanda and Ha, enable it to be established with almost complete certainty, however, that Ruhaga was the name of the hero of the second lot of tales. It can therefore be assumed that Ruhinda was the name of the hero of the first lot. How, then, can the confusion have arisen, both in the tales and in the proverbs? At a given moment of the past, the proverb must have been applied to one only of the two kings, and bore reference to a particular situation: that in which two kings were each trying to conquer the other's country, and a choice had to be made as to which to give allegiance to. This interpretation is supported by the translation of the proverb, which runs: 'Long live Ntare and Ruhinda (or Ruhaga)' followed by the phrase: 'the country does not recognize two kings'. Now traditional tales tell us that this situation occurred twice in Burundi's history. What more natural than that persons experiencing the second situation should have been reminded of the first precisely because of the existence of the proverb, and that they should have adapted the proverb to meet the situation with which they were faced? This being the case, the original version is the one containing the name Ruhinda, since it has been proved that Ruhaga was the hero of the second situation. The confusion that later arose both in the tales and in the proverbs is quite simply due to the similarity between the two situations, to faulty transmissions of the tales, and to the free adaptation of the proverb containing the name Ruhinda to one containing the name Ruhaga, and the subsequent existence of the two side by side. This example, which I have purposely gone into in some detail, shows how various indications in combination can show which of two testimonies is the genuine one.

3. Results obtained by the comparative method

The comparative method is without any question extremely useful, and adds greatly to our knowledge about historical documents and the information they convey. It is above all useful in enabling archetypes to be established which represent an earlier stage of a tradition. It is true that archetypes are not the equivalent of the actual testimonies handed down from one informant to another in the chain of transmission. They are no more than a reconstruction of a testimony of this kind, and between the two there is all the difference that exists between an actual fact and a hypothesis. But such a hypothesis, if the reasoning it is founded upon is flawless enough, can approximate very closely to the unknown fact. It can serve, not only as a synthesis and an abstract of the various related traditions from which it is reconstructed, but also as a basis for the comparison of the testimonies concerned. The construction of an archetype from these testimonies involves comparing all the variant versions and endeavouring to understand how and in what order they have come about. Comparison of the archetype with the testimonies shows the possible or probable distortions the tradition must have undergone within an interval of time that is sometimes known, but more often unknown. Moreover, the comparison supplements the information already obtained concerning the quality of transmission of the tradition, and such information as has been collected about the likelihood of distortion of the tradition. The results obtained from the comparative method consist, in fact, in procuring an overall check on the critical methods already used, and in the supplementary evidence which it provides.

So far it has been tacitly accepted that the comparative method should be applied only to traditions of the same type, belonging to the same literary category, in order to establish whether or not there is a direct relationship between them. But it can also be applied to different types of testimony and different categories of traditions. The only kind of relationship which can then be established is either one which results from diffusion, or one which results from two separate traditions having been transmitted by a single observer or a single informant in the chain of transmission, so that the number of possible relationships between them is lower.

If use of the comparative method is extended to include comparison of oral traditions with other historical sources, this increases the chances of establishing that traditions are completely independent, and this in turn further adds to the usefulness of the comparative method, for the main aim here is to establish whether independent sources do or do not agree in their accounts of the same events. When there is complete concordance between independent sources, the chances that the events described did actually happen are very much increased, and almost amount to certainty, especially if the sources are as different in kind as they could possibly be. When there is disagreement between them, further examination of each type of source—that is, a revision of the critical examination that has already been made of each one—will put one in a better position to discern the bias that may have led to a distortion of facts in one or other of them. One thing the comparative method does not do—or at any rate, not often—is to establish that one source contains more 'truth' than another. For instance, discrepancies between two genealogies usually mean that both are biased in the interests of the group concerned.[7] But when the sources under comparison belong to different categories of oral tradition, or when one of them is an oral tradition and the other some other kind of historical source, then it quite often happens that analysis of the historical content will enable a choice to be made as to which of the two sources is nearer to the truth, so that the other can then be seen to be falsified or distorted, and this fact must then be stated and an explanation sought for the presence of the distortions. A third result obtained by the comparative method is that the various sources examined supplement each other so that a better idea is gained not only of the events described, but of the whole historical perspective.

This frequently happens when nineteenth-century written sources are compared with oral traditions. The written sources are the work of foreigners who, while being well aware of the historical importance of the arrival of Europeans upon the scene, yet do not sufficiently take into account the incidents attendant upon this event and the effects it produced. The traditions for their part reflect the native point of view, and give a good description of what the intrusion of strangers meant to their society, although they often fail to realize what changes the arrival of the Europeans would bring about. Comparison of the two sources enables one to arrive at a more complete picture of the whole occurrence. For example, a Protestant missionary source describes how a dispute broke out between a Kuba king and his son, who had turned Protestant. Shortly after he had done so, a revolt arose and the mission was burnt down. The tradition states that the son wanted to dispossess his father with the aid of the missionaries, for since his society was matrilineal he could not in the ordinary course of events have succeeded his father. His claims to succession were not only rebellious, but implied a profound change in the customs of succession. Apparently the missionaries did not know that the society was matrilineal, and supported the pretender because he was a Protestant. The outcome was that the king had the mission destroyed, which resulted in a general rebellion on the part of the Kuba against the independent state. The sources complement each other in such a way as to provide a general picture of the whole course of events. Each, taken separately, would only have given a truncated version of this or that aspect of the matter. The choice of events worth recording made by each person giving a historical account of them can thus be corrected by the comparative method in a way which cannot be accomplished by the use of any other technique.

4. Summary

This chapter concludes my description of the techniques of historical methodology that can be applied to oral traditions. Having discussed the meaning and the distortions of the individual testimony in the two preceding chapters, I have in this one centred the discussion on an examination of the weight to be attached to a testimony as an account of the events described, including in this discussion an analysis of the kind of information contained in the testimony, and an account of the application of the comparative method for the purpose of controlling and supplementing the information already obtained by other means. Wherever the comparative method can be used, this is the best way of establishing the extent to which a tradition is a true reflection of the events described. The discussion provides a striking illustration of the axiom that in history one can only arrive at probabilities—never at certainties.

The next chapter is devoted to the more general question of historical knowledge—its characteristics, limitations, and possibilities. The characteristics of the various types of oral traditions are discussed, and then the features which characterize all oral traditions. Lastly, something will be said about the means at the disposal of the historian for mitigating the limitations of the information that can be derived from oral traditions alone.

CHAPTER VI

Historical Knowledge

M AN's knowledge of the past is limited to the amount of information that can be derived from the sources at his disposal. The historian is like someone whose only way of viewing a landscape is by looking at photographs. He can see everything that is revealed by the photograph, but has no idea what exists beyond the field of vision covered by the camera. True, he can infer from the photograph that probably such and such a detail at the edge of the picture continues beyond his field of vision, but he cannot be sure. Also, if the camera happens to have focused on the only factory chimney in the area, the observer may be misled into thinking that the main feature of the country is its industrialization, although in fact the reverse may be the case. The historian is in exactly the same position as regards the past. He only sees certain aspects of it, from which he may to some extent make extrapolations; but he can never know more than what his documents have preserved for him.

Moreover, his documents—particularly if they are indirect accounts, as is the case with oral traditions—are biased. Every photograph of the past has been made with a special kind of camera, fitted with a lens that is suitable for a given situation. Each type of historical source not only has its own limitations, but also its own particular way of seeing things—its own particular bias. The existence of such a bias means, however, that each type of source has its own advantages as a means for conveying information about the past, just as each type of camera is specially adapted for one kind of photography and not for another. Genealogies are useful for establishing chronological data, aetiological myths may be of help in studying the history of diffusion or the introduction of cultural traits, and the humblest tools and utensils among archaeological finds may enable a picture to be built up of everyday life—and so on.

A study of the limitations, bias, and particular uses of each source—of its main features, in short—can be carried out at different levels: at the level of the individual testimony, at that of the type of traditions to which the testimony belongs, and at that of oral tradition as a whole; and it is at this last level that I propose to proceed here. As far as each individual testimony is concerned, intelligent application of historical methodology will reveal its main features. Here, I shall deal in the first section with the typology of traditional sources and the characteristics of each type. The second section will be devoted to the characteristics of oral tradition in general. The third will discuss the scientific disciplines which the historian can use as an auxiliary aid to enable him to go beyond the limitations inherent in oral traditions. These scientific disciplines have their own bias and their own limitations, but they are of a very different order from those of oral traditions. By comparing widely different historical sources, bias can be detected and corrected, and a more rounded view of the past can be arrived at. To return to my photographic metaphor, comparison of oral sources with other kinds of historical sources is a little like juxtaposing and superimposing a number of photographs one with and upon the other, so that a larger area of the landscape can be seen, and seen more clearly.

I. TYPES OF TRADITIONS AND THEIR CHARACTERISTICS AS HISTORICAL SOURCES

So far no one has drawn up a typology of oral traditions, and there is such a lack of adequate data for doing so that it is, I hope, scarcely necessary to say that the typology I propose here can in no way be regarded as final. It has, however, become apparent that an attempt must be made to give a description of the various types, if only to emphasize the fact that there are certain clearly distinguishable categories, each with its own limitations, its own bias, and its own particular uses for providing a knowledge of the past. The only way to get an all-round picture of oral tradition as a historical source is to describe the various types which occur.

The sub-sections which follow are devoted, first to the typology itself, and then to a discussion of the various types of source: formulae, poetry, lists, tales, and commentaries.

1. The typology

The various possible criteria of classification have already been dealt with.[1] Those which will be used as a basis for the following typology are: the purpose, the significance, the form, and the manner of transmission of the testimony. The psychological attitude adopted towards a tradition, and the literary category to which it belongs, are neither of them criteria which permit of forming clear-cut classifications. But both factors are important for the establishment of a typology because they are factors which play a part in historical sources of all kinds. For this reason, I have not made it a hard-and-fast rule to exclude them altogether in elaborating my proposed typology. Justification for using these criteria is provided by the fact that when applied to oral traditions, they enable attention to be drawn to certain factors which are of primary importance in assessing their characteristic features. The use of one criterion alone cannot reveal the characteristic features of any one particular type of tradition. It is only by taking account of all criteria, including those which do not lend themselves to the formulation of clear-cut classifications, that the possibility arises of making generalizations about types.

Oral traditions can be divided into five categories, which in turn can be subdivided into types. The resulting typology is shown in Table III.

The categories are discussed in the following sub-sections, in each of which one of the types belonging to them is outlined, and its relative worth as a historical source discussed.

2. Formulae

These consist of certain stereotype phrases used in various special circumstances. The phrase forms part of an action of

TABLE III

The typology of oral traditions

A	B	C
Category	*Sub-category*	*Types*
I. Formulae		Titles
		Slogans
		Didactic formulae
		Ritual formulae
II. Poetry	Official	Historical
		Panegyric
	Private	Religious
		Personal
III. Lists		Place-names
		Personal names
IV. Tales	Historical	General
		Local
		Family
	Didactic	Aetiological myths
	Artistic	Artistic
	Personal	Personal memories
V. Commentaries	Legal	Precedents
	Auxiliary	Explanatory
	Sporadic	Occasional comments[2]

some kind, and its significance lies as much in its wording as in the use made of it in the appropriate circumstances. Thus the reply to a magic formula pronounced for the purpose of driving away the rain will only have value if it has been correctly *formulated* so as to bring about the intended and desired result. This explains why it is that formulae are transmitted with very great accuracy. They often contain archaic elements which are no longer understood by the informants, but which are nevertheless retained precisely because of the inherent characteristics of formulae as such. It must also be understood that any inaccuracy in repeating a formula is immediately threatened with sanctions, if only in the sense that the purpose for which it has been pronounced may not be achieved.

Sources of this kind are of great value, because they are fixed texts which, although privately transmitted, are nevertheless transmitted with great accuracy. Their function has little influence on the text. Since they are not aimed at recording history, and are merely an instrumental factor in the situations in which they are used, they may be regarded as sources of an archival character.

Their usefulness to the historian lies in the light they throw on the history of ideas, but it is usually impossible to assign them with any accuracy to a particular period of the past. If they contain any incidental historical information, this is likely to be trustworthy, because it has been transmitted unintentionally.

(a) Titles

Titles are formulae describing a person's status. They are seldom likely to contain any historical information. An isolated instance among the Yoruba has been recorded: the title *Maye balogun* recalls that a certain Maye once played the role of chief in one of the wars waged by the town of Ibadan. *Balogun* means leader of the army.[3]

A title preserves—as do many names as well—a memory of the past; but for the historian, titles can only be used as auxiliary sources, because the past facts to which they bear reference require to have fuller details supplied by some form of commentary. A title in itself is no more than a medium for recording that such a situation did at one time exist.

(b) Slogans

Slogans describe the character of a particular group of people, belonging either to a family, to a clan, to a district, or to a country. They often contain eulogistic features. Sometimes they supply information about the past history of the group. Among the Kuba, one of the variant versions of the Ndoong clan slogan: *Ndoong aBieeng* ('Ndoong stemming from the Bieng'), refers to their past history. Usually slogans are recited on occasions when the special characteristics of the group concerned are highlighted.

Any value that slogans may have for the historian depends primarily on the extent to which the original wording has been preserved. In spite of the fact that they come under the category of fixed texts, they are nevertheless mostly transmitted without any special schooling, and there may be a wide variety of versions. Frequent repetition is here no guarantee of accurate reproduction of the content, as is proved by the examples quoted earlier in the discussion on the textual comparison of testimonies. Furthermore, slogans can often only be understood in the light of accompanying explanatory commentaries. In general, they are sources from which information can be extracted about the family, clan, district or country which they characterize.

(c) Didactic formulae

Under this heading come proverbs, riddles, sayings, and epigrams. They are regarded as the storehouse of ancient wisdom. Unlike other types of formulae, they are meaningful in themselves, and sometimes contain historical information. 'Ponder the death of Gaha and mend your ways', say the Yoruba, to whom the meaning of the phrase is quite clear—namely, that injustice is punished. The meaning becomes clear as soon as it is known that Gaha, who was in charge of the administration at Oyun, was burnt alive by the people of the town because of the cruelty of his administration over a number of years.[4]

Didactic formulae, like titles, only give a clue to facts, the details of which have to be filled in from commentaries. 'What are the hoes that Woot forged?' ask the Bushongo, the answer being: 'The feet of men'. The riddle would be incomprehensible if one did not know the myth which tells how Woot forged the feet of men. Some proverbs are useful sources for legal history,[5] but most of them are restricted to dealing with the moral norms of a society. They are, therefore, useful as a means of discovering what these norms were. But since it is usually impossible to date a proverb with any accuracy, it can only give generalized information about the past.

(d) Ritual formulae

These are formulae used in either religious or magic rites. It is commonly believed that if they are not repeated word for word, supernatural sanctions will fall, not only on the person who recites them, but on everyone else involved in the ceremony. The texts of formulae of this kind are therefore learnt with special care, and indeed they are usually spoken by specialists: priests, water-diviners, sorcerers, or layers of spells. A special sub-type of the ritual formula is the *judicial oath*, which is used as a form of ordeal.

Ritual formulae always contain information about the history of religion, and in addition often convey other kinds of historical information.[6] They are transmitted with special care because of their ritual nature, and this adds to their trustworthiness. Among some peoples, oaths preserve the memory of an important event of the past.[7] The oath merely alludes to such an event, a more detailed account of which must be sought in a narrative source.

3. Poetry

Under poetry I include all traditions in fixed form, the form and content of which are considered to be of artistic merit in the society within which they are transmitted. They are similar to formulae in that they are composed in fixed form, but the significance attached to them is of an entirely different order, for while formulae are used purely instrumentally in the performance of an act of some kind, poetry must, both in form and content, fulfil aesthetic demands. Moreover, it is because of its artistic merit that poetry becomes a tradition to be transmitted. Its preservation and transmission is often in the hands of specialists, and the mode of expression must comply with certain fixed laws and conventions. Its social significance is also subject to conventions, although this varies according to whether the poetry in question is official or private. Official poetry is either straight propaganda, or else awakens feelings which, in the eyes of the community as a whole, ought to be aroused and meditated upon. Private poetry, on the other hand, expresses the feelings of private individuals. Nevertheless, both these sub-categories have one feature in common, namely, that as poetry, they depend far more than any other type of tradition upon the effect which they have upon the feelings of the audience, and that in order to obtain this effect, formal expression of the content plays as great a role as the actual content itself. This importance of the formal structure of a poem accounts for the fact that so many poems are full of padding, metaphors, and stereotype phrases.

In assessing the value of poetry as a historical source, it must be remembered that its psychological function and its aesthetic qualities distort the facts described. Furthermore, the kind of historical information transmitted by poetry is usually of a rather vague, generalized nature, and it is often impossible to attribute it to any definite period of the past. But poetry can be used as a historical source, mainly because it gives indications of the psychological attitude adopted by certain people towards certain historical events. This is particularly true of private poetry. Official poetry is more likely to convey the attitudes and behaviour patterns which society wants to impose upon its members.

(a) *Historical poetry*

Historical songs and poems are intended to provide an account of historical events. They are often composed for propaganda purposes. A particularly striking example of poetry of this kind is furnished by the Incas, among whom poems were composed on themes laid down by the government,[8] but it is not found everywhere. In one of the Mbuun clans, the clan history is recited to the accompaniment of songs and dances,[9] but it would appear that the performance is not carried out for propaganda purposes, although the underlying intention may be to add to the clan's prestige. When historical poetry is of a popular nature, it becomes folk-song. According to W. Bauer, wars, or the death of famous men, form the themes of such folk-songs, and he remarks that their aim is to stir up loyalties, or to ridicule, or arouse compassion, or awaken hatred, and that they are full of allusions to forgotten events, so that, although these events are preserved in the songs, they become distorted, and may in the end be omitted altogether.[10] No mention is made in ethnological literature of the popularized versions of history found in songs such as these, but Bauer's remarks concerning them could be applied to the whole of traditional historical poetry, except that it treats of a far wider range of themes than those he mentions.

Since historical poetry is usually composed for propaganda purposes, it can be used for studying the political attitudes of the group which gave birth to it. But its value as a historical source is diminished by its propaganda aims, which give rise to major distortions in the account of the facts, and also by the fact that it is so full of allusions which often can no longer be interpreted, that it cannot be used for purposes of analysis of the events which it describes.

(b) Panegyric poetry

A poem of praise is certainly not composed for the purpose of recording history. Poetry of this kind is composed either during the lifetime of the person concerned, or immediately after his death.[11] It is a category of poetry which is strictly bound by rules of the poetic art, and its outstanding characteristic is a liberal use of stereotype phrases indicating the exceptional virtues of the person who inspired the poem. These poems are also rich in metaphors, as is illustrated by the following song for the chief of Nkwanta:[12]

Tromu Kwasi (Bongo antelope born on Sunday, a reference that kings are sons of the sun), whose origin no one knows,[13]
King of the dark forest,
The leopard at his door,
Dua Yaw, King of thousands of Bonos,[14] Nkwantahene,[15] great Lord of old,
Adu Kwao (name of a plant with numerous offshoots), whose offshoots are many,
Gyameradu (name for a person who killed his father-in-law or mother-in-law, possibly a reference to the founder's marriage with a daughter of a conquered Brosa chief or queen-mother).

It is obligatory to use a large number of stereotype phrases in this category of poems, so the poems serve as a source of information about the social ideals prevalent at the time when they were composed. Moreover, although the poems themselves give very little precise information about historical events and refer to them mostly by allusions, they are accompanied by a commentary which gives more detailed information. Any attempt to study the poem itself in order to learn something about the history of the institution to which the person whose praises are sung belonged comes up against the difficulty of deciding whether a statement is merely a stereotype phrase, or one which describes actual facts. This is well illustrated by a poem of praise for the Zulu king, Shaka. It is known that what the poem says corresponds with reality, yet it consists almost exclusively of stereotype phrases. It runs as follows:

> You have destroyed, destroyed the tribes!
> Where will you make war now?
> Hei! Where now will you make war?
> You have conquered kingdoms.
> Where now will you make war?
> You have destroyed, destroyed the tribes!
> Where will you make war now?
> Hurrah, hurrah, hurrah.[16]

In evaluating these poems as historical sources, one must remember that the form strongly influences the content, not only because of the purely formal rules that must be followed, or because stereotype phrases are obligatory, but also because in many of them a special vocabulary must be employed, and certain particular ideas, and no others, expressed.

(c) *Religious poetry*

This type includes stereotype forms of prayer, hymns, and dogmatic texts. The characteristic feature of this kind of poetry is the care which is taken to ensure that it is transmitted accurately, together with the fact that it usually belongs to an esoteric tradition. Another fact worth noting is that this is a form of literature produced by a class of specialists—the ministers of the religion in question. Often texts of this kind are accompanied by traditional commentaries, such as those found in New Zealand.[17]

Like all other traditions connected with religion, those belonging to this category are transmitted with care, transmission being in the hands of specialists. Usually therefore little distortion arises. Traditions of this kind supply information about religious life and about past world conceptions. But their particular value lies in the light thrown by hymns and prayers on the feelings of those who composed them towards the supernatural world. Occasionally they also provide information about

events of the past which are not specifically religious in character. For instance, prayers to local spirits are the most important
Luapula source for a knowledge of local history.[18]

(d) Personal poetry

Contrary to the foregoing types, poetry of this kind plays no
part in public life. It is composed in order to give free expression
to the feelings of the person who composes it. Transmission of
testimonies of this kind usually occurs only in an irregular way,
and distortions of all kinds, due to the artistic tastes in fashion
at the time, are liable to creep in.

But this category expresses better than any other the individual's attitude towards life. It can thus be used as a source
for the history of feelings and ideas. But one has to be on one's
guard against distortions due to adapting the tradition to the
tastes of the day. When a poem has not been rearranged, it
shows the feelings and cultural ideals of its author, as is demonstrated by this funeral lament of a Sioux woman for her husband
killed on the field of battle:

> Braver than the bravest,
> You sought for glory at the gates of death.
> Did you have no thought
> For the lonely one who weeps at home?
> Did you have no thought for me?
> Braver than the bravest,
> You sought for glory rather than for love.
> Dear one, I weep, but I am no coward.
> My heart laments you,
> My heart laments you, as I think of you.[19]

4. Lists

Lists contain the names either of places or of persons. Although
a list may be an established one, the names are not always in
the same order. Lists are usually preserved by specialists belonging to some institution, and pronounced on the occasion of
some public ceremony, such as the death or the accession of a
chief. They generally form an official tradition intended as a
historical record, although the facts recorded are mostly used
to support claims to political, social, or economic rights. In

many societies, this is a highly venerated type of tradition, and in some—for example, among the tribes on the Luapula—the same names are transmitted from generation to generation, and a person who inherits a name inherits all the rights and obligations of the person who bore it before him.[20] Their whole history is so much built up around these names that it is even thought that the alliances and enmities which exist nowadays between the bearers of inherited names are the same as formerly existed between the first bearers of the names.

The reliability of this type of source cannot be taken for granted. They are usually transmitted with care, but they are official traditions, as often as not used in the defence of political, social, or economic interests. This explains why lists—especially lists of the names of persons—lend themselves so readily to falsification. Lists are normally the only available sources for compiling a chronology, and if, upon examination, a source is found to be reliable, it can be invaluable from this point of view.

(a) Place-names

Lists of place-names fall into two groups: those which give the names of places passed through during a period of migration, these places being unknown to the informant, and those listing places which are known to the informants. The names in the first kind of list often get confused, but the main aim of a testimony of this kind is to record history. In the second group, the names are easily remembered, because the places that bear them are there to act as reminders, and the recording of history is a secondary matter. The main aim of testimonies of this kind is usually to maintain and defend rights to land.

Lists giving names of places that are no longer known are seldom distorted intentionally, but sometimes a name will be omitted, or the order transposed. As soon as it is a matter of names of places known to the informants, a knowledge of the geography acts as a mnemonic device for accurate memorization of all the names in the right order, but distortions frequently occur in defence of claims to land. Lists of place-names are the main sources for the study of migrations, and sometimes for obtaining information about the demographic structure of the past.

(b) Personal names

These occur in two forms: as lists, and as genealogies. Both, however, together constitute a single type of tradition, for lists can be regarded as genealogies reduced to their simplest form of expression. It is a type of tradition which is never primarily aimed at recording history. The historical data it contains are only used for the vindication of rights. It is strongly influenced by the social structure. This accounts, among other things, for the fact that many genealogies have the same generation depth. A typical example of this is found among the tribes on the Luapula, where all genealogies have a generation depth of from four to seven generations, many genealogies being truncated so as not to go beyond the seventh generation, except for the royal genealogy, which, unlike the others, is faithfully recorded and which goes back for nine generations.[21] This state of affairs has a sociological explanation. Among the Bushongo, the situation is even more clear-cut. Apart from the genealogies of the chiefs, and in particular those of the king, no other genealogy goes back as far as the sixth generation. On the other hand, the royal genealogy has a depth of more than fifteen generations. The reason for this is that commoners have no interest in preserving their genealogies over a span of more than four or five generations. The same situation is found in Burundi, where the only genealogies of over three generations in depth are those of the king and of certain religious functionaries. In Rwanda, the same phenomenon exists, but it is less marked, because many Tutsi families are genealogically connected with the royal house, and trace their ancestors back to the royal genealogy.

Genealogies are sources in which distortions are very prone to occur, because they form the ideological framework with reference to which all political and social relationships are sustained and explained. Because of the functions they fulfil, they undergo many alterations, and are frequently telescoped. On the other hand, they are sources which readily provide mythical explanations for the creation, for the relationship between supernatural beings, and for the origin of various social groups. The Greek pantheon provides a well-known example. Genealogies are, by their very nature, official traditions. They are transmitted with care when they have any political or social significance. Apart from their uses in establishing a chronology, they can also provide information about the political and social development of a country, and mythical genealogies do the same for the history of religions and of ideas. Furthermore, genealogies are often the sole source available for studying demographic development.

5. Tales

All of these are testimonies which have a free form of text—that is, which are composed in prose; but the category as a whole contains very diverse types, the only common feature of which is that all are in narrative form, which entails a certain arrangement of the subject-matter and a special internal structure. The divergence between the various types has led me to propose four sub-categories: historical, didactic, artistic, and personal tales. There is one other feature which tales have in common: all record history to some extent, but this aim is subordinate to another, the main aim being either to instruct, edify, give pleasure, or vindicate rights.

Because of their intentionally historical nature, tales are generally less trustworthy than other types of source. But in contrast to formulae, poetry, lists, and commentaries, they are the only sources which give a detailed account of a series of events. They alone contain a historical perspective. The various types of tale are of very unequal value, simply because they are so different. Historical tales are mainly useful as sources of information about military, political, social, institutional, and legal history. Didactic tales provide information about cultural values. Artistic tales have, on the whole, little value except for the history of psychological attitudes, whereas tales containing personal recollections can be used as sources of information for all forms of history.

All historical tales are official traditions aimed at recording history. They are recited by specialists on ceremonial occasions, and are transmitted within a particular social group. Three types can be distinguished: those concerning general history, those concerning local history, and those concerning family history.

154

(a) *Tales concerning general history*

Tales of general historical interest mainly concern tribal history. Among certain tribes such as the Kuba, testimonies of this kind are a separate type, but this is not the case elsewhere, where general history consists of episodes from different local histories, put together into a more or less coherent whole.[22] Even so, the general history of the tribe is often identical with the history of the ruling house. Several writers maintain that general history is only found in centralized societies—that is, in states—and never among tribes with a political structure which depends entirely upon kinship links.[23] Examples of this type of historical tale are found among almost all peoples without writing.[24]

They are always official traditions, and thus extremely prone to distortion in defence of public interests. But they give a general survey of the past history of the people concerned, and show the main lines of development. Without some such general survey it is difficult to fit the various local narratives into a general framework. Occasionally sources of this kind are merely compilations of secondary sources, in which case they cannot be regarded as trustworthy. Others are simply the history of a ruling social group. The history of Burundi is that of the dynasty, and the same is true of Rwanda, of the Kuba tribes, and of the peoples of the Ashanti Confederacy and of other states. One cannot accept the facts contained in these histories as applying to the whole population, but they can be compared with the versions supplied by local traditions.

(b) *Tales concerning local history*

These differ from the foregoing not only because they recount the past of small local units within a state, but also because they do not as a rule go very far back into the past, and they are transmitted with much less care, for there are no proper specialists for this purpose, and their recital is not subjected to the same strict control as is that of the tales concerning general history. They usually narrate the history of a family, a clan, or a village.

This type of tale is at times disappointing as a source, because

155

the information given is of such purely local interest that it throws little light on history as a whole. On the other hand, the information such as it is is usually more exact and coherent than in general histories. The best thing to do is to treat general and local historical tales together, so as to bring out more clearly the links between them.

(c) Tales concerning family history

These deal with the past history of lineages. In many societies which have no centralized forms of government, they replace general histories. Very often these family tales are no more than the outgrowths of genealogies. They explain why two branches of a family have separated and no longer live together. Tales of this kind contain many stereotype phrases.[25] Family traditions do not, however, disappear in societies with state organization. They may even become the general history of the society, either because the family history in question is that of the dynasty, or because the general history consists of a number of family histories. In addition to dynastic traditions, most of the important families whose members hold official positions preserve a knowledge of their family history. It is noticeable that such family histories all tend to follow the same lines, being designed to vindicate the family's privileged position and establish some sort of a link with the ruling house. A common type of Kuba family history runs: Our ancestor killed an animal and brought it to the king, who thanked him and said: 'Thanks; you will become a chief', or 'you will be given an official position in your village'. In Rwanda, the Abaskyete are said to owe their important position to the fact that their ancestor Byskyete saved a queen-mother from death. And in both countries many other instances of this kind occur. Family histories also often contain traditions of migrations from other villages, or localities usually not very distant.

These sources, when they are neither general nor local histories, are mainly useful as explanations of and commentaries to genealogies. They must of course be approached with the same caution as genealogies, with the further proviso that one must be on one's guard against stereotype phrases. They are often still more useful as checks on official sources, whether these consist of general or local traditions, or as checks on the history of migrations. By combining and comparing all the family histories of the various sections of the Kuba clans it was possible to arrive at a clearer picture of the tribal origins. The same thing could be done, although less completely, for Rwanda and Burundi. The results would in turn provide a very accurate check on the traditions concerning general history. Family histories are valuable sources if used in this way. Their value may, however, be reduced owing to the fact that often unimportant family traditions are untrustworthy because of poor transmission. In such cases, they are similar in nature to personal recollections.

(d) Myths

Didactic tales are testimonies designed to instruct. They attempt to explain the world, the culture, the society. When such explanations are given in terms of religious causes, the tale in question is a myth. Myths are often recited during a rite which recalls and enacts the myth itself.[26] Most myths concern events which are not thought of as having happened in the past, but in a time which is sacred and which exists either beyond or side by side with profane time. This question has had many studies devoted to it.[27] Feder classifies myths of this kind along with aetiological myths and legendary lives of heroes and saints,[28] but this classification is wrong, because myths not only have a didactic and moral purpose as do aetiological myths and the lives of heroes and saints, but also deal with, and interpret, the relations between the natural and the supernatural, and are concerned with all that part of religious life that lies beyond the moral order.

Because of their religious character, myths are transmitted with care. They are very valuable sources for the history of religion, particularly for the history of beliefs. They contain hardly any information about the history of any particular cult, except for a few details here and there about certain archaic features. Whenever such facts are recorded, they are usually reliable. But since myths are for the most part designed to supply explanations, one must be on the watch for possible anachronisms.

157

(e) *Aetiological myths*

This is the type of tale which sets out to explain the origin of cultural traits and natural features without bringing in religious factors. It can be divided into four sub-types: local legends, tales about natural phenomena, popular etymologies, and tales about cultural traits.

A great deal is known about local legends through European folklore studies.[29] Local legends supply an explanation for some particular feature of the landscape. A Kuba example is provided by the explanation given for a circular depression in the treeless plain of Iyool, which is said to be the place where, at the end of hostilities over a struggle for the throne, people danced with such exuberance that the ground sank beneath their feet. The place where the drums were placed is still pointed out to this day.

In contrast to local legends, tales concerning natural phenomena are not regarded as historical. An example is the story of the dog who discovered the sun. The sun, furious at having his hiding-place uncovered, said: 'None of those who looked for me could find me. You alone have found me. That is why you will henceforth always be a thief.' Many Aesop's fables belong to this sub-type.

Popular etymologies are also familiar in European folklore. A Kuba example concerns the name of a village called Bulek. A certain king had suppressed a revolt in the village, which he then gave the name of *bulek*, 'the act of overcoming', based on the saying: the king has overcome all the villages.

Tales about cultural traits deal with the origins of institutions, customs, etc. Several Tetela genealogies show Oluba and Okuba as being the brothers of the ancestors of several Tetela lineages. The Luba and the Kuba are descended from them, and an explanation is thus provided for these tribes being neighbours of the Tetela.[30]

Aetiological interpretations also occur in other types of source, particularly in tales of artistic merit.

Baumann has aptly remarked that aetiological myths are the sources best suited for providing accurate information about cultural history.[31] They do indeed often contain memories of features that no longer exist. They are indispensable for studying the history of the cosmological concepts of a people. Unfortunately few of them are reliable as sources, because they have been so much adapted to their aim, which is to instruct or edify. The information to which Baumann refers consists for the most part of details which have no bearing on the moral which the author wants to draw.

(f) Tales of artistic merit

These form a whole sub-category, and not merely a type within a sub-category, because their artistic merit is such as to distinguish them quite clearly from all other categories of tales.

The main purpose of these tales is to please the listener. Everything else is subordinated to this. The historical element is often reduced to a mere background against which the tale unfolds, and it must in no way detract from the story itself. Indeed there is a tendency to supply historical details that are lacking, or touch them up if they are vague. Causes and motivations are invented, and historical personages are given a personality, or imaginary ones introduced. No particular status is given to minor characters, but well-known ones are made into ideal types. No hesitation is felt about combining several traditions if necessary, or about dividing up a single tradition into several parts. In short, violence is done to the facts, either by exaggerating them or by making them more exciting. These characteristics of the artistic tale have been fully described and discussed by various writers.[32] Most tales of this kind are transmitted without any form of control. The type includes three sub-types: the epic, the legend, and the fable, according to whether the dramatic, the edifying, or the imaginative element is uppermost. The only reason for regarding them as sub-types rather than types is that the distinction between them is often vague.

Artistic tales are freely transmitted and often undergo numerous changes because of their aim, which is to please. Distortions may also arise because of didactic or moral purposes. Rationalizations and idealizations take place, and the need is felt to satisfy the demands of listeners for a climax, for excitement, and for a good ending to the story. All the writers who have dealt with this type of source have emphasized how untrustworthy it is.[33] But if a tale has been carefully transmitted, it can serve as a source for the history of the psychological attitudes of a people. Such tales are rare, however. Most tales merely express the ideals and ways of life of the present.

(g) Personal recollections

These are traditions which are transmitted without control, and which are simply preserved in the memory of the informant. Because of their mode of transmission, they usually have no more than a few links in the chain, which must all be traced in order to assess the reliability of the source. The transmission takes place either within a family or a neighbourhood. Usually the story is told in order to enhance the prestige of the person telling it.

Facts supplied by traditions of this kind are often astonishingly detailed, at least when the information is reliable, and very diverse. They are sources which can be used for studying a fairly recent period of the past for all kinds of historical research. As falsification rarely occurs, they are extremely trustworthy. They can best be used for finding out about economic, demographic, and social aspects of the past, but are less useful for supplying information about political or institutional matters, unless the informant is specially qualified to speak of them.

6. Commentaries

All sources of this kind have two features in common: they are presented in the form of brief pieces of information, and they are either supplementary to other sources, or are closely connected with a particular situation and are only transmitted in the context of that situation. They can be extremely useful if the information they contain is reliable, because usually there is nothing to cause distortions, and they are so brief that transmission does not require any special care. They are never primarily aimed at recording history, having either a legal or a didactic purpose.

The distinction between the types is however clear-cut, and depends upon the circumstances in which they are used, legal precedents being used in courts of law, explanatory commentaries with reference to a tradition, and occasional comments in all other circumstances.

These micro-traditions are of inestimable value as source material for historical research of all kinds, as the discussion of the types will show.

(a) Legal precedents

These are traditions which supply directives for solving legal problems. A precedent creates law. This legal type of commentary can be treated in the same way as written archival sources. Usually there is no formal technique of transmission, but that does not mean that transmission is inaccurate, because the parties interested in solving the problem exercise a control. Traditions of this kind include not only decisions on legal problems of the past, but may also encompass questions of procedure, others concerning institutions, etc.

In so far as the strictly legal traditions are concerned, they come under strict control by the judges and the parties concerned. Their transmission is thus controlled and accurate. As archival sources they can be regarded as trustworthy in the highest degree. But they do not give any historical perspective and say nothing of historical developments. Nor can they be assigned to any definite period of the past. Like didactic formulae, they are ageless. They can however be used with great advantage in the study of law and institutions.

(b) Explanatory commentaries

Explanatory commentaries are recited at the same time as the historical traditions to which they are attached. Their transmission is therefore linked with that of the other tradition, but only partially, for they are designed to throw light on those parts of the other testimony which are unintelligible, and when a listener fails to understand these parts, he may ask for an explanation—in which case the commentary is transmitted—or he may not, in which case the narrator will probably not supply the commentary, which may lead to its being lost. It may then happen that, to replace this lost commentary, which arose from the explanations given by one or by several informants in the chain of transmission of the other tradition, a false commentary is later invented. Suppose that a poem or a proverb has in the course of time lost its explanatory commentary because no one has asked for it. Then comes a time when a listener asks questions, and the narrator does not know what to reply, for he himself does not understand what he is narrating. If he is intelligent, he will be inclined to invent a hypothetical explanation, which will then pass for the real explanation and will be the only one handed down to future generations. Thus a false commentary is created, which has had no facts to go upon, but which provides explanations for various things—perhaps elucidating the meaning of an archaism, pointing out the historical significance of place-names or personal names, or explaining poetic allusions or double meanings. These explanations always refer to a word or a group of words in the other testimony, and each of these separate comments explaining a word or a group of words in the tradition to which the commentary is attached must be regarded as a separate tradition. Each of these separate traditions is quite brief, is transmitted accurately and without falsification, and is rarely distorted, unless it should be entirely re-invented.

Commentaries are extremely useful. Hardly any fixed text or poem would be intelligible without them. But most people who make use of oral sources fail to realize that commentaries are quite separate traditions from the traditions they accompany, and this constitutes a danger, as is shown by the following example. It has been said that a proverb, being invariably a fixed text, can always be regarded as genuine. A proverb often quoted by the Rundi runs: 'It is cracking at Nkoondo'. As the meaning of this is not exactly clear, the proverb has an accompanying explanatory commentary, which says that it refers to the battle fought by the regent Ndivyaariye against the rebel Twaarererye at Nkoondo, in which the rebel was defeated. One is tempted to accept all this as historical fact. But further research will show that there are other versions of the commentary, some of which say that it was King Mweezi who fought against Ndivyaariye, while others say no, he fought against Macoonco, etc. The existence of these various versions shows that the commentary was not regularly transmitted along with the proverb, and that new ones were invented. The only point on which all agree is that Nkoondo was a battlefield. One cannot therefore be too careful, and one must recognize those parts of a tradition which consist of explanatory commentary whenever they occur, to avoid the risks of making errors of judgment with regard to the validity of sources. The only way to find out what commentaries are genuine is to compare the various versions that are current. But here again one must apply the principle: in the absence of precise indications to the contrary, one must accept the evidence provided by a source as being reliable.

(c) Occasional comments
It sometimes happens that, when taking a stroll, my curiosity was aroused about the origin or layout of some feature in the landscape, but any questions about it usually elicited the reply: 'We do not know'. Occasionally, however, I was given a brief answer which, though laconic, was nevertheless traditional. A Kuba example: 'The maize was brought by Shyaam', and a Rundi example: 'The royal clan is umuhaanza, umuhiiza', will serve as illustrations. Comments of this kind are clearly only transmitted in answer to a chance question. Their content is not regarded as being of much importance, since all it does is to provide some information of secondary importance in order to explain something. They exist primarily as a record of historical facts rather than to provide explanations, and they undergo little alteration, being simply the stereotype answer to a chance remark. Since they depend on chance for their transmission, one comes across very few of these comments. Most of them get forgotten after a short space of time, resembling personal recollections in this respect.

Sources of this kind are of great interest to the historian. They are comparable in value and in characteristics to archaeological evidence. Whatever the nature of the remark, it remains almost invariably the same, and sometimes important information is provided. The two examples quoted above throw light on important developments in the history of the Kuba and of Burundi. The introduction of maize, a basic food crop, was an important event, which can be correlated with a population increase, evidence of which is found in other sources. We know enough about the royal clan of Burundi to enable us to link it with other clans, particularly with clans in the southern part of the country, this being the area which we know, from other sources, to have been the place of origin of the dynasty. In both cases, the information provided is of interest. In the first, it adds something to the explanation of an already known historical occurrence, and in the second, it serves as a check on facts already known.

But where these traditions are of most interest is in the sphere of cultural history. They are the best sources of information about the diffusion of cultural traits, of ideas, and even of institutions.

7. *Summary*

The foregoing description of the various types of oral tradition is no more than a rough outline, and must be understood as such. A more detailed study, containing a sufficient number of examples to illustrate the possible variations of a single type, would require a whole book. My aim here was restricted to suggesting a typology in order to draw attention to the diversity of types which exists, and to show that each type has its own usefulness, and provides one particular kind of information only. Each type of tradition also has its bias and its limitations. But their very diversity makes it possible to surmount the particular failings of each by comparing the information obtained from different types. Nevertheless all oral traditions have certain more general limitations and certain more pronounced tendencies towards bias, and these I shall attempt to demonstrate in the next section, for it is essential to go into the nature and scope of these factors more thoroughly, so as to be able to assess exactly what kind of information can be obtained from oral traditions.

2. HOW TRADITIONS ARE BIASED

All oral traditions are to a greater or lesser extent linked with the society and the culture which produces them, therefore all are influenced by the culture and society concerned, upon which their very existence depends. Usually it is not fully realized to what extent traditions are influenced by the culture to which they belong. For this reason I shall now draw a comparison between the oral traditions of Rwanda and of Burundi before going on to discuss in more general terms the tendencies towards bias found in traditions and to show that the bias is accounted for by the presence of certain institutions in the society concerned.

TABLE IV

Types of traditions in Burundi and Rwanda

BURUNDI   RWANDA

Vernacular name	Type	Type	Vernacular name	Class
umugani	non-historical tales	+	*umugani*	A
umugani	historical tales	+	*igiteekerezo*	
,,	aetiological myths	+	,,	
,,	personal recollections	+	*amakuru*	
,,	explanatory commentaries	+	*igiteekerezo*	A
,,	occasional comments	+	,,	
,,	eyewitness accounts	+	,,	
,,	local tales (1)	+	,,	
umugani	proverbs	+	*umugani*	
ururirimbo	folk-songs	+	*imbyino*	
		court songs	*indirimbo inaanga*	
		dynastic poetry	*igisigo*	
amazina	− (2)	warrior poetry	*icyivugo*	B
,,	− (2)	pastoral poetry	*amazina y'inka*	
	−	dynastic code	*ubwiiru*	
	−	(a) Poem	*igirage*	
	−	(b) Commentary	*igiteekerezo*	
	−	royal genealogy	*ubucurabwenge*	C

Legend: A : free texts; B: fixed texts; C: lists.
: identical; − : lacking.
1 : Local tales also include tales connected with particular institutions, such as those connected with the army, which Kagame classes separately. (A. Kagame, 'La notion de génération', pp. 36-40.)
2 : Panegyric *amazina* exist in Burundi, but almost never have a historical content.

1. Types of tradition and political organization, as exemplified by Rwanda and Burundi

The types of tradition which exist in these two countries are shown in Table IV.

The first thing that strikes one on looking at this table is that all the traditions found in Burundi also exist in Rwanda, but that Rwanda has many other types in addition. It is not difficult to show that the existence of these additional types is accounted for by the existence in Rwanda of political institutions which did not exist in Burundi. The political system of Burundi was not of the kind that favoured historiography. The country was governed by a royal family, the *abaganwa*, of which the king was the head. The political system was a fluid one. Each *umuganwa* possessed lands over which he had full jurisdiction. He sought to fight his neighbouring *abaganwa* for the aggrandizement of his own territory, and all the *abaganwa* were grouped into two or three blocs between which there was a balance of power. At the death of one of these chiefs, his son did not necessarily succeed as ruler of the province, for the province became a stake in the struggle for power between the other reigning chiefs. Moreover, each chief appointed his own sub-chiefs, and when he died, his successor dismissed all the old sub-chiefs and appointed his own men. If it is further noted that the boundaries of these provinces were constantly changing, one gets a general picture of a political organization that was essentially fluid and unstable. There was therefore nothing to foster the rise of oral traditions. There were no fixed provincial boundaries, and so little likelihood of local traditions arising; no important families apart from that of the king, and so no family histories, or hardly any. Lastly, there was no central government which might have given rise to official historians such as the *abiiru*. Indeed, there was a strong bias against history in Burundi. If the equivalent of the *abiiru* had existed, they would have upheld the power of the king, and this none of the *abaganwa* would have welcomed. The king was *primus inter pares* and not the sole centre of power. It was in everyone's interest to forget about history, whether it were the chief in his province, the sub-chief who had been dismissed, or the king himself, who relied now upon one faction, and now upon another. An old chief told me that no one at court was interested in history. The political system makes this easily understandable. The only kinds of oral tradition found here are folk traditions: stories enjoyed as such, songs, and proverbs. Moreover, there were no specialists for the transmission of traditions. Even the guardians of the dynastic tombs or of the royal drum were no more expert in traditions than their fellow countrymen.

In Rwanda, the situation was entirely different. The king was in command of everything. He governed through the great Tutsi families, to whom he gave semi-hereditary fiefs which had more or less fixed boundaries. Government was carried out by means of direct administration, backed by an organized military force, and supported by the clientage system known as *ubuhake*, connected with the ownership of cattle. The following diagram shows the connection between this form of political organization and its accompanying wide variety of oral traditions. The power of the king was exalted and legally justified by the *ubwiiru*, the *ubucurabwenge*, and the *ibisigo*.

The *ubwiiru* was the royal ritual and legal code; the dynastic genealogy vouched for the legitimacy of the reigning monarch and enhanced his prestige as the descendant of a long line; and the *ibisigo* were eulogies—propaganda poetry for exalting the power of the king. The *indiriimbo inaanga* and the *icyiivugo* were the traditions concerned with the army, and the *amazina y' inka* were connected with the army, just as family histories were connected with the great families, and the local histories with the various administrative units and with institutions such as the army. As for the common people, they cultivated the same types of tradition as those found in Burundi: tales, folk-songs, and proverbs.

The tales form a somewhat complex pattern. There are the *igiteekerezo*, which are of a popular variety enjoyed by the whole population on account of their artistic merits. Others are less widely known, and derive from the court, more particularly from the *abacurabwenge*, who have to be acquainted with historical tales as well as with genealogies. Some probably derive from the *abiiru* themselves. The nobles liked listening to dynastic tales, which encouraged clients who were seeking favour to learn them. The same complexity is found among the sub-types of other categories—for instance, songs. All traditions are either linked with certain social groups which have political signifi-cance, or else they are folk traditions, in which case they are also found in Burundi. The following diagram shows in graphic form the points I have been discussing.

DIAGRAM II

Oral traditions and political organization

B U R U N D I

```
┌─────────────────────────┐
│     ROYAL FAMILY        │
└─────────────────────────┘
```

Royal sites and aetiological myths

Fluid administration

```
┌─────────────────────────┐
│         PEOPLE          │
└─────────────────────────┘
```

Historical tales
Aetiological myths
Personal recollections
Explanatory commentaries
Occasional comments
Eyewitness accounts
Proverbs
Folk-songs

RWANDA

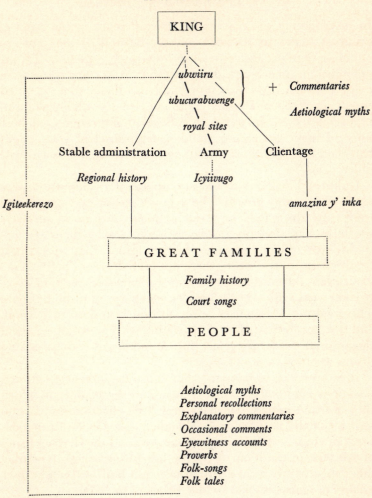

Legend:

Words in capital letters: Political classes.
Words in roman type: Political organization.
Words in italics: Types of tradition.

| : Lines showing political relationships.

| : Lines showing links between types of tradition.
....

2. *The limitations of oral tradition*

In investigating the reasons for the difference in the types of tradition found in Rwanda and in Burundi, I was able to establish that the difference can be entirely explained by the difference in their political organization. If a comparison were made between these two states and the Kuba state, it could equally well be established that most of the differences can be accounted for in terms of political organization, but here some of them, appearing mainly on the level of what might be called folk traditions, would be found to be due to cultural differences.

Cultural differences would also appear if a comparison were made with pygmy groups. The pygmies do not have any official traditions, since they have no political institutions properly speaking, and the only traditions found among them are folk traditions,[34] which provides further proof that specialized traditions only arise where there is a high degree of political organization. But even within the categories of folk tradition, comparison would discover differences which are cultural in origin. These cultural differences apply to oral traditions in general, and are not restricted to folk traditions. For instance, royal slogans in drum language are only found in areas where talking drums are used, and not elsewhere.

It is, however, to be noted that cultural differences between traditions often only affect the form and the manner in which they are transmitted, and have very little effect on the characteristics of the type as such. Whether a slogan be drummed, sung, or spoken, it remains a slogan, with all the characteristics of this type of tradition. A pygmy tale of the artistic type may differ in structure from a Rundi tale, but both will retain their quality of texts designed to give pleasure to people.

It follows, therefore, that it is political structures and, to a lesser degree, social structures which give rise to traditions other than folk traditions. All such traditions have political or social functions, and hence suffer from the bias imposed by the function they fulfil. But there is more to it than this. Each type of society has in fact chosen to preserve the kind of historical traditions suited to its particular type of structure, and the historical information to be obtained by studying these traditions is restricted by the framework of reference constructed by the society in question. This defines the limitations of such traditions, which only folk traditions can escape. Unfortunately, however, the latter provide a random selection of facts which often do not enable one to trace history very far back into the past, the only exceptions being songs and proverbs—and here the commentaries are usually inaccurately transmitted.

The result of all this is that the kind of history to be obtained from traditional accounts is mainly the history of states with a political organization. It is characteristic that Westermann should have chosen to give the sub-title *Staatenbildungen südlich der Sahara* to his *Geschichte Afrikas*. In areas where there were no states, the only data he found were data of varying degrees of reliability concerning migrations. Generalizing from this, one can distinguish between the different kinds of historical information provided by oral tradition as a whole. One can speak of the history of states, the history of segmentary societies, the history of towns, and the history of micro-societies, according to the type of tradition dealt with, and their main characteristics can be indicated.

The history of states will be found to go fairly far back into the past, to be well transmitted, and to furnish a wide variety of information. Federations of states, states not completely centralized, and neighbouring micro-states will have a wider variety of traditions than a highly centralized state. In states of this kind there will, therefore, be more opportunity of comparing different traditions, and thus of arriving at a better knowledge of past events than in a highly centralized state.

The history of segmentary societies will not go so far back into the past, will be less accurately transmitted, and will be almost exclusively based on genealogies and family traditions, in addition to which some lists concerning migrations and some myths will also be found. But great difficulty will be encountered in reconstructing the tribal history because the traditions will be so stereotyped as to be almost meaningless.

The history of towns will have the special feature of existing alongside written documents. All the towns of the world have known writing, except those of Yoruba and Benin. Even if writing is known, oral traditions, in the form of tales of marvels, genealogies, and family traditions, will be found alongside the written chronicles, as is instanced by East African towns such as Mombasa, Lamu, and Kilwa.

The history of micro-societies—that is, societies in which there is no social group larger than the extended family, or several extended families (a camp)—is pretty well non-existent. Traditions are carelessly transmitted, do not go far back, and are always of a folk nature.

One could add to the list of different kinds of history which I have drawn up by including for instance the history of societies with age-grades, or by distinguishing between the history of villages and the history of micro-states larger than villages, etc. In fact, each type of society has its own character-istics which are reflected in its traditions.

The examples which I have given are merely intended to support the following statement: Oral traditions are conditioned by the society in which they flourish. It follows therefore that no oral tradition can transcend the boundaries of the social system in which it exists. It is spatially limited to the area cir-cumscribed by the geographical boundaries of the society in question, and limited in time to that society's generation depth. The historical information that can be obtained from oral traditions is therefore always of a limited nature and has a certain bias. This is equally true of many written sources, and written and oral sources are very much alike in this respect. In both cases, the factor which most imparts bias and imposes limitations is the political system.

The question arises whether the historian can find a way to overcome the limitations of the traditions he is dealing with. I think he can. He can make use of the traditions of other societies, if they are relevant and reliable, or he can refer to written sources—also mainly belonging to other societies—or he can supplement the historical information supplied by the traditions he is studying with the findings of a number of auxiliary disciplines, which, despite their own limitations, will enlarge the field of possibilities.

Before going on to discuss the contribution of these auxiliary disciplines, I must once more draw attention to one consequence of the limitations inherent in oral traditions. It has been said that it is only possible to reconstruct the history of peoples who have reached the stage of state organization, and that even then the historical perspective is likely to be very distorted, since the history of states which have perished perishes with them without a trace.[35] It must be admitted that this objection is not without foundation. But I hope that I have made it clear in this section that folk traditions exist everywhere, and also that there are other kinds of oral tradition besides state traditions—notably those belonging to segmentary societies, which are found throughout the whole world. The validity of Professor Fage's argument can, however, only be proved by putting it to a practical test. I have the feeling that historical research carried out in depth in societies without state organization might reveal much more of their history than has been commonly supposed to be possible. But the experiment has yet to be made.

3. THE CONTRIBUTION OF AUXILIARY DISCIPLINES

Historical source material can be supplied by disciplines not directly connected with oral tradition to supplement the information found there. In theory all scientific disciplines can be used in this way, for all have some bearing on history. Thus entomology can supply useful information concerning the history of Rwanda, for a study of the insect fauna in one part of the country shows that for ten centuries at least the region has always been a savannah, so that it was suitable pasture land in the past, which confirms the information supplied by the oral traditions. Astronomy is used more and more as an auxiliary scientific discipline for establishing chronological data. If a tradition says that an eclipse occurred under such and such a chief, and if the number of generations since his reign is known, then the eclipse can be dated accurately.

There are, however, four disciplines in particular which the historian will find more useful than any others when studying the history of peoples without writing. These are, archaeology, cultural history, linguistics, and physical anthropology.

In the following sub-sections I shall discuss the contribution each can make to the furthering of our historical knowledge.

These are the disciplines which, in conjunction with oral traditions, form the resources used by the ethnohistorian, according to the views of members of the American school.[36]

1. Archaeology

Archaeology can throw light on certain aspects of the past, especially on migrations and on material culture. It is, however, often impossible to link the information obtained from oral traditions with any definite archaeological finds. No oral traditions survive from neolithic times. For later periods, it is sometimes possible to establish a link between traditions and certain material objects of archaeological interest. In Rwanda, farmers when ploughing sometimes turn up objects buried in the ground which differ in shape from similar objects of the present day. They are said to have belonged to a people who have died out: the Renge. Further examination of the tradition concerning the Renge has shown that these iron objects did not—in the opinion of some people at least—belong to the Renge culture.[37] What must have happened is that inhabitants of the region must have reported these archaeological finds to another tribe whose oral traditions claimed that they used to own the land before the first conquerors occupied it. This supposition is confirmed by the fact that in certain regions of Burundi that border upon Rwanda, objects belonging to the same prehistoric culture are found, but are here attributed to the Abahoondogo and not to the Abarenge, the reason being that here the traditions recall the Hoondogo and not the Renge.

It not infrequently occurs that traditions arise because of visible archaeological remains. A local legend arises in order to explain their presence. But usually such legends are of no validity whatsoever.

The biggest problem in the use of archaeological evidence is the identification of names preserved in traditions with protohistoric cultures. It is very hard to know if these names can be identified with any particular culture, and one seldom arrives at any satisfactory results. For instance, throughout the region of the Great Lakes in Central Africa one finds traditions which refer to the 'Bachwezi', who, a long time ago, founded an empire which has since disappeared, while in Uganda there are the remains of large dikes and canals, almost all of them circular in shape, which are popularly believed to have been constructed by the 'Bachwezi'. The remains are on such a scale as to lead to the assumption that they must have been constructed by large numbers of labourers, probably slaves, which presupposes the existence of an organized state. Since the traditions maintain that the Bachwezi founded a state, there is some reason to suppose that they were in fact responsible for these large-scale public works.[38] But there is room for doubt, for people might have arrived at such an assumption from the appearance of the remains, and invented a tradition about a powerful kingdom in order to explain them. It is not probable, but quite possible.

It is only by chance that one can sometimes exclude the hypothesis that an archaeological site has given rise to a tradition. A good example of such a chance occurrence—although it is true the chance was foreseen—occurred in Nkole, where the traditions maintained that a certain site, which had clearly been occupied by an earlier people, had served as residence for two different kings at some distance apart in the dynastic genealogy. Excavations showed that, unknown to the inhabitants of the region, a second site lay buried beneath the first one, which was very much smaller than the first. Thus the tradition was correct in maintaining that the place had been twice occupied, and very probably it also gave the correct names to the kings that were said to have lived there.[39] This example can also be used to illustrate the relation between archaeology and tradition. Tradition indicates sites suitable for archaeological excavation. It was thanks to archaeology that the vast burial grounds on the shores of Lake Kisale in Katanga were discovered. They belong to a culture which knew the use of iron and copper, and the vast extent of the burial grounds indicates a concentration of population such as to lead one to suppose that the place must almost certainly have been an important centre in an organized state. Now the oral traditions of the Luba lineages, particularly those inhabiting Katanga, have for their part always insisted that their empires and kingdoms all descended from a prototype that was situated in the region of

Lake Kisale. Here, therefore, there is a striking similarity in the data supplied by the different sources available.

Archaeology can supply data which make it possible to identify proto-historical cultures with tribes whose memory is preserved in traditions, and in addition it can provide useful information about migrations and trade—information which can be deduced from the diffusion of certain techniques, pottery being of particular interest in this respect. Here, too, there are data which may agree with those provided by tradition. Archaeology supplies direct historical evidence, although the historical context for archaeological finds often remains unknown. But the objects can be dated, and archaeology can explore far further back into the past than any other of the humanist disciplines. For all these reasons, archaeology is the most necessary and the most useful of the auxiliary disciplines that the historian of oral traditions can make use of.

2. The methods of cultural history

These are the methods used by ethnologists when they attempt to establish the relationship between two cultures and the evolution each has gone through by comparing the cultural traits common to both. They are somewhat similar to archaeology, because both are connected to some extent with diffusion. The great difference between them is that cultural history is not confined to the diffusion of material objects, but includes all cultural traits, so that the data which it handles are not material data only, as is the case with archaeology, but all evidence, material or otherwise, of an earlier state of affairs. Archaeological evidence, consisting merely of the material objects of earlier times, is more direct.

The cultural-historical method starts from the assumption that common cultural traits can only be accounted for in two ways: either by independent evolution or separate instances of the same invention, or by common origin, whether this be because both cultures derive from the same parent culture, or because one has borrowed the cultural trait from the other, or both have borrowed from a third. The cultural trait provides a unit of comparison, and is regarded as the molecule of culture—

the smallest possible separable part of a thing or an institution.

This method can be applied—and has been applied—in three different ways. The diffusion of a single trait throughout the world can be studied, the diffusion of a large number of traits within one continuous and narrowly limited geographical area can be studied, and the distribution of a large number of traits over much wider areas—over a whole continent, or throughout the world—can be studied.

The study of the distribution of the xylophone in Africa, and more specifically of the various names given to it, is an example of the first of these methods. A comparison of Javanese and African xylophones shows that they are related, and that they probably originate in Indonesia, for the instrument is too complicated to have been invented in two separate places. Its distribution in Africa and a study of the names given to it further show that it was diffused from several centres on the coast, especially the east coast. Study of the names shows that diffusion took place rapidly, and that it was the Portuguese who introduced the instrument into Africa, except in one small area—the region round Malindi.[40]

The second method applies the well-known principle of age-area, also used in the study of dialects. If it is found in a given area that a form A of the trait being studied is widespread throughout the whole area or a major part of it, while in the centre of the area a form B is found, then A is older than B, for there could have been no direct diffusion of A from one place to another without passing through the place where B is found, whereas if this place used to have A, it is clear that diffusion has occurred and that B is an innovation that has replaced A. Kroeber has an excellent discussion on this method, in which he shows how he was able to trace the evolution of religious rites in California by following the geographical distribution of the various existing rites. He was thus able to postulate for each place a series of *cultural strata*, that is, of successive cultural stages explained by the existing distribution of the various cults.[41]

The third method has been mainly used by the Vienna school of cultural history.[42] The only point on which it differs from the second method is that here cultural strata are established on a world scale. Thus the culture of the pygmies in Africa and of the negritos in Malaysia preserve the remains of the oldest cultural stratum in the world. Graebner and Schmidt, who developed this method, used two kinds of criteria: a quantitative one, which concerns the number of cultural traits common to two cultures (the greater the number of common traits, the greater the probability of diffusion or of a common cultural ancestry); and a qualitative one, which concerns not the number of traits, but the internal complexity of such traits or groups of traits. If the game of chess is found in different cultures, the likelihood is that this game will not have been invented twice over separately, but will have been diffused from one culture to the other, for it is so complex in character that it is scarcely imaginable that it could have occurred twice in the history of human inventions. It should further be noted that in the counting of traits carried out during application of the quantitative criterion, traits linked together by causal relations do not have the same weight numerically as traits which are entirely independent of each other. If in two cultures the two traits: complicated hair-style, neck-rests, are found, this will be regarded as less significant than if, for example, neck-rests were found along with distortion of cattle's horns, because in the first case, neck-rests can be explained by the need to avoid disarranging the complicated hair-style. A final point worth noting is that there are some traits which, by a process of survival or of culture-lag, have survived the destruction of a culture and have been incorporated in those which followed. Thus the existence of knives made of jet among the Kuba, the meaning of which has been entirely forgotten, is a case of survival. Traits of this kind are much the most useful for the establishment of cultural strata.

The methods of historical ethnology have been much criticized by the upholders of all other schools of social anthropology. The criticisms brought against them may be summarized as follows:

1. It is difficult to know how to define a cultural trait, for no trait can be regarded as a single indivisible element. A table, for instance, consists of a number of elements, so does the leg of a table, one of its elements being the joint, which again has several elements including the tenon. The tenon would seem to be indivisible, but it is made of a particular kind of wood,

is stuck in a certain way with a certain kind of glue, etc. And this example is a material trait. In the case of non-material traits, each one can be regarded from various points of view. In fact, it would appear that it is always a complex of traits that comes under consideration, and that they are selected somewhat arbitrarily.

2. No one is familiar enough with any culture to be able to draw up a list of all its cultural traits. Each culture contains at least five thousand traits, and probably many more. Comparisons are therefore made between various elements chosen at random.

3. Often comparisons have been made of large complexes traits when the complexes are not really comparable. The matriarchate, for instance, is not identical in the various cultures in which it is found. It is, in fact, an institution which is different in each of the cultures where it exists.

4. No statistical method has ever been used in calculating the number of traits, nor has any statistical method been invented which would be valid for calculating the comparative importance of traits of different kinds: survivals, traits assessed by the qualitative criterion, traits functionally interconnected, independent traits. No unit of measurement has been evolved for comparing them.

5. The possibility of independent invention has not been sufficiently taken into account.

6. It has been shown that the principle of 'age and area' is not always valid. The principle is based on the assumption that cultural diffusion operates in concentric circles, but dialectology has shown that this is not necessarily the case. Moreover, the principle assumes that the diffusion of traits occurs everywhere at the same speed, and this is directly contradicted by what we know about the mechanisms of acceptance and integration of foreign elements in a society or culture.

7. The complexity of cultural history does not permit of even a minimum degree of probability when reconstructing cultural strata. The Kuba culture has during the past three centuries come under the influence of small tribes who have introduced what is probably a very large number of cultural traits that have gradually been integrated into what is now the present-day

Kuba culture. In addition, the Kuba culture has probably made independent inventions of its own. This supposes a very large number of strata. The Kuba example illustrates the hypothetical nature of most of the historical reconstructions of this kind. The most superficial calculation leads one to the conclusion that even in the most favourable circumstances the chances of any exactitude being reached in a hypothesis of this kind are extremely low.

The foregoing discussion is aimed at showing that the various methods of cultural history are, for one thing, not adequately elaborated, and, for another, extremely difficult to apply. Moreover it is to be feared that they only occasionally arrive at satisfactory results in the sense of offering a more likely explanation than any other hypothesis. In my opinion, it is only in the rare cases when the diffusion of one trait over a limited area is studied, or in certain special cases of the diffusion of cultural complexes within a given area, that the cultural-historical method can provide historical information that goes beyond mere speculation. It is precisely because of the highly speculative nature of the method as it is practised that I have discussed the matter at some length. Too often it has presented as historical fact what is no more than a fantasy of the imagination.

3. Linguistics

Historical linguistics attempts to establish a genetic link between languages and groups of languages. While an affinity of language provides insufficient grounds for assuming ethnic affinity, one can, however, sometimes deduce that behind a genetic relationship between several languages lies an ethnic relationship. Thus historical linguistics mainly provides information concerning the history of migrations, and sometimes enables one to arrive at very accurate results. Greenberg, in his study on the classification of African languages, has shown that Bantu is related to the Sudanese languages, and, curiously enough, to one branch of the Benue-Cross group.[43] From this it can be inferred that the Bantu originated in the region of the river Cross, whence a large number of existing tribes have come. From the geographical distribution of the group it can further be established that the Bantu migration occurred much more rapidly than that of other tribes.

Other branches of linguistics, such as dialectal geography, onomastics, and toponymy, can also supply historical information. It is not yet possible, however, to work with data of this kind, because linguistic study of most of the languages of pre-literate peoples is not far enough advanced. A number of works give etymologies that are facile and superficial. Hence it is not perhaps irrelevant to emphasize the fact that one must have a thorough knowledge of the languages from which the words come if any serious results are to be expected from comparative studies.

Lexicostatistical dating is a technique used by linguists in an attempt to find out exactly when differences arose between languages belonging to the same genetic group.[44] It was found that the basic vocabulary of a language is built up in an empirical manner, and that it changes only very gradually. A statistical calculation can be made of the percentage of words in a basic vocabulary which are replaced by others within a given period. Comparison of the vocabularies of the different languages can then indicate exactly when the differences between them arose. The technique, however, has not yet been fully worked out, and moreover it has not yet been accepted as valid by linguists in general. But some indication of its potentialities is given when we learn that its application has shown that Mongo and Rwanda have been separate languages for thirty-two centuries.[45]

4. Physical anthropology

One of the scientific tasks of this discipline is to determine the differences and affinities between the various peoples of the world. It appears, however, that the adaptation of the 'human animal' to its environment has so much influence on racial differences, that it is difficult to determine which differences are due solely to genetic factors. Moreover, the results arrived at are so generalized that they are of little interest to historians.[46]

There are instances when it can be demonstrated that a genetic difference exists, if, for example, two peoples living within the same biotope show marked differences in physical type. An instance of this kind is found among the Kuba, where it has been proved that the Bushongo and Kwa tribes are genetically different. On the historical level, it can be deduced from this that the Kwa are, and always have been, a separate tribal group.[47]

5. Summary

The first thing to note about the historical information that can be obtained from oral traditions is that it varies according to the type of tradition. A survey of the typology of traditions and an outline of the characteristics of each type show that the types vary widely, and that all have a given historical bias which imposes certain limitations, but which gives each type its own particular usefulness in providing information about certain particular aspects of the past. Next, oral tradition as a whole can be shown to have its limitations, as well as certain tendencies towards bias due to the influence of the political system— which accounts for the very existence of many traditions—and also due, to a lesser extent, to cultural factors. The limitations of the information that can be derived from oral traditions are real, and must be accepted by the historian; but he can attempt to make up for them by using data supplied by other historical sources, such as written documents, and the disciplines of archaeology, cultural history, linguistics, and physical anthropology. Each of these disciplines furnishes data which in themselves are limited; but by putting together all the available information, the area of the past about which we can acquire some knowledge is greatly extended. Nevertheless, even if all these techniques are used, we can never arrive at a complete knowledge of all the events of the past. We can never do more than touch upon a small part of past history—namely, that part which has been preserved in the various surviving historical documents. But this statement must not be taken as an excuse for abandoning the study of history on the grounds that perfection can never be attained.

CHAPTER VII

The Interpretation of History

IN the foregoing chapters I have attempted to show that oral traditions are historical sources which can provide reliable information about the past if they are used with all the circumspection demanded by the application of historical methodology to any kind of source whatsoever. This means that study of the oral traditions of a culture cannot be carried out unless a thorough knowledge of the culture and of the language has previously been acquired. This is something which is taken for granted by all historians who work on written sources, but it is too often apt to be forgotten by those who undertake research into the past of pre-literate peoples.

In these final remarks I shall make several observations about the interpretation of the facts obtained. The layman is too often inclined to entertain a completely false idea as to the powers of the historian, and is apt to regard any historical reconstructions offered as absolutely valid. He fondly imagines that written sources reveal events of the past which can be accepted as fact, but considers that oral sources tell of things about which there is no certainty—things which may or may not have happened. He forgets that any historical synthesis comprises an interpretation of the facts, and is thus founded upon probabilities.

I must apologize in advance to those historians who are only too familiar with the reflections which are here offered for their perusal. I make them in order to refute a prejudice which is commonly found among all those who have raised objections to the use of oral traditions as a historical source.

There is no great difficulty in accepting the proposition that history is always an interpretation. An example will prove the point better than abstract argument. If a Rwandese source tells us that a certain king conquered a certain country, what does this statement mean? It may mean that a cattle raid was carried out in enemy territory and was highly successful; or that the chief or king of the enemy country was deposed or killed, and his territory annexed, in theory, by Rwanda, while local government was left as it was; or it may mean that the conquered chief remained in power, but recognized the suzerainty of the king of Rwanda. Or yet again, it may mean that the king of Rwanda occupied the country, incorporated it as part of the states over which he ruled, and replaced the administration from top to bottom. Any one of these possibilities could be inferred from the statement, and this is still leaving out of account the subsidiary question as to whether the measures taken were temporary or final. That stating the problem in this way is not merely the sign of a Byzantine finicalness is shown by the following factual example from Rwanda. A certain King Ndabarasa conquered Gisaka, a country bordering on Rwanda. This meant in effect that he carried out several raids there with the intention not only of bringing back cattle, but also of weakening the military power of the enemy and disorganizing the government—a project in which he succeeded. His great grandson, Mutara Rwogera, also 'conquered' the same country, and succeeded in killing or exiling all the various chiefs who ruled there, thus ending the country's existence as an autonomous state. But it was his successor Rwabugiri who first founded administrative centres there of the kind found in Rwanda, and who appointed Rwandese to high government posts. In 1901, Rwabugiri's son was faced with a rebellion there, and it was not until this ended in 1903 that all the native chiefs and sub-chiefs were deprived of their rights, and the entire administration was taken over.

Thus every historian is obliged to interpret the sources he is dealing with. He does not and cannot have an unlimited knowledge of history, and there is usually more than one interpretation possible of the facts at his disposal. In addition, the historian adds something of his own to these facts, namely, his own particular flair, which is something more akin to art than to science. The only concession to history as a scientific discipline he can make here is to ensure that he discloses what his sources are, so that his readers will be informed as to the reasons for the choice he has made in his interpretations of the texts.

Interpretation is a choice between several possible hypotheses, and the good historian is the one who chooses the hypothesis that is most likely to be true. In practice it can never have more than a likelihood of truth, because the past has gone for good and all, and the possibility of first-hand observation of past events is forever excluded. History is no more than a calculation of probabilities. This is true not only as far as the interpretation of documents is concerned, but for all the operations of historical methodology, and above all for the most important ones. How shall one decide whether a statement is an error, or a lie, or is 'veracious'? Each of the three hypotheses has a varying degree of probability, and the historian will choose the most probable one. Or if, in comparing two texts, resemblances between them are found, the historian must judge whether the resemblances imply that the texts have a common origin or not. Here again what he does is to assess possibilities and weigh probabilities. Historical science is a science of probabilities.[1] Nor is it the only science of this kind. A large number of present-day scientific disciplines make use of the concept of chance and of probability.

From what has been said, it follows that there is no such thing as 'absolute historical truth', and no one can formulate an 'unchanging law of history' on the basis of our knowledge of the past. The truth always remains beyond our grasp, and we can only arrive at some approximation to it. We can refine our interpretations, accumulate so many probabilities that they almost amount to certainty, and yet still not arrive at 'the truth'. We can never hope to understand everything, and indeed do not even understand all that we experience personally. We cannot arrive at a full understanding of the past because the past is something outside our experience, something that is other. It has been said that it is possible to describe historical events because history is a science which deals with mankind, to which we ourselves belong, whereas a scientific description of bees does not make sense, since we cannot imagine what it is like to be a bee. This is true. But it is also true that we cannot understand the past because the men who lived then were different from us, and however great an effort we make, we cannot ever completely enter into the mentality of someone else. We can never understand his motivations, and thus we can never pass judgment on them.

What the historian can do is to arrive at some approximation to the ultimate historical truth. He does this by using calculations of probability, by interpreting the facts and by evaluating them in an attempt to recreate for himself the circumstances which existed at certain given moments of the past. And here the historian using oral traditions finds himself on exactly the same level as historians using any other kind of historical source material. No doubt he will arrive at a lower degree of probability than would otherwise be attained, but that does not rule out the fact that what he is doing is valid, and that it is history.

In Search of Oral Traditions

HERE I wish to discuss the practical problems which the fieldworker encounters when in search of oral traditions. This is a field of research in which any claim to be able to lay down firm rules which, if followed, would infallibly lead to the discovery of the material sought, would be entirely illusory. One can only point to certain practical rules which arise from the methods that must be adopted if any useful work is to be done. I mean, by this, the rules that follow from the requirements of historical methodology. A tradition is of very little use as a historical source unless all the relevant preliminary investigations have been carried out and the testimonies collected systematically, since otherwise there are no proper means available for testing its reliability. Too often in the past people have been content to collect traditions at random, record them carelessly, and study them out of context, although it is only in their context that they can be fully understood.

If reliable information is to be obtained, one must first get to know the environment in which the traditions have arisen. Next, informants must be found and selected, and their testimonies collected in a systematic way. Lastly, the testimonies must be recorded in writing in an accurate manner, and notes made of any subsidiary information that might throw light on them. These are the points which will be discussed in the various sections of this appendix, and I shall conclude with some remarks on the presentation of the material for publication.

1. Getting to know the environment

Every tradition arises and is preserved within a particular cultural environment, and is modelled after the cultural pattern. It is part and parcel of the culture, and the removal of a tradition from its context is a form of amputation. To understand a tradition, therefore, it is necessary to know the culture which gives rise to it.

The first requirement is a knowledge of the language in which the information provided by traditions is conveyed, for without a knowledge of the language the meaning cannot be grasped. It is more or less impossible to collect traditions in a language other than that in which they have been transmitted. This is obvious in the case of fixed texts, but it is also true of free texts. If the informant has to try to translate them into another language, he will not find it easy to express what he wants to say. Moreover, he will come up against special difficulties of translation, because the concepts he wants to express do not exist in the culture to which the language he is translating into belongs, or because he cannot find an equivalent for the subtle shades of meaning of his mother tongue in the foreign language. He therefore translates carelessly and inaccurately. The fieldworker, then, must either have a thorough knowledge of the language of the original, or else have an assistant who knows it perfectly, and in whom he can trust. In any case, he must reproduce the tradition in its original language, and this presupposes that a linguistic study of the language has already been made prior to the collection of traditions.

If, however, he knows the language, but is unacquainted with other aspects of the culture, the traditions will still remain unintelligible. The whole emphasis of the present study lies on the importance of the influence of culture and society on every aspect of tradition. Thus the historian cannot dispense with the aid of the social anthropologist, and must make a careful study of the social system and of the main cultural features before turning his attention to his historical studies, for otherwise he will be unable to understand how or why traditions exist, nor will he be able to grasp their content.

Once he has become familiar wth the language and with the

culture in general, his first task as fieldworker will be to find out what types of traditions exist in this culture and to analyse the characteristics of each type—what its purposes, functions, and psychological significance are, what its outward form is, what literary category it belongs to, and how it is transmitted. Once he has collected all this information, he will know where to look for traditions. If he is not fully documented about them, he will be unable to proceed to the later stages of his work, for how can he collect his sources systematically if he does not know something about the object of his search? If he does not know whether traditions do, in fact, exist in this society, and if so, what type of traditions they are? The following examples will show the need for following this rule.

Among the Lozi the site of the royal tombs is known, and each tomb is guarded by a descendant of the deceased, who preserves what is remembered about the main events in the life of the deceased.[1] In order to study the history of the royal house it is therefore necessary to visit each of the tombs and closely question the guardians. In the Akan States, many traditions are preserved by priests who live in sacred places known as *piesie*, which are usually situated near rivers and streams.[2] Here again it is necessary to find out where these places are and to go there to hear the priests recite the traditions.

The fieldworker does, however, come up against obstacles which he will not find easy to surmount. A major difficulty consists in the fact that the recognized literary categories do not cover all types of testimony, for testimonies sometimes turn up in unexpected places. For instance, the Kuba *ncok* songs are usually performed when the persons taking part in a masked dance are dressing. In the Akan States, the state oath contains echoes of historical events.[3] In New Zealand, the lullabies known as *oriori* are full of historical allusions,[4] and the same applies to Rundi lullabies.[5] Herskovits witnessed a group dramatization of a theme relating to the past performed by negroes in Paramaribo,[6] and so on. One can never be sure where one might unexpectedly come upon a testimony. The only hope of getting on to the right track is to enter into the life of the group one is studying and become acquainted with their daily routine over a long period.

2. *The search for informants*

Not everyone is capable of supplying the historical information one is in search of. One must find informants whose status is such as to have equipped them with the requisite kind of information. The Bushongo hit the nail on the head when they say: 'Listen to the words of the smith, do not listen to what the man who works the bellows has to say'.

The fieldworker is met with two possibilities: either a tradition is handed down by specialists, or it is transmitted by ordinary channels. In the first case, he must of course find out about the tradition from the specialists and from them only, for outsiders will only know it fragmentarily and from hearsay, whereas the specialists will have learnt it in a systematic manner. There are vast numbers of traditions of this kind, of which the Kuba tribal traditions and the dynastic poems of Rwanda provide examples. Indeed, transmission by specialists is much more frequent than is generally supposed, and once one knows that a tradition is transmitted in this way, and knows which social group it is connected with, there is no problem in obtaining reliable information. One could even go so far as to say that most traditions belong to a particular group and concern the past history of the group, so that if the fieldworker wants to find out about the past of any social group, all he needs to do is to make enquiries from the members of the group. This procedure has, however, one drawback, which is, that it will be only official traditions that will be recorded in this way. It is much more difficult to know where to look for private traditions, especially personal recollections. Only the collaboration of the inhabitants themselves can lead to their discovery. A method of control for assessing the reliability of informants which was found useful among the Kuba was to make enquiries concerning the reputation and trustworthiness of those who had contributed private testimonies.

When traditions are transmitted haphazard without the intervention of specialists, their discovery is a much more difficult problem. The first thing to do is to make investigations as to whether there may not after all be some methods of transmission that are more common than others, and whether there may not be some semi-specialists of a sort. Do not fathers, for instance, transmit what they know to their children rather than to some other person? Are not traditions more often transmitted within a village or a neighbourhood than to somewhere outside such an area? In a caste society, does not transmission occur more readily between those who serve the same master? Semi-specialized channels of transmission of this kind can be discovered by finding out when, why, and how traditions are recited and learnt. In Rwanda, for instance, clients learn the dynastic tales in order to curry favour with the masters they serve, and thus transmission of these tales mostly occurs within the middle strata of the population who are in contact with the aristocracy without themselves belonging to it. The aristocrats like listening to these traditions, but do not themselves learn them.

In the case of traditions for which there are no specialists of any kind, one has to choose one's informants very carefully. Informants who have second-hand knowledge of a tradition are to be avoided. Schoolchildren are not usually good informants, because they have learnt what they know from people who are still alive, and it is they to whom one should turn, since this enables one to go one link further back in the chain of transmission.

Another type of informant to be avoided is someone who has left his customary environment. Very often he is no longer familiar with the culture to which he formerly belonged, and what is of even more frequent occurrence is that people of this kind have acquired a foreign mentality which will profoundly distort their testimonies. Included in this class of informants are those who transmit traditions belonging to groups other than their own, or traditions from distant parts. Often they are not acquainted with the main topographical features of the region where the events they relate took place, and they are prone to make mistakes in place-names. In addition, they are inclined to reinterpret the tradition in terms of their own culture or their own group.

A third type of informant to be avoided—and the worst of the lot!—is the man who has derived his information from a number of different sources in order to get to know the history of his society. He creates a personal version of this history in which all the contradictions of the sources he has used are obliterated, and to which he has added his own interpretations. His testimony is quite worthless, because it is second-hand, and it is necessary to go back to all the traditions he has used in order to be able to evaluate it.

Who, then, can be said to be a 'good' informant? A good informant is someone who still lives the customary life, who recites traditions without too much hesitation, who understands their content but is not too brilliant—for if he were, one would suspect him of introducing distortions—and who is old enough to have acquired some degree of personal experience of his cultural environment. In short, a good informant is the common man who has reached a position which enables him to be conversant with traditions.

There are no precise indices for discerning good informants, and any that might come to mind would be merely superficial. Age and sex, for instance, are of no importance in deciding the choice of a good informant. The Kuba believe that women cannot know much about tradition because of their sex, which excludes them from taking part in public affairs, but in this they are mistaken. The old women of a clan lineage are often those who best know the clan history.

An actual example of this occurred among the Loody clan of the village known as 'Little Loody'. The head of the village and of the clan knew much less about their traditions than his sister, but it would have been shameful for him if a woman had spoken of them and thus shown up his ignorance. The difficulty was resolved by the following gambit. The chief and his sister were both present, but it was the sister who spoke, on the pretext that the recital of traditions exhausted the head of the clan beyond measure.

The kind of people who are good informants in one society are not necessarily so in another, and this is one of the reasons why it is impossible to lay down an ideal type of informant. Much depends on the kind of behaviour expected on the part of certain members of a society by its other members. This behaviour pattern influences the attitude of the informant towards his testimony more than might be expected at first sight. Thus young Tutsi or Hutu[7] who transmit dynastic tales are taken seriously. They are certain to have stuck to the version of the tale which they have heard, and may be expected to follow the style of the court even more closely than the version which has been transmitted to them. The Twa, on the other hand, are regarded as clowns, and it is expected of them that they will make people laugh. Thus they take every opportunity of distorting, expanding, and adding to the tale they are telling, interpolating it with allusions or biting remarks, and accompanying it with a special form of mime. Clearly the Twa of Rwanda would not make good informants. But it does not necessarily follow that the Kwa—like the Twa, a pygmy tribe, but found among the Kuba—are equally poor informants.

Once the informants have been found, they then have to be persuaded to recite the traditions they know. Being human beings, it is reasonable to expect them to co-operate with the fieldworker, but they may, on the contrary, do everything to hinder him in his work. So it is essential that he should gain the confidence of the people he is working among, and that he should make clear to them what his aims are, so that they will not ascribe other purposes to his being there. And that may take time. Sometimes one has to wait a long time before any perceptible progress is made, simply because one has not yet gained the people's confidence. During my residence at the capital of the Bushongo I had to wait several months before being able to collect a single reliable testimony, because nobody knew what this stranger was up to, nor what the reactions of superiors or equals might be if anyone should give information about traditions. It was not until the king himself had testified that contact was established and others followed suit. But even so, no Bushongo ever volunteered information, for this would be a form of behaviour incompatible with their feelings of self-respect. They have a proverb which illustrates this: 'Enquire from those who know; then they will tell you about it'. At the beginning of my investigations they adopted a passive attitude, and when they later became more co-operative, they never did more than indicate the best people to apply to for information.

In Burundi and Rwanda the problems were different. There, the collaboration of some people could be obtained, but not that of others, and I came across instances where it was impossible to record traditions because the informant was hostile, and nothing would persuade him to depart from this attitude.

3. The systematic collection of sources

The fieldworker must endeavour to find all the testimonies that exist concerning the facts he is interested in—that is, concerning the whole past history of the culture he is studying, since this is what he is usually hoping to reconstruct. There are several cogent reasons for enunciating this rule that *all* testimonies must be collected. If all the testimonies in question derive from one and the same tradition, they must all be collected because it is necessary to know all the existing variants of a tradition in order to estimate as accurately as possible what its actual content is and how reliable it is. Thus it is essential to contact all the informants who know the tradition one is studying, or rather, all the informants who know different versions of it. If the testimonies one is seeking belong to different traditions, it will be in the interests of historical research to collect the greatest possible number of them, because they will all throw light upon each other, and will together make it possible to arrive at a more accurate reconstruction of the past. Here, the more complete the collection of material, the greater the chances are of arriving at an accurate reconstruction of the past.

Obviously these demands are sometimes difficult to satisfy, especially when traditions are widely known by a large number of people, as is of course the case with traditions which are transmitted without the intervention of specialists, but which is also true of traditions which are transmitted by a large number of specialists. In Rwanda, for instance, the number of poets who specialize in the transmission of the dynastic poetry is round about a hundred. Together they can produce about 900 testimonies, although the number of traditions transmitted is no more than around 180. One therefore has to record four or five versions of each poem, which means there is four or five times as much work as there are traditions to collect. This work could of course be cut down by collecting one version only of each tradition, but the accuracy of the final results would be much reduced.

Burundi offers an example of a country with traditions which are not transmitted by specialists. The total number of informants able to tell the forty or so traditional tales might be reckoned at about 8,700. This would mean collecting about 2,175 testimonies for each tradition. Needless to say, the effort required to collect so many testimonies would be far greater than the results would justify. Moreover, it would still be impossible to be sure of having collected all the testimonies in existence. This is not the case in Rwanda, where one can be certain of the total number, since the informants there are specialists, who are restricted in number.

Clearly in the case of the traditions of Rwanda already mentioned one must collect all the testimonies, since it is possible to do so. Wherever traditions are in the hands of real specialists, one can find out who they are. One can exclude informants who have acquired their knowledge from another specialist who is still alive, and take only his testimony. Later, one can often divide the specialists into groups of those who have derived their knowledge from the same parent source or from the same chain of transmission. One thus obtains a classification of testimonies before recording them, and the work can be carried out in a systematic way. I need scarcely add that in order to find the specialists one must be familiar with the methods used for the transmission of traditions, and be able to count on the co-operation of the people. I have already laid sufficient stress on this point.

Where no specialists exist one can proceed in a number of different ways. The only method that must never be adopted is to collect a number of testimonies chosen at random, and select the content which is common to the largest number of them—in other words, establish a random sample. In fact, the various testimonies are not equal in value, whereas a random sample is based on the assumption that the data studied are of equal value. But actually, ten versions of a tradition may be further removed from the proto-testimony than an eleventh that has been better preserved.

It is best to use one or other of the following methods. In a small area where there is a large number of informants who know the traditions, collection of testimonies should continue until no further variant versions are found and it is reasonable to suppose that none exist. This fulfils the demands of the rule that all testimonies must be collected, for what the rule really means is that not all the testimonies, but all the variant versions, must be collected.

Where a very large number of informants are scattered over a wide area, there are two ways of solving the problem. The first is to plan a careful selection of samples—a method which is to be specially recommended when the number of informants is out of all proportion to the number of traditions, as in Burundi. What one must do is to draw up a list of the places where a thorough search must be made, the choice of these places depending upon how one can best find all the variants, or as many of them as possible. The first places on the list will be those where historic events have taken place, for informants there usually know more about them than is the case elsewhere. Next come the places where one may expect to find semi-specialists. In Burundi these would be the former sub-chiefdoms which came directly under the rule of the king, and the neigh-bourhood of the site of the royal tombs. The list will be com-pleted by including a series of places at a regular distance apart from each other, since one of the factors that give rise to variant versions is geographical distribution. The further a tradition is diffused from its centre of origin, the more variants will be found. This criterion has to be differently applied according to the type of population distribution encountered—that is, whether the people live in villages, or scattered over the countryside. In the case of villages, it is not difficult to set up a norm for the choice of places to investigate, while with a scattered population one will have to come to whatever arrange-ment is most suitable. A further factor that must be taken into account when selecting one's sample is the possible existence of geographical or social barriers which might prevent or hinder the diffusion of traditions.

Once the method of selecting samples has been decided upon, a thorough study must then be made of the places selected and as many informants found as possible. This is important, because often two contradictory traditions will overlap in the borderland between two areas of diffusion, and in this borderland variants of both traditions must be selected. The two traditions may be outwardly similar in form, and this may have led to a number of changes having been made in the various traditions within the area in order to bring them into harmony with each other.

If the selection of samples has been well planned and nothing occurs during fieldwork to cast doubts upon its efficiency, one may rest assured that the correct choice of places to investigate will guarantee success in collecting all the variants, or at least all the important ones. A further advantage of having worked systematically is that one is always in the position to reconsider the list of samples and decide whether it should be extended so as to increase the chances of discovering all the variants, or cut down, either because no new variants come to hand, or because of some practical problem that may arise.

The other method is as follows. If the area is a wide one, and the number both of informants and of traditions is large, the best procedure is to undertake a preliminary investigation before actually embarking on the recording of testimonies, in order to collect all the information required for deciding upon the selection of samples. Rwanda is a case in point. Here, there may be as many as 400 traditional tales and probably something in the region of 10,000 possible informants for them, or an average of over twenty for every tradition. But some of these tales are very widely known, and hundreds or even thousands of testimonies could be collected, whereas others are rare, either because they are local, or because they are family traditions. In a situation of this kind, one must begin by making a systematic investigation of the whole area to be covered in order to find out likely informants, whose names and status must be noted, as well as the title, or a brief outline, of their testimonies. Analysis of the results of this preliminary investigation will enable one to find out where the rare testimonies are to be found, and also which informants have the best knowledge of the more specialized types of tradition. It will also show if there is any correlation between semi-specialists of this kind and some social factor.

After this analysis has been made, a list can then be drawn up of the traditions which are transmitted by more or less specialized informants, and then informants can be selected on the basis of their particular specialization, even if this is simply a question of knowing rare traditions. One must also take into account the same factors as had to be considered when following the other procedure for the selection of samples—namely, places of historic interest, the geographical distribution of variants, and the existence of barriers to diffusion.

This method of selecting samples is much more likely to produce good results than the method mentioned earlier, whereby one attempts to collect all possible versions; but its drawback is that it takes much more time and energy. In Rwanda, the preliminary investigation alone took nearly two years, and even so only about seventy per cent of the informants that would eventually be required were discovered during that time.

In each research project, a decision has to be made as to what is practicable, and the degree of accuracy one hopes to attain—dependent upon the circumstances connected with the traditions one is in search of, and the time and financial means at one's disposal—must be gauged. Each project has its own particular problems, and each requires a different application of the technique of sampling. One must not feel that the time spent on the preliminary investigation is wasted, even if it takes as long as the actual collecting of traditions. The same applies to any kind of historical research. It is the subject-matter studied that determines the methods to be used.

4. How to record one's sources

Attention has already been drawn to the fact that when a fieldworker confronts an informant, a new social situation is created which gives rise to a certain amount of tension, and this may have an unfortunate effect on the testimony he gives.[8] This means that one must do one's best to ensure that the circumstances are as favourable as possible when recording traditions. One should try to see that the informant is as relaxed as possible, and that he makes no attempt to distort his testimony in order to please the fieldworker, and thus find favour with him for his own advantage.

In order to ensure that the informant will be at his ease, one should either be already acquainted with him, or have created a favourable impression through some third party, so that he will feel neither afraid nor over-confident. This is not very difficult to arrange. But what is sometimes a more tricky matter is to know where the best place would be for recording a testimony, and to get all the circumstantial details right. This is important, because the place, and the reactions of the informant as to whether other people are present or absent, etc., may have a greater influence on the testimony than one might think. For instance, the Kuba tribal chiefs and the members of their councils were approached at the capital, where they were staying in order to attend a national council meeting. Each tribal group was questioned separately, and testified readily. But soon it appeared that there were some traditions which they could not tell at the capital, either because certain persons who, according to custom, must be present at their recital, were not there, or—a more curious reason—because they could not tell, in strange surroundings, traditions which contradicted those preserved by the tribal council of the district they were visiting. It was clear that behind this second reason lay a certain amount of fear and political caution; and if, in spite of that, their testimony had been recorded, it would certainly have been falsified.

One must, therefore, take full account of all such attendant circumstances, the most important of these being, of course, the customs that must be observed when traditions are recited. A group testimony, for instance, cannot be recited unless all the members of the group are present. Thus when the Kuba king was asked to tell the history of his people, he confined himself to giving a few evasive replies. Later, he assembled his council in the palace one day and gave a public lecture which was recorded on tape, and which was a reproduction of the national tradition which is recited by the king at one of his coronation ceremonies. Afterwards he expressed his displeasure that the magnetic tape on which the recording had been made should have been played in places where people who were not members of the council could hear it.

Another Kuba custom is the *kuum*, the preliminary discussion at which the members of the council appoint a 'speaker', and at which they go over the tradition before it is performed in public.

Among the Akan, sacrifices to the ancestors have to be made before certain traditions are recited, so that the fieldworker must be supplied with a sheep or a cask of rum for this purpose.[9] Among the Bushongo, the secrets of initiation cannot be told unless one has first given the initiators some home-brewed palm wine, this obligation being of a religious nature. Also among the Bushongo, the *muyum*, the guardian of the national fetishes, cannot tell their history unless certain precautions have been taken. First, he must obtain the consent of the ancestor of the king whose spirit is associated with these fetishes. Then, the recital must take place at night, in an unfrequented spot, and in the presence of the relics. These few examples show that the recital of a testimony often has ritual accompaniments, and the fieldworker must be careful to comply with the ritual, which will in any case guarantee that the testimony will be recited accurately and without distortions.

But it is not enough merely to ensure that the informant should find himself in circumstances which will allow him to testify in a normal fashion: he must also be prevented from feeling tempted to give false testimony in order to gain favour from the fieldworker. Several methods exist for getting round this difficulty, and everyone will find his own. There is, however, one general rule, and that is, that the informant must not know whether the fieldworker is or is not interested in his testimony, for if he does, he will distort it. Hence good informants must not be rewarded more highly than bad ones. The amount paid must be reckoned according to the number of hours spent on the work, or on some other objective or customary basis, and never according to the quality of the work. In addition, during the recording of the testimony, one must adopt a sympathetic attitude towards the informant, without, however, revealing one's real feelings. In Rwanda and Burundi, where I recorded testimonies on magnetic tape, I pretended that I did not understand a word of the language. The clerk who was with me would explain to the informant what he had to do, and then the informant could recite the testimony as he wished. Since he was under the impression that I did not understand what he was saying, he felt that how he said it was unimportant, and he had no particular motive for distorting the tradition. It should be further noted that with fixed texts the attitude of the fieldworker is less important, since the text is invariable. But his attitude again becomes important when he starts recording the explanatory commentaries.

How should a tradition be recorded? It can either be written down by hand, or recorded on tape. The great advantages of recording on tape are as follows: it gives the exact wording of the testimony, and allows the informant to speak at the speed and in the rhythm natural to him without any interruptions, since the fieldworker cannot ask questions during the recording. But there are some disadvantages too. With a fixed text, or one which has accompanying commentaries, it will still have to be written down after the tape-recording, along with the commentaries. Again, some informants are too old for their voices to be clearly audible on tape. Finally, reading back the tape takes almost five times as much time as writing down the whole thing in the first place. The conclusion to draw would seem to be that it is preferable to record on tape all fixed texts, where the words themselves are part of the tradition, even if they have to be recorded a second time in writing, which incidentally provides an opportunity for assessing the reliability of the informant. As regards free texts, the best plan is to record a number of variants on tape, and take down the rest in writing. The variants recorded on tape will give some idea of the nature of the testimony as it sounds when spoken, but, since the words in a free text do not form part of the tradition, there is no need to record the exact wording of every version. One final piece of advice: after some time has elapsed, it is advisable to make contact again with the most important informants and write down once more the traditions they know, so as to test their powers of memory. A recording on tape is not necessary for the purpose of carrying out a check of this kind.

But it is not enough merely to record the testimony. All the other information which the historian will require later must also be noted down—and in the first place, the explanatory commentaries. I said earlier that the fieldworker must avoid asking questions, and that if he did ask any, the replies to them must be regarded as separate testimonies. This is all very well, but in practice there are often occasions when one cannot avoid asking questions. What one must then do is to avoid asking *leading* questions, and limit oneself to making vague, general enquiries which leave the informant free to provide whatever explanations occur to him.

The next thing to be done is to make a note of all the necessary subsidiary information, which is best done by means of a questionnaire. This auxiliary documentation must supply the name, genealogy, social position, and address of each informant, the place and the date of the recording of the testimony on tape or in writing, and the method of transmission used; and, whenever possible, the same information supplied for the final informant should be supplied for all the links in the chain of transmission. Information should also be supplied about the manner of reciting the testimony, the degree of frequency of recital of the tradition, the degree of specialization, what controls are exercised over the recital of testimonies, mnemonic devices used during apprenticeship, and the specific function and particular purpose of each tradition. Finally a note should be made of any psychological characteristics of the informant, should there be occasion to do so, and of the amount he received in payment, so as to give some indication as to what advantage the informant may have derived from testifying. The type of questionnaire one must draw up in order to obtain the required information will vary according to the society in which one is working, and to the type of tradition being studied.

5. *Summary*

The foregoing can be summed up briefly.

The various stages in the search for oral traditions are as follows:

First of all the language and the culture of the people whose past history is to be investigated must be studied.

Next comes a general survey of the extent to which traditions exist in the society in question, after which some soundings should be made to discover what types of tradition there are, what their special characteristics are, and in particular what methods of transmission are used. One will then be able to plan one's work in a methodical way, and can proceed either to make a systematic collection of every existing tradition, or decide upon a system of sampling which will indicate the lines of research to follow. If a pilot survey is carried out too hastily, the fieldworker will in the end waste as much time correcting or recasting his system of sampling as he would have spent if he had not been negligent about the preliminary investigation. As regards the recording of testimonies, the best results will be obtained by creating as favourable an atmosphere as possible, by taking down the text in the language in which it has been transmitted with the greatest possible accuracy, whether this be done by writing it down or by recording it on tape, and by collecting all the auxiliary information necessary for the subsequent application of the methods of historical criticism to the material collected. It will have been gathered from the foregoing survey that if search for oral traditions is carried out along the right lines, it is apt to be a protracted affair which can at times become extremely tiresome. But the results will be a real contribution to our knowledge of history, and they can only be obtained by making such an effort.

I should like to conclude by giving some practical advice about the publication of material. The scientific level of existing publications of oral traditions, or of general works based on oral traditions, is, as a rule, not very high. Nevertheless, if only certain elementary rules were followed, useful work could be produced. An edition of original texts should include an indication of variant versions. When the texts are fixed texts, the same rules can be applied as those established for the publication of written sources. As far as the publication of free texts is concerned, the notation of variants raises some technical problems. The variants must be shown either in diagrammatic form, or indicated by key initials with full documentation on the whole range of variants in theme, plot, episodes, and setting. In either case, the texts must be preceded by a commentary and accompanied by a *stemma codicum* which will show the relationship between the various versions.

In his comments on the texts, the author must allow his readers to follow his ideas step by step, and must provide them with all the necessary information concerning the texts. He must also inform his readers of any choice he may make between alternative versions, or any interpretations he himself makes of important points in the text, with full documentation of his reasons for doing so, for the golden rule of all scientific publications is that the reader must be in a position to be able to check the author's statements.

Notes

(The full titles of the works referred to are given in the bibliography. In the notes, only the author's name is given, together with a shortened form of the title if more than one work by the same author is listed in the bibliography.)

CHAPTER I

1. See the works by H. Delehaye and F. Lanzoni.
2. R. Bloch, p. 125, gives the following explanation for this attitude: 'But, as we have seen, even for the most distant periods of the past, traditional legends do not provide any information of value on the course of events unless they are submitted to careful examination and confirmed by evidence from the positive sciences, such as archaeology, before they are accepted'. [Trans. of French text.]
3. G. Dumezil, pp. 119-25.
4. E. Bernheim, *Einleitung in der Geschichtswissenschaft*, 1908/6, p. 217.
5. *Idem*, pp. 494 and 504.
6. *Idem*, p. 486.
7. This stipulation shows that it was mainly European oral tradition in its published form that the writer had in mind.
8. E. Bernheim, pp. 382-4.
9. *Idem*, pp. 494-504, where he is in agreement with J. Engel, *Ueber die Arten der unbewussten Geschichtsentstehung* (Nauen, 1879), a work which he supplements.
10. *Idem*, p. 503.
11. A. Feder, pp. 61-5 and 199-204. The discussion makes it clear that it is mainly European tradition that is under consideration.
12. *Idem*, pp. 203-4.
13. W. Bauer, pp. 236-45.
14. Cf. J. D. Fage.
15. R. Oliver, 'The Traditional Histories . . .', 'A Question about the Bachwezi', 'Ancient Capital Sites', and 'The Royal Tombs'.
16. R. A. Hamilton (ed.), pp. 15-27 and 41-70.
17. *Ibidem*, p. 11.
18. A. Van Gennep, p. 165: 'One should therefore remain sceptical about reconstructions of historical events based on traditions'. [Trans. of French text.]
19. *Idem*, pp. 267-94.
20. E. S. Hartland, pp. 428-34 and p. 456, note 32.
21. R. Lowie, *Journal of Amer. Folklore*, pp. 165 and 167.
22. *Idem, op. cit.*, p. 167.

23. R. B. Dixon and J. R. Swanton, *Amer. Anthr.* 16, p. 376.

24. R. Lowie, *Amer. Anthr.* 17, p. 598.

25. R. B. Dixon and J. R. Swanton, *op. cit.*, p. 376.

26. R. B. Dixon, *Amer. Anthr.* 17, p. 599 (Dr. Dixon's reply. Dr. Swanton's reply is on the same page.)

27. A. A. Goldenweiser, pp. 763-4. His views are summed up as follows: 'Poor evidence is poor evidence but it is evidence', p. 764.

28. E. Sapir, pp. 395-7.

29. M. Herskovits, 'Anthropology and Africa', p. 230.

30. *Ibidem*, p. 232: 'The validity assigned to traditional mythical history, which often reaches beyond anything that the most confirmed euhemerist would claim, has also bedevilled the serious student of African ethno-history'.

31. C. E. Fuller, pp. 127-8. His study entitled *An Ethnohistoric Study of Continuity and Change in Gwambe Culture* (Ph.D., Dept. of Anthropology, North Western University, 1950) has unfortunately not been available to me.

32. D. Tait, p. 209.

33. W. Muehlmann, pp. 206-7.

34. F. Graebner, pp. 52-4; G. Van Bulck, *Beiträge . . .*, p. 198.

35. G. Van Bulck, *op. cit.*, p. 198.

36. R. Mortier, p. 35.

37. H. U. Beier, pp. 17-25.

38. P. Mercier, pp. 92-5.

39. The English functionalist school is one of the dominant trends in present-day ethnology. Founded by A. R. Radcliffe-Brown and B. Malinowski, it maintains that a society or a culture forms an integrated whole, the parts of which are structured in such a manner as to help maintain the social system as a whole. The role thus performed by the parts in relation to the whole is known as their *function*.

40. E. E. Evans-Pritchard, 'Social Anthropology: Past and Present', p. 121.

41. A. R. Radcliffe-Brown, *Structure and Function in Primitive Society*, pp. 3 and 49-50.

42. This aspect has been particularly emphasized by M. Fortes in *The Dynamics of Clanship . . .*, p. 23, and 'The Significance of Descent . . .', p. 370.

43. I. Wilks, 'Tribal History and Myth', and probably I. Wilks and E. Collins, *Memory to Myths. A Study in Oral Tradition*.

44. E. E. Evans-Pritchard, 'Social Anthropology . . .', p. 121. This writer has also published several articles on Zande history which are mainly based on oral traditions. Cf. 'A historical introduction to a study of Zande society', 'The origin of the ruling clan of the Azande', 'A history of the kingdom of Gbudwe'. He has used traditional material for reconstructing the Zande military organization of the nineteenth century. Cf. 'Zande warfare' and 'Zande border-raids'. He believes that in studying the political systems of African kingdoms, the historical dimension must be taken into account as well as sociological data. Cf. 'A historical introduction to a study of Zande society', p. 1.

45. P. C. Lloyd, pp. 20-8.

46. A. W. Southall, pp. 139-45.

47. J. Van Velsen, pp. 105-8, and also the works by Barnes, Bohannan, Cunnison, Middleton, Read, and Wilson cited in the bibliography. These writers emphasize the distortions of traditions due to their sociological function, but all of them consider that traditions nevertheless contain historical information of real value. They are in fact close to those who adopt a functionalist position, such as Fortes and Wilks, the only difference between them being that the latter maintain that the function creates the tradition, whereas the former think that it only distorts it.

48. A. A. Nicholson, p. 609.

49. K. Luomola, p. 773; R. Linton, p. 180.

50. Cf. R. Romero Moliner. This writer only deals with African oral traditions, but his remarks have a wider implication. The absence of a chronological system in Africa has been deplored by D. Westermann, p. 17, who, despite the resulting confusion and the mistakes made in dating, nevertheless overestimates the value of African traditions. With regard to Polynesia, a number of authors have thrown doubt on the validity of the genealogical lists that form the basis of the chronological system there. Cf. R. Heine-Geldern, p. 336; H. J. Fletcher, pp. 189-94; J. F. G. Stokes, pp. 1-42; P. Buck, pp. 21-4.

51. *Notes and Queries on Anthropology*, p. 40.

52. E. Meyerowitz, *Akan Traditions of Origin*.

53. C. von Fuehrer-Haimendorf, pp. 158-9.

54. E. Meyerowitz, pp. 15-17 and in notes *passim*.

55. *Idem*, pp. 19-22. The only other works known to me where this has been done are two by A. Kagame, in which he studies the typology of the historical sources of Rwanda. Cf. *La Poésie dynastique au Rwanda*, particularly pp. 1-30, and *La Notion de génération . . .*, ch. i, pp. 9-44.

56. E. Meyerowitz, p. 46.

57. *Idem*, p. 46.

58. *Idem*, p. 93.

59. *Idem*, pp. 124-9.

60. Cf. J. Goody.

CHAPTER II

1. W. Bauer, p. 244, and E. Bernheim, p. 494, make the same distinction. They use the following terms: 'direct testimony' for eyewitness account, and 'indirect statement' for a reported statement. Bernheim puts oral tradition in the category of direct testimonies on the grounds that both are communicated orally. It is, however, better to classify oral traditions and eyewitness accounts separately, because each has special characteristics.

2. Cf. p. 162 for two other examples of contradictory traditions known by the same informant.

3. For the formal structure of the testimony, see Ch. III, section 2.

4. J. Jacobs and J. Vansina, p. 7. Also, pp. 5-7: 'We have indicated to those whose work it is to take up the words of the king. And/you/notables/if you have anything to say, then say it', says the king. At the end he asks: 'My mother's clan, is it not thus?' 'The mountains are thus, are thus', is shouted in reply. The king continues: 'And you, come along. Confirm what I have said.' The dignitaries *mbeem* and *mbyeeng* rise and declare that he has spoken the truth. [Trans. of original text.]

5. E. Meyerowitz, p. 115.

6. J. Jacobs and J. Vansina, p. 15.

7. A. Kagame, *La Poésie dynastique* . . ., pp. 22-4; E. Meyerowitz, p. 20.

8. H. Lavachery, p. 37; R. Lowie, *Social Organization*, p. 197; K. Luomola, pp. 772-89; E. Best, pp. 57-84; E. S. C. Handy, p. 20.

9. G. C. Vaillant, p. 117; J. Soustelle, p. 102; H. B. Nicholson, p. 609; L. Baudin, 'La formation de l'élite . . .', p. 109; J. H. Rowe, 'Inca culture . . .', pp. 201-2.

10. E. S. C. Handy, p. 20.

11. *Notes and Queries*, p. 204. A good example is provided by an official called the *baba elegun* of the town of Ketu (Yoruba), whose duty it is to know its history by heart. The office is hereditary in the Oyede family, and the information is transmitted from father to son. The traditions are recited at the enthronement of each new ruler. On that occasion, the *baba elegun* receives a reward if he succeeds in reciting them without a mistake. If he fails, he is punished by supernatural sanctions. Cf. S. O. Biobaku, 'The wells of West African history', p. 19.

12. D. Westermann, p. 406. Also pp. 15-16.

13. A. d'Arianoff, pp. 14-15; A. Kagame, *La Notion de génération* . . ., pp. 9-44.

14. A. Kagame, *La Poésie dynastique* . . ., p. 39, note 35.

15. E. Meyerowitz, pp. 19-20.

16. E. Best, pp. 73 and 65.

17. R. Lowie, *Social Organization*, p. 202.

18. D. Westermann, p. 1; L. Frobenius, pp. 343-4. The latter recognizes the importance of the lists of ancestors, but makes no mention of the sanctions attached.

19. A. Kagame, *La Poésie dynastique* . . ., pp. 22-4.

20. G. C. Vaillant, p. 117; J. Soustelle, p. 199.

21. R. Lowie, *Primitive Society*, pp. 224-32; *Idem, Social Organization*, pp. 131-4.

22. I. Cunnison, *History on the Luapula*, p. 5.

23. A. Kagame, *La Poésie dynastique* . . ., pp. 22-3.

24. B. Malinowski, *Argonauts* . . ., pp. 291 and 185-6.

25. Cf. L. Baudin, 'La formation de l'élite . . .', pp. 107-14; J. H. Rowe, 'Inca culture . . .', pp. 201-2; *Idem*, 'Absolute chronology . . .', p. 272; H. B. Nicholson, p. 609.

26. R. Karsten, p. 113. A chapter is devoted to the subject, pp. 128-37. See also L. Baudin, *Der socialistische Staat der Inka*, pp. 48-50, and the bibliography he gives. Also pp. 103-7.

27. L. Baudin, *op. cit.*, p. 49.

28. E. Elisofon, p. 129.

29. See P. Verger. See also M. Herskovits, *Dahomey*, pp. 330-1, on the mnemonic value of the attributes ascribed to the umbrellas of the nobles.

30. H. Lavachery, p. 37.

31. E. Meyerowitz, pp. 29-32.

32. A. Kagame, *La Poésie dynastique* . . ., p. 39, note 35.

33. There is a photograph of a sword of this kind in E. Torday, p. 192, fig. 276e.

34. A. B. Attafua, pp. 18-20.

35. *Ibidem,* pp. 18-20.
36. J. Gorju, p. 112.
37. I. Cunnison, *History on the Luapula,* pp. 35-8.
38. *Ibidem,* p. 10.
39. L. Frobenius, p. 344.
40. Cf. J. Gorju, pp. 83, 87, 107-9; R. Oliver, 'Ancient Capital Sites . . .', and 'The royal tombs . . .'; M. Wilson, *Communal rites of the Nyakusa,* pp. 42 and 70-85; *Idem,* 'The early history . . .', p. 175; A. E. Jensen, p. 94, note 3.
41. Thus the dynastic poets of Rwanda first learn a melody, and only after they know it well do they learn the words of the poem which they wish to remember. One of them actually said that the melody served as a means of remembering the words.
42. D. Westermann, p. 16; E. Meyerowitz, p. 19.
43. Among the Mongo of the Congo, for example. Cf. A. de Rop, pp. 178-9.
44. L. Stappers, 'Toonparallelisme . . .', mentions examples from the Luba of the Kasai. Poetic forms also have a mnemonic value.
45. Cf. Ch. IV.
46. A Feder, p. 203; D. Westermann, pp. 16-17; J. Gorju, p. 113. The last two writers give examples of feats of memorization reaching to the extent of mastering a list of several hundred names.
47. For N. J. van Warmelo, three hundred years is the limit of validity of a tradition. R. Lowie, *Social Organization,* p. 163, and E. S. Hartland, p. 434, set this limit at two hundred years. A. Feder, pp. 62-3, suggests a classification of traditions according to their depth in time, basing himself on the same argument.
48. Valid traditions can sometimes go very far back into the past. F. Boas, 'The Folklore of the Eskimo', p. 512, cites the example of the Eskimos of Greenland who remember wars they fought against the Normans (1379-1450), and the Eskimos of southern Baffinland, who still retain memories of the visit of Frobisher (1576-8). E. Meyerowitz, pp. 29-32, shows that in the state of Takyiman some traditions go back to 1295. In the case of certain South African tribes, M. Wilson, 'The early history . . .', pp. 173-8, shows that there too tribal traditions enable us to trace the course of history back until about 1300. Finally, I myself have been able to provide proof that the Kuba of the Kasai still remember the coats of mail worn by the Portuguese on the Congolese coast before 1525.
49. R. Lowie, *Social Organization,* p. 202.
50. A. Kagame, *La Poésie dynastique . . .,* p. 27.
51. G. Dieterlin, 'Mythe et organisation . . .', pp. 39-40.
52. Cf. Ch. V, section 2.

CHAPTER III

1. On the subject of intentional and unintentional testimonies, see M. Bloch, ch. ii, a and b.
2. There is no question here of any claims being made to these places, because they are too far away from the area now inhabited by the Bushongo.
3. A. Kagame, 'Le code ésotérique de la dynastie du Rwanda'.

4. The esoteric traditions of the priestly schools in New Zealand are a good example of sacred traditions. Any error committed by a priest in the recital of a ritual text would probably result in the death of the priest. No criticism of the content of these traditions was allowed. Cf. E. Best, pp. 65-73.

5. Among the Lugbara, for example. Cf. J. Middleton, pp. 193-9.

6. R. Linton, p. 187.

7. The next chapter discusses in detail the distortions which arise due to the purposes pursued, and, even more, the functions fulfilled by a tradition.

8. E. Bernheim, pp. 257-9; A. Feder, pp. 62-3; W. Bauer, p. 161.

9. A suggestion for a classification of literary categories according to form only, discounting content, is discussed by A. de Rop, pp. 8-14. Such an attempt would come up against almost insurmountable difficulties. What is more, de Rop includes the internal structure as part of the form of a text, which shows how complex a matter the classification of categories is.

10. A. van Gennep, p. 74.

11. M. Herskovits, *Man and his Works*, pp. 414-18.

12. W. Bauer, p. 161.

13. A. Feder, p. 62.

14. A. Feder, pp. 62-3.

15. M. Jousse, 'Le style oral . . .', and the discussion on pp. 15-16 of A. de Rop, 'De gesproken woordkunst . . .'.

16. L. Stappers, pp. 99-100.

17. Cf. A. Coupez and T. Kamanzi; A. Coupez; P. E. Boelaert, pp. 348 and 365; L. Stappers, 'Eerste geluiden . . .', pp. 97-110. Apparently rules do exist in Bushongo poetry, but nobody has yet succeeded in finding out exactly what they are.

18. A. Kagame, *La Poésie dynastique . . .*, pp. 13-14.

19. The title is part and parcel of the tale, which is not always the case.

20. The king here is Ruganguuza.

21. This is the nameless king who wants to kill Ruganguuza.

22. This is the site of a sacred forest. The whole passage is a warning. The rain symbolizes the advancing army. Rainmaking is something that can only be done by kings, and a change of dynasty is forecasted here.

23. The *inyaambo* cows symbolize the kingship.

24. Ruganguuza wakes up.

25. This is the pretender to the throne that enters Ruganguuza's chamber.

26. A structural analysis can be carried out with any tale. The methods employed and the theory of narrative structure are illuminatingly discussed by V. Propp with reference to Russian folk-tales.

27. See Ch. IV, section 1, where a Rundi example is given.

28. B. Malinowski, 'The Problem of meaning in primitive languages'.

29. P. Tempels.

30. R. van Caeneghem, *Hekserij bij de Baluba van Kasai*.

31. Personal communication from M. A. Coupez.

32. J. A. Barnes, 'History in a changing society', p. 2.

33. P. C. Lloyd, p. 27.

34. G. Van Bulck, 'De invloed van de Westersche cultuur . . .', p. 293.

35. A. de Rop, pp. 12-13.

36. E. R. Leach, p. 29, thinks that primitive peoples are trained to think poetically, and that they cultivate an aptitude for making and under-

standing ambiguous statements. In many parts of Asia, lovers conduct their courtship by reciting verses which are apparently innocent but which contain declarations of love. Leach concludes from this that: 'People who use language in this way become highly adept at understanding symbolic statements'.

37. A. Kagame, *La Poésie dynastique* . . ., pp. 14-19.

38. P. Denolf, pp. 399-425; R. van Caeneghem, *Over het Godsbegrip* . . ., pp. 29-30.

39. A. Kagame, *op. cit.*, pp. 63-4, and personal communications.

40. P. Denolf, pp. 568-70. The quotations come from p. 569.

41. E. Bernheim, pp. 356-8; A. Feder, p. 64; W. Bauer, pp. 240-1; H. Delahaye, pp. 30-41; F. Lanzoni, pp. 74-85.

42. P. Denolf, p. 29; I. Cunnison, *History on the Luapula*, p. 19; M. Planc-quaert, p. 88.

43. Folklorists have been studying the distribution of folklore motifs for the past hundred years. There is an international index of these motifs which is constantly being revised and added to. The motifs of some tales, such as Cinderella, are found to have a world-wide distribution.

44. J. P. Crazzolara, p. 10.

45. R. Mortier, part II, pp. 129 and 132-3.

46. I. Cunnison, *History on the Luapula*, pp. 11-14.

47. H. Baumann, *Schöpfung und Urzeit* . . ., pp. 260 ff., mentions the Larusus, Masai, Nyoro, Yao, Ngoni, Ila, Luyi, Mambunda, Subiya, Umbundu, Kimbundu, Zulu, Ronga, Xhosa, Hottentot, Sotho, Hausa, Kerri-kerri, Mossi, Ashanti, Mende, Kpelle, and the Kabyles. To these should be added the Kuba and the Yans. Cf. R. de Beaucorps, *Les Bayansi du Bas-Kwilu*.

48. This motif is found among the Ganda, Nyoro, Rwanda, and Rundi. In Burundi a striking example is found of how an existing motif can be applied to a new situation. About 1900, Kilima, a pretender to the throne, contested the rights of King Mweezi of Burundi. Kilima was a stranger, with no kinship connections in the country. He made use of the stereotype formula of claiming to be a son of one of the wives of Ntare, the father of Mweezi, and maintained that his mother had had to hide him in her native country so that he could escape from the enemies who wanted to kill him. His story was believed by one section of the population, and the Kilima rebellion was thus legitimatized in their eyes. If Kilima had won, future historians would have found that this stereotype account formed part of the official history of his reign; but by comparing it with motifs from other interlacustrian countries, they would have been able to infer that Kilima was the founder of a new dynasty.

CHAPTER IV

1. The ideas about society and functions discussed here are mainly taken from A. R. Radcliffe-Brown, *A Natural Science of Society*.

2. M. Herskovits, *Man and his Works*, p. 419; W. Muehlmann, pp. 206-07, mentions other examples.

3. E. Meyerowitz, pp. 21-2.

4. R. Oliver, 'The traditional histories . . .', pp. 111-12.

5. E. Meyerowitz, pp. 21-2, 84 note 2, 106 note 3, 109.

6. J. A. Barnes, 'History in a changing society', pp. 4-6.

7. B. Malinowski, *Argonauts*, pp. 291-8. The song was a property that could be sold.

8. A. Kagame, *La Poésie dynastique* . . . , pp. 158-9.

9. *Ibidem*, p. 157; pp. 22-4.

10. D. Westermann, p. 17.

11. P. Denolf, I, p. 27 f.

12. R. Lowie, *Journal of Amer. Folklore* (1917), pp. 164-5.

13. R. Romero Moliner, pp. 44-7, stresses this.

14. Cf. M. P. Nilsson, pp. 1-336, where examples of ecological time-reckoning taken from many different peoples are given. On the subject of concepts of time, cf. E. E. Evans-Pritchard, *The Nuer*, pp. 96-104; P. Bohannan, pp. 251-4; I. Cunnison, *History on the Luapula*, pp. 29-31; J. Middleton, p. 194. Among the Lugbara, 'events that do not recur are not put on a measured comparative scale'.

15. See J. Daelman, and L. Denis.

16. Cf. M. P. Nilsson, pp. 324-6, for the market-week; E. E. Evans-Pritchard, *The Nuer*, pp. 104-8; P. Bohannan, pp. 254-62; I. Cunnison, *History on the Luapula*, pp. 31-5.

17. A. W. Southall, p. 148.

18. J. Middleton, p. 194; B. Malinowski, *Argonauts*, pp. 300-1.

19. D. Westermann, p. 17.

20. B. Malinowski, *Argonauts*, pp. 299-303.

21. G. Van Bulck, 'De invloed . . .', p. 29.

22. Cf. p. 102.

23. The following Kuba proverb shows that a capacity for critical judgment exists: 'After people have imagined something, and have recited it in public in an exaggerated manner, their descendants (that is, informants later in the chain) have overdone it still further when telling the tale'. But this proverb applies mostly to weird sounds made while telling a story.

24. B. Malinowski, *Argonauts*, p. 301.

25. J. Middleton, pp. 191-5.

26. M. Eliade, pp. 40-67.

27. R. Firth, *The Work of the Gods* . . .

28. J. Vansina, 'De handelingen der voorouders . . .', pp. 282-3.

29. Cf. I. Cunnison, *History on the Luapula*, p. 5. He notes that among the Luapula peoples official history coincides with dynastic history. The same is true for the Kuba and for Rwanda. In the Kuba chiefdoms, moreover, the official history of each chiefdom is the history of the chiefly clan, just as the history of the country is the dynastic history.

30. A. van Gennep, pp. 267-71.

31. Cf. p. 44.

CHAPTER V

1. P. Denolf, p. 415.

2. J. H. Rowe, 'Absolute chronology . . .', p. 272.

3. M. Herskovits, *Man and his Works*, pp. 414-26; F. Boas in all the works mentioned in the bibliography.

4. E. Meyerowitz, pp. 21-2.

5. *Idem*, pp. 21-2.

6. I. Cunnison, *History on the Luapula*, pp. 1-10.

7. J. van Velsen, p. 107; I. Cunnison, *op. cit.*, pp. 21-2.

CHAPTER VI

1. Cf. Ch. III, section 1.

2. Cf. J. Vansina, 'La valeur historique . . .', p. 59, where a slightly different typology is given. This one is an improved version.

3. O. Biobaku, 'The wells of African history', p. 19.

4. O. Biobaku, *op. cit.*, p. 19.

5. Cf. W. Bauer, p. 243, where he quotes proverbs concerning Prussian law. L. de Sousberghe thinks that the Bantus do not have any legal proverbs. G. Hulstaert does not consider this to be the case with Mongo proverbs (cf. pp. 7 and 718 under the word 'droit', and pp. 758-9 under the word 'jugement', and in several other places as well). Although it is often difficult to decide whether a proverb merely has the character of a moral exhortation, or whether it refers to a specific legal matter, the Rev. Father Hulstaert would seem to be right. A proverb such as: 'The plant *Boerhavia diffusa* cannot walk, it is a scrap of material that has made it spread' can only refer to the fact that legal responsibility lies with the principal in any transaction, even if he is not to blame for any infringement of the law. This proverb certainly refers to legal matters and is not simply a rather vague or generalized moral injunction. Cf. G. Hulstaert, p. 414, No. 1588.

6. An example is provided by the magic formula employed by the Mbuun for making rain: 'I beseech thee: Go to the Kwilu of Pombo of Zombo, which receives many small tributaries. Ngul of Kaam. The Mbuun of Mbanza Wemba have chased away the men of Samba (lit. the hut containing the chiefly insignia of the Samba). They wear little pads on their heads. The mountains lie at their feet.' The names date from the migratory period of the Mbuun, and furthermore, the memory of a quarrel with the Samba is preserved in this formula. Cf. J. M. de Decker, p. 27.

7. As, for instance, the royal oath of the Ashanti, which recalls the defeat and death of Osei Tutu, the founder of the Ashanti Confederacy. Cf. E. Meyerowitz, p. 34, and M. Manoukian, p. 41.

8. L. Baudin, 'La formation de l'élite . . .', p. 111.

9. J. M. de Decker, p. 105.

10. W. Bauer, pp. 242-3.

11. Such as the Bushongo *ncyeem ingesh*.

12. Cf. E. Meyerowitz, p. 120.

13. The chiefs do not disclose the secret of their origin.

14. The Bono kingdom was the most ancient of the neighbouring kingdoms.

15. The chief of Nkwanta, one of the Akan states. The song was composed in his honour.

16. E. von Sydow, p. 172.

17. E. Best, pp. 57-84.

18. I. Cunnison, 'Perpetual kinship . . .', and *History on the Luapula*, pp. 33-4, for the names of persons, p. 42 for the names of places. The writer expresses the opinion that the name is the hero and the preserver of history. The same is true, although to a lesser degree, of the Kuba. O. S. Biobaku, in 'Myths and oral history', p. 14, says that among the Yoruba names of places are 'retentive of history'.

19. E. Best, pp. 57-84.

20. I. Cunnison, *History of Luapula*, p. 10.

21. I. Cunnison, 'History and genealogies . . .', p. 29. Cf. P. Bohannan, M. Fortes, and also E. E. Evans-Pritchard, *The Nuer*, pp. 192-248.

22. I. Cunnison, 'History and genealogy . . .', and *History on the Luapula*, pp. 1-10, 41-2.

23. M. Fortes, *The Dynamics of Clanship* . . ., pp. 11-12, and A. W. Southall, pp. 138-9.

24. Cf. an example given by J. Vansina, 'De handelingen der voorouders', which is a tale known throughout the Bieng tribe.

25. Cf. J. Middleton and D. Tait, *Tribes without Rulers*, and J. P. Crazzolara, *The Lwoo*. The first of these works describes various types of society without state organization; the second gives numerous examples of Lwoo family histories containing stereotypes. Examples of family traditions are to be found in almost all historical studies by social anthropologists.

26. Typical instances of this are found in Australia. For the Murnghin, see R. M. Berndt and W. L. Warner; for the Arunta, see B. Spencer and F. J. Gillen, part I, pp. 67-390.

27. Cf. B. Malinowski, 'Myth in primitive society'; H. Baumann, *Schöpfung und Urzeit*; M. Eliade, pp. 40-6 and the bibliography, p. 142.

28. A. Feder, p. 64.

29. E. Bernheim, p. 355; A. Feder, p. 62. The latter restricts the category of aetiological myths to local legends.

30. P. Stanislas, pp. 124-30.

31. H. Baumann, *Schöpfung und Urzeit*, pp. 334-84, and 'Ethnologische Feldforschung . . .', p. 162.

32. See F. Lanzoni, A. van Gennep, H. Delehaye (in particular pp. 1-67 and 84-5), E. Bernheim. The last is based on J. Engel, *Ueber die Arten der unbewussten Geschichtsentstehung* (Nauen, 1879), a work which I have not been able to procure. A. Feder (pp. 203-4) faithfully follows E. Bernheim. W. Bauer (pp. 237-8) draws special attention to the anecdotal nature of tales. These writers call tales of artistic merit either sagas or legends, and are not always rigorous in maintaining a clear distinction between aetiological myths and tales of artistic merit.

33. F. Lanzoni, pp. 34-6, mentions, as illustration, the biographies of Pilate and Belisarius. See also H. Delehaye, pp. 84-5, E. Bernheim, pp. 494-502, A. Feder, pp. 203-4, W. Bauer, pp. 237-8.

34. C. M. Turnbull, 'Legends of the BaMbuti'.

35. J. D. Fage, 'The investigation of oral tradition . . .'.

36. M. Herskovits, 'Anthropology and Africa . . .'.

37. J. Hiernaux, pp. 351-60.

38. S. Cole, pp. 280-4, pl. 16, and M. Posnansky, *Museum Archaeological Project*.

39. M. Posnansky, *Progress and Prospects* . . ., pp. 32-6.
40. J. Nicolas.
41. A. Kroeber, *Anthropology*, pp. 564-8.
42. F. Graebner; W. Schmidt; G. Van Bulck, *Beiträge* . . . .
43. J. Greenberg, pp. 88-106.
44. M. Swadesh, 'Diffusional Cumulation . . .', pp. 1-21; 'Lexico-statistic dating . . .', pp. 452-63; 'Towards greater accuracy . . .', pp. 121-37.
45. A. Coupez, pp. 85-7.
46. Cf. W. C. Boyd, pp. 488-506; M. Bates, pp. 700-13. W. Boyd (p. 506) establishes the existence of six races, based on an analysis of blood groups—two in Europe and one in each of the other continents.
47. J. Hiernaux, pp. 719-27.

CHAPTER VII

1. Cf. M. Bloch, pp. 60-5.

APPENDIX

1. A. E. Jensen, p. 94 note 3.
2. E. Meyerowitz, p. 15.
3. E. Meyerowitz, p. 34.
4. K. Luomola, p. 777b. They contain praise of the heroic deeds of the baby's ancestors, in order to teach him to be worthy of them.
5. Rundi lullabies may contain allusions to the baby's parents or grandparents, and are then a source of information about the family history.
6. M. Herskovits, *Man and his Works*, p. 431.
7. The people of Rwanda are divided into three castes: the Tutsi, the Hutu, and the Twa.
8. Cf. Ch. IV, section 3.
9. E. Meyerowitz, p. 21.

Bibliography of Works Cited

ATTAFUA, A. B., 'Traditional history', *Transactions of the Gold Coast and Togoland Historical Society*, 1952, I, 18-20.

BARNES, J. A., *Politics in a Changing Society*, London, 1954.

— 'History in a changing society', *Human Problems in British Central Africa* (Rhodes-Livingstone Institute Journal), 1952, XI, 1-9.

BATES, M., 'Human ecology', in *Anthropology Today*, by A. L. Kroeber and others (Chicago, 1953), pp. 700-13.

BAUDIN, L., *Der sozialistische Staat der Inka*, Hamburg, 1956. Trans. from the French by J. Niederehe.

— 'La formation de l'élite et l'enseignement de l'histoire dans l'empire des Incas', *Revue des études historiques*, 1927, 83, pp. 107-14.

BAUER, W., *Einführung in das Studium der Geschichte*, Tübingen, 1928.

BAUMANN, H., *Schöpfung und Urzeit des Menschen im Mythus der Afrikanischen Völker*, Berlin, 1936.

— 'Ethnologische Feldforschung und kulturhistorische Ethnologie', *Studium Generale*, 1954, VII, 151-64.

BEIER, H. U., 'The historical and psychological significance of Yoruba myths', *Odù*, 1955, I, 17-25.

BERNDT, R. M., *Kunapipi. A Study of an Australian Aboriginal Religious Cult*, Melbourne, 1951.

BERNHEIM, E., *Lehrbuch der historischen Methode und der Geschichtsphilosophie. Mit Nachweis der wichtigsten Quellen und Hilfsmittel zum Studium der Geschichte*, Leipzig, 1908.

BEST, E., *The Maori* (Memoirs of the Polynesian Society V), Wellington, 1924, 2 volumes.

BIOBAKU, S. O., 'The problem of traditional history with special reference to Yoruba traditions', *Journal of the Historical Society of Nigeria*, 1956, I, 43-7.

— 'Myths and oral history', *Odù*, 1955, I, 12-17.

— 'The wells of West African history', *West African Review*, 1953, XXIX, 304, pp. 18-19.

BLOCH, M., *Apologie de l'histoire ou le métier d'historien* (Cahiers des Annales 3), Paris, 1952.

BLOCH, R., *Les Origines de Rome*, Paris, 1946.

BOAS, F., *Race, Language and Culture*, New York, 1940.

BOELAERT, E., 'Premières recherches sur la structure de cinq poésies Lonkundo', *Comptes rendus des séances de l'Institut Royal Colonial Belge*, 1952, XXIII, 348-65.

BOHANNAN, L. A., 'A genealogical charter', *Africa*, 1952, XXII, 301-15.

216

BIBLIOGRAPHY OF WORKS CITED

Bohannan, P., 'Concepts of time among the Tiv of Nigeria', *South-Western Journal of Anthropology*, 1953, IX, 251-62.

Boyd, W. C., 'The contribution of genetics to anthropology', in *Anthropology Today*, by A. L. Kroeber and others (Chicago, 1953), pp. 488-506.

Buck, P. H., *Vikings of the Sunrise*, Philadelphia, 1938.

Cole, S., *The Prehistory of East Africa*, London, 1954.

Coupez, A., 'Application de la lexicostatistique au mongo et au rwanda', *Aequatoria*, 1956, XIX, 85-7.

Coupez, A., and Kamanzi, T., 'Rythmes quantitatifs en poésie rwanda', Folia sci. Afr. centr. 3 (1957), 58-60.

Crazzolara, J. P., *The Lwoo*. Part I: Lwoo Migrations. *Museum Combonianum*, 1950, 3; 1951, 6; 1954, 8.

Cunnison, I., 'History and genealogies in a conquest state', *American Anthropologist*, 1957, 59, pp. 20-31.

— *History on the Luapula. An Essay on the Historical Notions of a Central African Tribe*, Rhodes-Livingstone Papers, Lusaka, 1951.

— 'Perpetual kinship: a political institution of the Luapula peoples', *Human Problems in British Central Africa* (Rhodes-Livingstone Institute Journal), 1956, XX, 29-48.

Daeleman, J., 'Dag- en jaarverdeling bij de Bakoongo', *Aequatoria*, 1958, XXI, 98-101.

D'Arianoff, A., *Histoire des Bagesera, souverains du Gisaka* (Mémoires de l'Institut Royal Colonial Belge, Classe des Sciences Morales et Politiques, Série in-8°, Livre XXIV, fascicule 3), Brussels, 1952.

Davidson, B., 'The fact of African history', *Africa South*, 1958, II, 44-9.

de Beaucorps, R., *Les Bayansi du bas-Kwilu*, Louvain, 1933.

— *Les Basongo de la Luniungu et de la Gobari* (Mémoires de l'Institut Royal Colonial Belge, Classe des Sciences Morales et Politiques, Série in-8°, Livre X, fascicule 3), Brussels, 1941.

De Decker, J. M., *Les Clans Ambuun (Bambunda) d'après leur littérature orale* (Mémoires de l'Institut Royal Colonial Belge, Classe des Sciences, Morales et Politiques, Série in-8°, Livre XX, fascicule 1), Brussels, 1950.

Delahaye, H., *Les Légendes hagiographiques*, Brussels, 1905.

Denis, L., 'La supputation du temps et le calendrier chez les Bakongo', *Congo*, 1938, II, 481-9.

Denolf, P., *Aan den rand der Dibese* (Mémoires de l'Institut Royal Colonial Belge, Classe des Sciences Morales et Politiques, Série in-8°, Livre XXXIV, unique fascicule), Brussels, 1954.

De Rop, A., *De gesproken woordkunst van de Nkundo* (Annales du Musée Royal du Congo Belge, Série in-8°, sciences de l'Homme: Linguistique, Vol. 13), Tervuren, 1956.

de Sousberghe, L., 'L'étude du droit coutumier indigène. Méthode et obstacles', *Zaïre*, 1955, IX, 339-58.

Dieterlin, G., 'The Mande creation myth', *Africa*, 1957, XXVII, 124-38.

— 'Mythe et organisation sociale au Soudan français', *Journal de la Société des Africanistes*, 1955, XXV, 39-76.

Dixon, R. B., 'Primitive American history, Discussion and correspondence', *American Anthropologist*, 1915, XVII, 599. (See also under Swanton, J. R.)

DUMEZIL, G., *L'Héritage indo-européen à Rome*, Paris, 1949.

ELIADE, M., *Das Heilige und das Profane. Vom Wesen des Religiösen*, Hamburg, 1957.

ELISOFON, E., and FAGG, W., *The Sculpture of Africa*, London, 1958.

EVANS-PRITCHARD, E. E., *The Nuer*, Oxford, 1950.

— 'Zande border-raids', *Africa*, 1957, XXVII, 217-31.

— 'Zande warfare', *Anthropos*, 1957, LII, 239-62.

— 'Social anthropology: Past and present', *Man*, 1950, Vol. 198, pp. 118-124.

— 'The origin of the ruling clan of the Azande', *South-Western Journal of Anthropology*, 1957, XIII, 322-43.

— 'Zande historical texts', *Sudan Notes and Records*, 1955, XXXVI, 123-45.

— 'A history of the kingdom of Gbudwe (Azande of the Sudan)', *Zaïre*, 1956, X, 5, pp. 451-91; 7, pp. 675-710; 8, pp. 815-60.

— 'A historical introduction to a study of Zande Society', *African Studies*, 1958, XVII, 1-15.

FAGE, J. D., 'Some notes on a scheme for the investigation of oral tradition in the Northern Territories of the Gold Coast', *Journal of the Historical Society of Nigeria*, 1956, I, 15-19.

FEDER, A., *Lehrbuch der geschichtlichen Methodik*, Regensburg, 1924.

FIRTH, R., *The Work of the Gods in Tikopia* (Monographs on Social Anthropology No. 1), London, 1940, 2 volumes.

FLETCHER, H. J., 'The use of genealogies for the purpose of dating Polynesian history', *Journal of the Polynesian Society*, 1930, XXXIX, 189-94.

FORTES, M., *The Dynamics of Clanship among the Tallensi*, London, 1945.

— 'The significance of descent in Tale social structure', *Africa*, 1944, XIV, 362-85.

FOSBROOKE, H. A., 'The Masai age-group system as a guide to tribal chronology', *African Studies*, 1956, XV, 188-206.

FROBENIUS, L., *Kulturgeschichte Afrikas*, Zürich, 1954.

FULLER, C. E., 'Ethnohistory in the study of culture change in Africa', in *Continuity and Change in African Cultures*, ed. W. R. Bascom and M. J. Herskovits (Chicago, 1958), pp. 113-29.

GOLDENWEISER, A. A., 'Heuristic value of traditional records', *American Anthropologist*, 1915, XVII, 763-4.

GOODY, J., 'Ethnohistory and the Akan of Ghana', *Africa*, 1959, XXIX, 67-81.

GORJU, J., *Entre le Victoria, l'Albert et l'Édouard*, Rennes, 1920.

GRAEBNER, F., *Methode der Ethnolgoie*, Heidelberg, 1911.

GREENBERG, J., 'Étude sur la classification des langues africaines', *Bulletin de l'IFAN*, 1954, XVI, 83-142; 1955, XVII, 59-108. Trans. from the English by C. Tardits.

HAMILTON, R. A. (ed.), *History and Archaeology in Africa* (Report of a conference held in July 1953 at the School of Oriental and African Studies), London, 1955.

HANDY, E. S. C., *Marquesan Legends* (Bernice P. Bishop Museum Bulletin No. 69), Honolulu, 1930.

HARTLAND, E. S., 'On the evidential value of the historical traditions of the Baganda and the Bushongo', *Folklore*, 1914, XXV, 428-56.

HAVEAUX, G. L., *La Tradition historique des Bapende orientaux* (Mémoires de l'Institut Royal Colonial Belge, Classe des Sciences Morales et Politiques, Série in-8°, Livre XXXVII, fascicule 1), Brussels, 1954.

HEINE-GELDERN, R., 'Some problems of migration in the Pacific', *Kultur und Sprache*, 1952, IX, 313-62.

HERSKOVITS, M. J., *Dahomey*, New York, 1938, 2 volumes.

— *Man and his Works*, New York, 1949.

— *Economic Anthropology*, New York, 1952.

— 'Anthropology and Africa: A wider perspective', *Africa*, 1959, XXIX, 225-57.

HIERNAUX, J., 'Note sur une ancienne population du Ruanda-Urundi: les Renge', *Zaïre*, 1956, X, 351-60.

HULSTAERT, G., *Proverbes Mongo* (Annales du Musée Royal du Congo Belge, Série in-8°, Sciences de l'Homme: Linguistique, Vol. 15), Tervuren, 1958.

JACOBS, J., and VANSINA, J., 'Nshoong atoot. Het konnigsepos der Bushong', *Kongo-Overzee*, 1956, XXII, 1-39.

JENSEN, A. E., 'Die staatliche Organisation und die historischen Ueberlieferungen der Barotse am oberen Zambesi', *Württ. Verein für Handelsgeographie*, 1932, L, 71-115.

JOUSSE, M., *Le Style oral rythmique et mnémotechnique chez les verbomoteurs* (Archives de philosophie II), Paris, 1924.

KAGAME, A., *La Poésie dynastique au Rwanda* (Mémoires de l'Institut Royal Colonial Belge, Classe des Sciences Morales et Politiques, Série in-8°, Tome XXII, fascicule 1), Brussels, 1951.

— *La Notion de génération appliquée à la généalogie dynastique et à l'histoire du Rwanda des Xe-XIe siècles à nos jours* (Mémoires de l'Académie Royale des Sciences Coloniales, Classes des Sciences Morales et Politiques, Nouvelle Série in-8°, Tome IX, fasc. 5 et dernier), Brussels, 1959.

— 'Le code ésotérique de la dynastie du Rwanda', *Zaïre*, 1947, I, 363-86.

KARSTEN, R., *La Civilisation de l'empire Inca*, Paris, 1949.

KROEBER, A. L., *Anthropology*, New York, 1948.

LANZONI, F., *Genezi e svolgimento e tramonto delle leggende storiche* (Studi e Testi, VIII), Rome, 1925.

LAVACHERY, H., *Vie des Polynésiens*, Brussels, 1946.

LEACH, E. R., 'Aesthetics', in *Institutions of Primitive Society*, ed. E. E. Evans-Pritchard (Oxford, 1954), pp. 25-38.

LIENHARDT, G., 'Modes of thought', in *Institutions of Primitive Society*, ed. E. E. Evans-Pritchard (Oxford, 1954), pp. 95-107.

LINTON, R., *The Tree of Culture*, New York, 1955.

LLOYD, P. C., 'Yoruba myths: a sociologist's interpretation', *Odù*, 1955, II, 20-8.

LOEB, E. M., *History and Traditions of Nive* (Bernice P. Bishop Museum Bulletin No. 32), Honolulu, 1926.

LOWIE, R., *Primitive Society*, London, 1949.

— *Social Organization*, London, 1950.

— 'Oral tradition and history: Discussion and correspondence', *American Anthropologist*, 1915, XVII, 597-9.

LOWIE, R. 'Oral tradition and history', *Journal of American Folklore*, 1917, XXX, 161-7.

LUOMALA, K., 'Polynesian literature', in *Encyclopaedia of Literature* (ed. J. T. Shipley), Vol. II, 772-89.

MALINOWSKI, B., 'Myth in primitive psychology', in *Magic, Science and Religion, and Other Essays* (Glencoe, 1948), pp. 72-124.

— 'The problem of meaning in primitive languages', in *Magic, Science and Religion, and Other Essays* (Glencoe, 1948), pp. 228-76.

— *Argonauts of the Western Pacific*, London, 1950.

MANOUKIAN, M., 'The Akan and Ga-Adangme speaking peoples of the Gold Coast', *Ethnographic Survey of Africa*. Part I. *Western Africa*, London, 1950.

MERCIER, P., 'Histoire et légende: la bataille d'Illorin', *Notes africaines*, 1950, XLVII, 92-5.

MEYEROWITZ, E., *Akan Traditions of Origin*, London, 1952.

MIDDLETON, J., 'Some social aspects of Lugbara myth', *Africa*, 1954, XXIV, 189-99.

MIDDLETON, J., and TAIT, D., *Tribes without Rulers*, London, 1959.

MORTIER, R., 'Historische legenden', *Aequatoria*, 1944, VII, 101-11 and 129-36.

MUEHLMANN, W., *Methodik der Völkerkunde*, Stuttgart, 1938.

NENE AZU MATEKOLE, 'The historical background of Krobo customs', *Transactions of the Gold Coast and Togoland Historical Society*, 1959, I, 133-40.

NICHOLSON, H. B., 'Native historical tradition', *American Anthropologist*, 1955, I, 595-613.

NICOLAS, F. J., 'Origine et valeur du vocabulaire désignant les xylophones africains', *Zaïre*, 1957, XI, 69-89.

NILSSON, M. P., *Primitive Time-reckoning*, Lund, 1920.

Notes and Queries on Anthropology, by a Committee of the Royal Anthropological Institute of Great Britain and Ireland, London (6th ed., 1951).

OLIVER, R., 'The traditional histories of Buganda, Bunyoro and Ankole', *Journal of the Royal Anthropological Institute*, 1955, LXXXV, 111-17.

— 'The historical traditions of Buganda, Bunyoro and Ankole', *Man*, 1954, LIV, 43.

— 'A question about the Bachwezi', *The Uganda Journal*, 1953, XVII, 135-7.

— 'Ancient capital sites of Ankole', *The Uganda Journal*, 1959, XXIII, 51-63.

— 'The royal tombs of Buganda', *The Uganda Journal*, 1959, XXIII, 129-33.

PLANCQUAERT, M., *Les Jaga et les Bayaka du Kwango*, Brussels, 1932.

POSNANSKY, M., 'Bweyorere, Ankole: 1 June-7 July 1959', *Museum Archaeological Project* (roneo of the Uganda Museum, Kampala).

— 'Progress and prospects in historical archaeology in Uganda. Discovering Africa's past', in *Uganda Museum Occasional Paper* 4 (Kampala, 1959), pp. 31-9.

PROPP, V., *Morphology of the Folktale* (Morfologia skazki), International Journal of American Linguistics Bulletin No. 24, 4), Bloomington, Indiana, 1958.

BIBLIOGRAPHY OF WORKS CITED

RADCLIFFE-BROWN, A. R., *A Natural Science of Society*, Free Haven, 1957.
— *Structure and Function in Primitive Society*, London, 1952.
READ, M. H., 'Traditions and prestige among the Ngoni', *Africa*, 1936, IX, 453-84.
ROMERO MOLINER, R., 'La historia en las culturas negroafricanas', *Cuadernos estudios africanos*, 1947, III, 43-55.
ROWE, J. H., 'Absolute chronology in the Andean area', *American Antiquity*, 1945, X, 265-84.
— 'Inca culture at the time of the Spanish conquest', in *Handbook of South American Indians*, ed. J. Steward (Washington, 1946), XI, 183-330.
SAPIR, E., 'Time perspective in aboriginal American culture', in *Selected Writings of Edward Sapir in Language, Culture and Personality*, ed. D. Mandelbaum (Berkeley, 1949), pp. 389-462.
SCHMIDT, W., *Handbuch der Methode der kulturhistorischen Ethnologie*, Münster, 1937.
SOUSTELLE, J., *La Vie quotidienne des Aztèques à la veille de la conquête espagnole*, Paris, 1955.
SOUTHALL, A. W., 'Alur tradition and its historical significance', *Uganda Journal*, 1954, XVIII, 137-65.
SPENCER, B., and GILLEN, F. J., *The Arunta. A Study of a Stone-age People*, London, 1927.
STANISLAS, P., 'Kleine nota over de Ankutshu', *Aequatoria*, 1939, pp. 124-30.
STAPPERS, L., 'Toonparallelisme als mnemotechnisch middel in spreekwoorden', *Aequatoria*, 1953, XVI, 99-100.
— 'Eerste geluiden uit de Luba-poëzie', *Kongo-Overzee*, 1952, XVIII, 97-110.
STOKES, J. F. G., 'An evaluation of the early genealogies used for Polynesian history', *Journal of the Polynesian Society*, 1930, XXXIX, 1-42.
SWADESH, M., 'Towards greater accuracy in lexicostatic dating', *International Journal of American Linguistics*, 1955, XXI, 121-37.
— 'Lexicostatistic dating of prehistoric ethnic contacts', *Proceedings of the American Philological Society*, 1952, Vol. 96, pp. 452-63.
— 'Diffusional cumulation and archaic residue as historical explanation', *South-Western Journal of Anthropology*, 1951, VII, 1-21.
SWANTON, J. R., 'Primitive American history. Discussion and correspondence', *American Anthropologist*, 1915, XVII, 599.
SWANTON, J. R., and DIXON, R. B., 'Primitive American history', *American Anthropologist*, 1914, XVI, 376-412.
TAIT, D., 'History and social organization', *Transactions of the Gold Coast and Togoland Historical Society*, 1955, I, 193-210.
TANGHE, P. B., *De Ngbandi. Geschiedkundige Bijdragen* (Bibliothèque Congo), Brussels, 1929.
TEMPELS, P., *Banto-filosofie*, Antwerp, 1946.
TE RANGI HIROA (P. Buck), *Ethnology of Manihiki and Rakahanga* (Bernice P. Bishop Museum Bulletin No. 99), Honolulu, 1932.
TORDAY, E., and JOYCE, T. E., *Notes ethnographiques sur les peuples communément appelés Bakuba. Les Bushongo* (Annales du Musée Royal du Congo Belge, D.: Ethnographie et anthropologie, Série III, tome 2, fasc. 1), Brussels, 1910.

TURNBULL, C. M., 'Legends of the BaMbuti', *Journal of the Royal Anthropological Institute*, 1959, Vol. 89, pp. 45-60.

VAILLANT, G. C., *The Aztecs of Mexico*, London, 1950.

VAN BULCK, G., *Beiträge zur Methodik der Völkerkunde* (Wiener Beiträge zur Kulturgeschichte und Linguistik, II), Vienna, 1931.

— 'De invloed van de Westerche cultuur op de gesproken woordkunst bij de Bakongo', *Kongo-Overzee*, 1936, II, 285-93; 1936-37, III, 26-41.

VAN CAENEGHEM, R., *Over het Godsbegrip der Baluba van Kasai* (Mémoires de l'Institut Royal Colonial Belge, Classe des Sciences Morales et Politiques, Série in-8°, Livre XXII, fasc. 2 et dernier), Brussels, 1954.

— *Hekserij bij de Baluba van Kasai* (Mémoires de l'Institut Royal Colonial Belge, Classe des Sciences Morales et Politiques, Mémoires in-8°, Nouvelle série, Livre III, fasc. 1, Ethnographie), Brussels, 1954.

VAN GENNEP, A., *La Formation des légendes*, Paris, 1910.

VANSINA, J., 'La valeur historique des traditions orales', *Folia Scientifica Africae Centralis*, 1958, IV, 58-9.

— 'De handelingen der voorouders. Een handschrift waarin de genesis der Bieng verhaald wordt', *Kongo-Overzee*, 1956, XXII, 257-300.

— See also under Jacobs J.

VAN VELSEN, J., 'Notes on the history of the lakeside Tongo of Nyasaland', *African Studies*, 1959, XVIII, 105-17.

VAN WARMELO, N. J., 'Grouping and ethnic history', in *Bantu-speaking Tribes of South Africa*, ed. I. Schapera (London, 1937), pp. 43-66.

VAN WING, J., *Études Bakongo, histoire et sociologie* (Bibliothèque Congo), Brussels, 1921.

VERGER, P., 'Note on the bas-reliefs in the royal palaces of Abomey', *Odù*, 1957, V, 3-13.

VON FUEHRER-HAIMENDORF, C., 'Culture history and cultural development', in *Current Anthropology*, ed. W. L. Thomas (Chicago, 1956), pp. 149-68.

VON SYDOW, E., *Dichtungen der Naturvölker*, Vienna, 1935.

WARNER, W. L., *A Black Civilization*, New York, 1937.

WESTERMANN, D., *Geschichte Afrikas*, Cologne, 1952.

WILKS, I., 'Tribal history and myth', *Universitas*, 1956, pp. 84-6 and 116-18.

WILSON, M., 'The early history of the Transkei and Ciskei', *African Studies*, 1959, XVIII, 167-79.

— *Communal rites of the Nyakusa*, London, 1959.

WRIGLEY, C. C., 'Some thoughts on the Bacwezi', *Uganda Journal*, 1958, XXII, 11-17.

Index